DRIVE FOR EQUAL ACCESS

DRIVE FOR EQUAL ACCESS

Access and Participation of Women and Girls to Nutrition
& Health, Education & Training, Science & Technology

Avinashilingam Institute for Home Science and Higher
Education for Women – Deemed University
Coimbatore, Tamil Nadu, India

Edited by

Minnie Mathew

and

Sayani Das

PARTRIDGE

Partridge India
1663 Liberty Drive
Bloomington, INDIANA 47403
USA

To order additional copies of this book, contact
000 800 10062 62
orders.india@partridgepublishing.com
www.partridgepublishing.com/india

CONTENTS

FOREWORD

It is my pleasure to introduce the book *'Drive for Equal Access'*, which evolved from the International Women's Day National Symposium in 2014, held at our esteemed all-women institution.

'Drive for Equal Access' depicts the **'drive'** for the very existence of the various social institutions of India, which strive to bring the gender justice through equality and equity in society as its functional and broader responsibility.

The book gives a pan-Indian understanding of girls' and women's struggles in all aspects of their living and being. Their health and nutrition needs, their education and employment needs, their science and technology needs are voiced by the nationally eminent gender scholars who participated in the symposium. The stories of struggles and achievements by grassroots women portrayed by the authors through their research-based micro-studies support the unanimous voices that demand for opportunity for girls and women's participation in development and empowerment.

The book sensitizes the readers towards 'gender justice' and raises critical issues that should be confronted by the decision-makers in public-private life. It is a good handbook on gender roles and relations for students, researchers, and policy makers. I strongly recommend this book as it is not only descriptive of the social status of women in contemporary Indian society, but it creates an urge in human minds to set a social change…

Dr. P.R. Krishna Kumar
The Chancellor
Avinashilingam Institute for Home Science and
Higher Education for Women – Deemed University
Coimbatore, Tamil Nadu, India

PREFACE

Gender roles and relations touch everyone's lives and vary with location, culture, class, age and time. The range of factors which influence gender roles and relations both positively and negatively need to be understood. This uneven phenomenon could cause concern if it negatively influences a particular gender, viz., 'the woman'. Consequently, the Women's Studies Centre at the Avinashilingam Institute for Home Science and Higher Education for Women (Deemed University) initiated a discourse on: 'Access and Participation of Women and Girls to Nutrition & Health, Education & Training, Science & Technology'. From what we already know, women are triply disadvantaged and have a lesser share of everything in this world.

The symposium offered a platform for young researchers to present their research findings and contribute to the existing pool of literature. The research papers brought out an array of information ranging from environment, women's health and nutrition, occupational health hazards, disabilities, skill development, quality of work life, micro-insurance and women's empowerment. These research papers were presented against the national backdrop of women's status and access to health and nutrition, education, science and technology.

The insights gathered through micro studies are crucial for reengineering the various factors in order to move towards affirmative action. What we brought together was the wisdom of experts and the insights from the field. Publishing the proceedings, we thought can provide future directives to policy and research. We therefore offer this bouquet to policy makers, programme designers and the business community who can consider the positive deviants to the way they work.

The book "Drive for Equal Access" has two major sections: The first part brings out the proceedings of the symposium with the rich content presented by experts of national renown. The second part includes the field studies which further enriched the profound exposition of expert presentations. Readers will appreciate the findings of the field studies when contextualized within the national and state circumstances articulated by the experts.

Dr. Minnie Mathew
Director, Women Studies Centre
Avinashilingam Institute for Home Science and
Higher Education for Women – Deemed University
Coimbatore, Tamil Nadu

ACKNOWLEDGMENT

We take immense pleasure to acknowledge the contributions of one and all, who worked with us a year before and after the international women's week national symposium of 2014 that focused on *Access and Participation of Women and Girls to Nutrition & Health, Education & Training, Science & Technology*, and was held in Avinashilingam Institute for Home Science & Higher Education for Women (Deemed University), Coimbatore, Tamil Nadu, India.

We begin with expressing our profound appreciation of our Vice Chancellor Dr. Sheela Ramachandran for her kind support at all stages of this initiative from organization to publication of the national symposium proceedings.

We extend our deep gratitude to the eminent nutritionists, educationists, economists, scientists, governmental and non-governmental representatives - Mr. Anoop Satpathy, Prof. Binod Khadria, Prof. Chandrika Basu-Majumdar, Dr. G. N. V. Brahmam, Prof. Gouri Srivastava, Prof. Ishita Mukhopadhyay, Dr. Jyoti Sharma, Prof. Karuna Chanana, Prof. Krishna Misra, Dr. M. Vijayalakshmi, Mrs. Madhvi, Dr. Prema Ramachandran, Dr. Rajan Sankar, and Ms. Sonia George. We are obliged to them for making the national symposium a truly pan-Indian conglomeration of scholars. We are grateful to the distinguished resource persons who worked together for bringing out the diverse concerns and offering imperative recommendations to help girls and women to gain equal access to health, education, vocation, and science and technology in India.

We are thankful to all the paper presenters, who shared their micro research and case studies relevant to the various themes of the national symposium: Health & Nutrition, Education & Dropout, Skills & Vocational Training, Science & Technology, Full & Decent Employment. Our heartfelt thanks to the paper contributors and authors for their cooperation in the publishing process.

We very much appreciate the generous funding we received for the two-day national symposium by the reputed national and international organizations – University Grants Commission (UGC), Indian Council of Social Science Research (ICSSR), Tamil Nadu State Council for Science and Technology (TNSCST) and Global Alliance for Improved Nutrition (GAIN). We also thank National Commission for Women (NCW) for allotting funds for us, which however we could not use due to all expenses adjusted from other sources.

Our special thanks to Dr. Rajan Sankar, GAIN, for making a major contribution to the symposium and supporting this publication. We are pleased to thank the Deans, Heads of the Departments, and Faculty Members who forwarded their assistance and extended participation in the national symposium to make it a success. We would like to credit our dear colleagues of Women's Studies Centre (WSC) for their unrelenting teamwork till the end.

Finally, we call upon the readers to participate in a journey with us to understand the nuances of gender issues existing in our society, whereby they can shed off their feelings of ignorance and drive themselves to create opportunities of equal access for girls and women of India.

Dr. Minnie Mathew
Sayani Das

PART I

National Symposium Proceedings

Report by Sayani Das

EXECUTIVE SUMMARY

UN Women official theme for International Women's Day 2014 was: Access and Participation of Women and Girls to education, training, science and technology, including the promotion of women's equal access to full employment and decent work.

In conjunction with the UN Women theme for 2014, Women's Studies Centre (WSC) at the Avinashilingam Institute for Home Science and Higher Education for Women (Deemed University) organized a two-day national level symposium from 13th - 14th March 2014 in Coimbatore, Tamil Nadu.

International Women's Week 2014 was observed by the national symposium, focal theme of which was to question and explore five critical objectives:

  - to reduce malnutrition and improve nutrition and health of girls and women

  - the status of education and dropout rates for girls and women

  - the status of need-based and skill-based vocational training programmes for women

  - participation of girls and women in science and technology

  - participation of women in gainful employment and women empowerment

The national symposium was aimed to bring together nationally distinguished gender scholars and achievers, and leading women professionals and policy-makers from diverse sectors -ministries, academia, Research & Development and Science & Technology based organizations, NGOs working for women, industries, and media to share - public opinions, research reports, and case studies. Discussions were initiated under panels based on the above cited five critical issues: 1) Health & Nutrition; 2) Education & Dropout; 3) Skills & Vocational Training; 4) Science & Technology; 5) Full & Decent Employment.

The symposium was greatly enriched by fifteen nationally eminent gender scholars, professionals and leaders - who chaired panels and shared their scholastic and empirical perspectives on the above mentioned themes. The eminent personalities opened the forum to debate and reflect the pressing issues: girls' and women's needs of and access to nutritional improvement and educational upliftment - their difficulties to health and educational achievement, their potentials and contributions to economic growth, their challenges to participation and decision making, and their roles in women empowerment. They exchanged ideas and experiences with the symposium participants; to inspire public opinions and discussions on girls and women empowerment; and to make valid recommendations towards women-friendly policies and practices in India.

The national symposium was also the first ever national level assembly of prominent gender scholars and leaders from diverse background, who marked the launch of 'National Gender Caucus' – a platform for gender scholars and practitioners to share common interests and act as a think-tank and pressure-group to improve the status of girls and women in India. National Gender Caucus was launched at the end of the national symposium, to facilitate networking across scholars, professionals, industrialists, entrepreneurs, policy makers, activists, and individuals; to recommend and impact women empowerment in India.

SYMPOSIUM THEMES

Theme 1: Health & Nutrition

In India the nutrition and health status of women is abysmally low. The patriarchal system prevalent in the society makes women the worst victims of poverty and malnutrition. It is due to women's multifaceted responsibilities such as - career, giver and protector. Girls in all Indian cultures are socialized from childhood to be self-sacrificing, offering others food first and take only if somebody chooses to share or if there is something remaining. In fact, women require good nutritional intake since they work at home as well as at the work place, in order to take care of their families. However, their contribution to work is ignored, so is their health and nutrition. This is in reality more among those women belonging to the low socio-economic classes, caste and ethnic minorities, urban slums and rural areas. It is a bitter reality that in India girls and women's health and nutrition is critically linked to social, cultural, religious, and economic factors. The poor health status of women in India is mainly due to her secondary status at home and in the society. Girls and women in India receive minimum benefits of healthy diet and nutrition and health care facilities. As a result, national data shows the 'level of anemia' among young girls and women ranges from 50-80 percent (National Family Health Survey, 2010). Nonetheless, anemia is a major reason for high maternal morbidity and mortality in India. Besides, there is a high prevalence of calcium and vitamin D deficiency among girls and women due to sources of which being expensive. This itself indicates that women are victims and not decision-makers.

Therefore, the important question that was raised in the symposium: whether pervasive malnutrition among girls and women of all ages could be effectively reduced and their nutrition status improved through alternative approaches and women-friendly policies.

Theme 2: Education & Dropout

Right to Education (RTE) has been promoted widely since 2009, yet school dropout prevails. To address the huge problem of dropouts, policy makers must counter the factors that lead girls and women to leave school/college at various stages. There is a combination of factors for girl children and young women dropping out of school/college. Most significantly, there are gender-ascribed duties like- i) household (domestic) work and ii) sibling care. Girls/young women from low-income group or below poverty level (BPL) families often are lady/mother/nurse of the household in the absence of their mother, engaged in remunerative work outside the house. Further, girl and woman students drop out for fear of gender based violence while commuting to schools/colleges located at far off places/other villages/towns for threat of safety and security and due to social sanction putting limits to their mobility. Above all, marriage of teenage girls and young women, or their preparation for marriage - is a stumbling block in continuity of girls' and women's education. Social attitudes towards advantages of education for girls and women are prioritized in the order of first, 'knowledge and good groom/marriage' and later, 'job and career opportunities'.

Hence, the symposium addressed the pertinent question: whether gender neutral/sensitive education system could be an effective means to prevent dropouts among girls and women students in India. Efforts towards gender unbiased curricula, gender sensitization, and women empowerment were stressed upon as women motivate the society, change social attitudes, and become role-models for other girls and women and their own children and family members.

Theme 3: Skills & Vocational Training

Despite the fact that the Indian economy has gained a considerable rate of growth in the last two decades, this growth rate is not uniform. Underemployment, low educational levels, high rate of dropouts, wide skill gaps, and lack or mismatch of vocational training and jobs are still prevalent. The skills shortage in India is a critical issue, reflecting imbalance of demand and supply in the market. Realizing the importance of vocational training and skill development programmes, the 11th Five Year Plan has established the PM's National Council for Skill Development (for framing policies), the National Skill Development Coordination Board (for coordinating the various skill development programmes), and finally the National Skill Development Agency (NSDA – a catalyst to enhance the skill development programmes).

Given these challenges, skills and vocational training can play a key role in helping adolescent girls and women get jobs or start-up micro-enterprises. Vocational training typically includes development of need-based and technical capacity, entrepreneurship and business skills, life and soft skills. The programme attempts to develop women as employable semi-skilled, skilled, and highly skilled workers for organized sector by offering them appropriate skill training facilities. Vocational training is targeted to develop the technical and business skills of girls and women on demand by employers and markets. There is a need to support a women-centred pedagogy for vocational and skills training so that it maximizes utilization of women's indigenous/local knowledge and expertise along with locally available techniques and production practices. Promotion of skills training in non-traditional fields for women will lead to gender equality and equity in society. There are calls for introduction of mentoring and specific trade-based learning; integrating business, self-employment and entrepreneurship opportunities; and training of women trainers in both formal and informal sector; for significant impacts in women and development.

The symposium therefore questioned: whether monitoring progress can increase women's participation and integration in training and employment (or) entrepreneurship in a socially equitable way.

7

Theme 4: Science & Technology

It is now widely recognized that education and career are not only the rights of girls and women, but also contributory factors to economic and social development of the nation-state. However, representation of girls and women in the field of science and technology from school education to professional career is still critically low in India. In recent years, there is negligible increase of women's participation in Science and Technology (S&T) profession. More representation is visible for women in the fields of life sciences and medicines; while women lack in numbers in the fields of genetics, agricultural sciences, engineering, and technology. Moreover, caste-wise there is a very poor representation of women in S&T under Scheduled Caste, Scheduled Tribe and Other Backward Class categories; and religion-wise, women from minority religions stay far away from S&T. There is also huge urban-rural gap among women in S&T. In fact, majority of women who become scientists are by default and not by choice, since women in S&T experience intersection of career and family life.

For all women, family commitments, particularly child rearing is foremost and critical and is major barrier to career development. However, more than the real issue, certain preconceived notions and gender stereotyping discourage young girls and women taking-up a career in S&T. Even for women who are in professional careers of S&T, suffer from patriarchal attitudes. Traditional values and norms that encourage men over women also retard women's progress in S&T.

Henceforth, it was timely to discuss in the symposium and understand the societal mindsets that unconsciously discriminate girls and women against science and technology as passion and profession. It was therefore important to identify and analyze the potential barriers to the entry and progress of women in S&T. It was also equally important to explore the flexibility and support in career for women scientists and technologists.

Theme 5: Full & Decent Employment

Women represent about 48 percent of the total population in our country. In the employment market, women's participation is even lower. National statistics show that out of the 472.9 million employed, population of women constitutes only about 129.1 million. Even of this, only about 6 million women are in organized sectors and 123 million are in unorganized sectors (Economic Survey, 2011-12). The societal value of women's work and non-conducive work environment in unorganized sector are critical issues in women's employment. Women juggle with the double burden - managing household work and complement family income. The complication and 'invisibility' of women's productive work and 'poor' conditions of work are now debated vocally. More appropriately, the 'triple burden' on women – paid work, housework, and child/elder care – influences to a great extent on the type of work and the availability of work for women in society. Moreover, the existing socio-cultural norms define 'acceptable' work and delimit women's participation and force them to engage in unorganized rather than organized sectors. Prime age group women (15-59 years) are engaged themselves in principal duties of domestic responsibilities. However, most vulnerable are the poor, illiterate and commonly women and girl children from rural areas.

Moreover, discrimination of women at the workplace is ever present in both unorganized and organized sectors. Some of the most relevant points to our theme are the working conditions and environment, duration and durability of work, lower earnings and wage gaps, labour rights and welfare, safety and security conditions at work. Widespread unregulated conditions at work lead to exploitation that manifested in different ways – gender-based harassment to sexual harassment. Gender discrimination, job-typing, and occupational segregation are not always explicit but exist implicitly, directly or indirectly, at home/work/community. Gender based discrimination in employment is profound and evident in the recruitment process, nature of work, opportunity of training and capacity building, evaluation of work performance, fixing of wages and incentives, denial to take-up rewarding work, denial of promotion, glass-ceiling to leadership position, sexual favours, and so on.

Thus pertinent was to inquire in the symposium, whether reproductive support and infrastructure facilities can improve gainful participation of young girls and women for decent and productive employment.

SYMPOSIUM REPORT

The national symposium on *"Access and Participation of Women and Girls to Nutrition & Health, Education & Training, Science & Technology"* which was aimed to commemorate 2014 International Women's Week, discussed five pressing objectives:

- to reduce malnutrition and improve nutrition and health of girls and women

- to reduce dropout rates of girls and women by promoting gender neutral education

- to introduce need-based and skill-based vocational training programs for women

- to increase participation of girls and women in science and technology

- to involve women in gainful employment and women empowerment

Distinguished dignitaries in the two-day national level symposium were renowned physician Dr. Rajan Sankar, Country Manager India & Senior Advisor South Asia of Global Alliance for Improved Nutrition (GAIN), nutritionists Dr. G. N. V. Brahmam (Retired Director, National Institute of Nutrition) and Dr. Prema Ramachandran (Director, Nutrition Foundation of India); eminent educationists Prof. Karuna Chanana (Retired Professor, Jawaharlal Nehru University) and Prof. Ishita Mukhopadhyay (Director of Women's Studies Research Centre, Calcutta University); prominent economist Prof. Binod Khadria (Professor, Jawaharlal Nehru University) and scientists Prof. Krishna Misra (Past General Secretary, National Academy of Sciences, India - NASI), Dr. M. Vijayalakshmi (Associate Director, Indira Gandhi Centre for Atomic Research). Other dignitaries were Prof. Gouri Srivastava

(Director of Women's Studies, National Council for Education, Research and Training), Prof. Chandrika Basu-Majumdar (Director, Women's Studies Centre, Tripura University), Dr. Jyoti Sharma (Principal Scientist, Department of Science & Technology), Mr. Anoop Satpathy (Fellow, V. V. Giri National Labour Institute), Mrs. Madhvi (Additional CEO, Tamil Nadu Corporation for Development of Women), Ms. Sonia George (General Secretary, Self Employed Women's Association-SEWA Kerala).

INAUGURAL SESSION

Honourable Vice Chancellor **Dr. Sheela Ramachandran** presided the inaugural ceremony and inspired women to be the 'change maker'. According to her, women signify power to nurture the future of society and nation-building; therefore, 'empowerment' is her 'right'. She stressed that the International Women's Day National Symposium was proposed as a target to achieve the 'empowerment objective' by opening a forum to dialogue, debate, and rethink women's issues from different perspectives through the voices of eminent scholars, professionals, academia, and students sharing the same platform and calling for justice, equality and equity of women in India.

Chief Guest **Dr. Rajan Sankar**, Country Manager India and Senior Advisor South Asia of Global Alliance for Improved Nutrition (GAIN) discussed the relationship between nutrition and women empowerment: "how good nutrition could contribute to women empowerment; and how women empowerment could remove malnutrition." According to Dr. Sankar, 'nutrition' is the central component for human, social, and economic development; and women are positioned at the centre of nutrition and everything in nutrition influences women's empowerment. Women in the family decide nutrition, health, optimum growth, learning and productivity of the family members and children. However, it is a contrary situation in India where women's position in the society as a 'disempowered being' causes maternal and child malnutrition.

Malnutrition is a major cause of child mortality (32 percent). In India, 7000 young children die from malnutrition everyday, while countless others live out of their childhood in a state of chronic malnourishment. According to Global Hunger Index (GHI, 2010), India alone represents less than 40 percent of the global underweight problem. This is due to its large population base and high proportion of children with under-nutrition. India has the largest number of stunted, wasted, and underweight children in the world. Malnutrition is therefore a 'silent crisis' and micronutrient deficiency (i.e., deficiencies in iron, zinc, iodine, and vitamin A) is a 'silent emergency'.

Seventy four (74.3) percent pre-school children in India suffer from anemia, which is even higher than 47 percent in Bangladesh and 20 percent in China. The effects of early malnutrition are non-communicable diseases, such as cardiovascular disease, diabetes, stroke and hypertension - which originate in "developmental plasticity," in response to under-nutrition during fetal life and infancy. Nutrient deficiency also affects children's cognitive, motor, socio-emotional development. Moreover, effects of malnutrition in childhood in turn affect productivity in adulthood.

Therefore, India is facing a larger public health problem and interventions like- micronutrient supplements need to be given to improve maternal and child under-nutrition. Improved nutrition increases productivity of family members. Henceforth, the primary target group for nutritional improvement in society is none but women. Thus, improved maternal nutrition can be a 'tool' for empowerment of women', which in return will improve child and adult nutrition in India.

TECHNICAL SESSION I: Health & Nutrition

The first session was on 'Strategy for Reducing Malnutrition and Improving Health of Girls and Women'. The session addressed micronutrient malnutrition, particularly-anemia, under-nutrition and obesity among girls and women. The session also argued for creation of universal nutritional awareness towards alleviation of malnutrition through a multi-level approach. The session was chaired by Dr. Prema Ramachandran, Director of Nutrition Foundation of India.

Dr. G.N.V. Brahmam, retired Scientist ('F') of National Institute of Nutrition, Indian Council of Medical Research, Hyderabad, presented a special lecture on the ***Nutritional Status of Rural Women & Adolescent Girls (Current Status and Way Forward)***. According to Dr. Brahmam, under-nutrition is strongly associated with morbidity and mortality, especially among women and young children. UNICEF Report of 2010 estimates approximately 60 percent of all childhood (among below 5 year children in developing countries) deaths are associated with malnutrition. Consequences of malnutrition go beyond morbidities and mortalities and extend to the cost of treatment, low productivity, lower economic output at various levels (individual, household, community, state, and nation). Nutritionally vulnerable groups for malnutrition and under-nutrition are: infants and young children (<5 years); adolescent girls; pregnant and lactating women; elderly and socio-economically deprived groups (SCs, STs, slum dwellers, rural poor). Household food security is a major issue in controlling malnutrition and under-nutrition - due to deficient intakes in food. All households should have access to culturally acceptable food with adequate quality, quantity and safety throughout the year. This will ensure active and healthy life for all members of the family. However, nutritional status is also determined by agro-climatic factors, demographic factors, socio-economic factors, physiological factors, socio-cultural factors, environmental factors, disasters, health care, pathological conditions, availability of and participation in developmental programmes.

Dr. Brahmam generated awareness through several vital statistical analyses. According to him, 'Micronutrient Deficiency Disorders' (Iron Deficiency Anemia – IDA, Vitamin 'A' Deficiency – VAD, Iodine Deficiency Disorders– IDD, Vitamin D Deficiency) are of public health significance. Challenges in this public health crisis remain despite the positive improvements in the demographic, socio-economic and health factors. It is because, the dietary intakes of the rural communities continues to be poor both in terms of quantity and quality. Infant and child feeding practices in India are sub-optimal. Intake of micronutrient rich protective food is grossly inadequate across age, sex, physiological groups. There is prevalence of low birth weight to about 22 percent, about 40 percent of below 5 year children are underweight, 45 percent are stunted, 20 percent are wasted. And about a fifth of adolescent girls, third of the women have Chronic Energy Deficiency. Micronutrient deficiencies such as Iron Deficiency Anemia, Vitamin 'A' Deficiency, Vitamin D Deficiency – all continue to be of public health significance. Moreover, coverage of target groups for Iron and Folic Acid and Vitamin A distribution is low. At the same time, there is prevalence of overweight or obesity among adults. Known risk factors for diet related chronic degenerative diseases such as Type 2 Diabetes, Hypertension and Cardiovascular Disease are about 20 percent. Nearly a fifth of adult population is found to be having hypertension.

Dr. Brahmam suggested several strategies toward possible solutions to the above mentioned challenges. His short term strategies included reinforcing supplementary nutrition programmes, in terms of quantity and type of supplement and coverage of target population and monitoring; immunization and health care services. His medium term strategies included micronutrient fortification of staple foods and food supplements. His long term strategies included the development and implementation of state specific nutrition policies and programmes; strengthening health and nutrition education, especially about optimal infant and child feeding; better nutrition during adolescence, pregnancy and lactation; promotion of healthy lifestyle practices. Dietary diversification, bio-fortification of foods, promotion of home gardening, through Krishi Vigyan Kendra (KVK) also formed part of his long term suggestions. According to him, environmental sanitation and personal hygiene including safe drinking water and programmes for economic development and income generating activities, especially at grassroots level are important. Nevertheless, population control remains an unabated long term strategy.

Dr. Minnie Mathew, Director of Women's Studies Centre in Avinashilingam Deemed University for Women, Coimbatore, Tamil Nadu gave a talk on ***Improving Hygiene Practices in Rural Women***. According to her statement, 30 percent of the total burden of diseases in the developing countries is due to the unhygienic household environment and individual practices. World Bank Report of 1993 estimates that 75 percent of all life years is being lost across the developing nations due to the lack of uncontaminated water supply, sanitation facilities and the prevalence of risky hygiene behaviour among citizens. The World Bank report further claims that the resultant consequence is not only serious public health issues; but also large economic and image losses for countries and their governments. Each year over 3 million children under the age of 5 die from Diarrhoea. Of India's more than 2.3 million annual deaths among children, about 3,34,000 are attributable to Diarrhoea. However, research has shown that better hygiene through hand washing, food protection and domestic hygiene; can reduce infant Diarrhoea to 33 percent. She emphasized on health education for rural women stressing on oral Hygiene, like- hand washing, bath, hair care, clean clothes and vaginal hygiene; and on the improvement of public services.

Chair of the health and nutrition session, **Dr. Prema Ramachandran**, Director of Nutrition Foundation of India (NFI) and Former Advisor of Health and Nutrition, Planning Commission (1993); quoted from the Constitution of India. The Article 47 affirms that, "the State shall regard raising the level of nutrition and standard of living of its people and improvement in public health among its primary duties". She stressed that India's nutrition policies and programmes should be based on the national situation analysis and appropriate research evidence-based intervention strategies. She highlighted the multi-pronged interventions undertaken by the Government of India for promoting food security and optimal nutrition through the following interventions: improving household food security; food supplementation to vulnerable groups; nutrition and health education to improve awareness so that the population can optimally access and utilize available services. She pointed out that the technical session was tailored to question and explore the first and fundamental objective of the symposium, namely to reduce malnutrition and improve nutrition and health of girls and women. This objective having universal importance, forms the basis for achieving the other objectives. She addressed her talk on *Nutrition Policies and Programmes in India* in three parts - food production, access to food and utilization (absorption).

National Programmes to Improve Food Production

At the time of Independence, India was not self-sufficient of food. Therefore, food production to adequately meet the hunger of growing population was given high priority. Green Revolution enabled India to become self-sufficient in food production within a decade. In the last four decades food grain production quadrupled and met the needs of the growing population. But pulse production was stagnant; and the demand and supply gap resulted in import of pulses. Cost of pulses soared and necessitated reduction in pulse consumption by general population. National Food Security Mission (NFSM) was launched in August 2007 - with the objective to increase production of rice, wheat and pulses. Over the last three years pulse production has increased by 2 tons per year. The National Horticultural Mission has focused on increase in fruits and vegetables which provide essential micronutrients. Currently, India is number 1 and 2 in production of vegetables and fruits respectively. Earning from export of fruits and vegetables is growing. But all segments of population, irrespective of families with economic capacities or constraints, show low per capita consumption pattern of vegetables and fruits. Low vegetable consumption is the primary reason for widespread micronutrient deficiencies among Indians. Horticultural mission has the mandate to focus on production, processing and marketing of low cost, nutrient rich vegetables, so that vegetables are available and affordable and the 'aware' population can buy and consume more vegetables. With the National Food Security Mission and National Horticultural Mission fully operational, the country is expected to remain self-sufficient in food production till 2030.

Food Security

Dr. Prema stated that mere self-sufficiency in production of food grains would in no way lead to household food security or improvement of health and nutritional status of individuals. Improvement of household food security, especially for the poor is the primary national concern. Therefore, national programmes focus on the administered prices of food grains to keep food grain costs low; food subsidy especially to poor and marginalized segments of the population and improving Public Distribution System (PDS) to improve access to subsidized food grains. The holistic strategy for the poor has been adopted in order to improve food security. Dr. Prema, suggested public distribution of essential goods like - subsidized food grains and programmes of food supplementation. Cost free services of safe drinking water, sanitation, education and essential health care should be based on people's needs and not to be dependent on their payment ability. These strategies could improve food security and result in decrease in under-nutrition and micronutrient deficiency among the poor.

Poverty Under-Nutrition Linkages

Dr. Prema presented the inter-relationships between poverty, under-nutrition and health as:

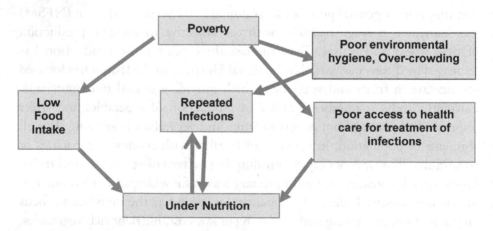

Macro- and micro-nutrient deficiencies are due to three primary reasons: i) low dietary intake because of poverty and low purchasing power; ii) high prevalence of infection because of poor access to safe-drinking water, sanitation and health care; iii) poor utilization of available facilities due to low literacy and lack of awareness. In the seventies and eighties, widespread 'poverty' in India - directly or indirectly - was the major factor responsible for high under-nutrition and micronutrient deficiencies and illnesses (mostly due to infections). Under-nutrition is associated with immune depression and repeated infections; and infections aggravate under-nutrition – it is a vicious cycle.

Poverty reduction therefore, continues to be a major intervention to improve health and nutritional status of women and girls in India. There has been a progressive decline in poverty. During 1993 to 2005 (11-year period), the average decline in the poverty ratio was 0.74 percent per year. However, it rose to 2.18 percent per year during the 7 year period from 2004 to 2012. Rate of decline in rural poverty is higher than urban poverty. Until 3 years ago India experienced high Gross Domestic Product (GDP) growth, which has been a major factor responsible for the poverty decline; the prevalence of hunger in India and South Asia is lower than Sub-Saharan Africa.

Five Year Plans and Food Security

The successive Five-Year Plans have outlined multi-sectoral programmes to combat poverty and food insecurity at national, state and household levels; bridge the energy intake gap among the vulnerable population; provide health care to reduce nutrition toll of infections; reduce under-nutrition and micronutrient deficiencies and improve nutritional status of the population. Since nineties, India has entered into the dual nutrition era whereby both under- and over-nutrition became major public health problems. Taking this into account the Tenth Five Year Plan adopted paradigm shifts. There was a shift from freedom from hunger and household food security to family nutrition security. Shift was from untargeted food supplementation to screening of all vulnerable persons. Mass identification of people with various grades of under-nutrition and appropriate management of their nutrition became the focus. Shift was from the lack of focused interventions on the prevention of over-nutrition to the promotion of appropriate lifestyles and dietary intakes for the management of over-nutrition (obesity). The Tenth Plan recommended the convergence in service delivery of vertical programmes and integrated comprehensive services for the improvement of nutrition and health status of common men, women, children and elderly persons. The Tenth Plan recommendations have been carried forward in the successive plan periods.

National Food Security Act

Since 2008 food inflation has become a major problem globally and in India. And from 2012 the Gross Domestic Product (GDP) growth rate has declined. Therefore, there has been a growing concern that continuous inflation of food price might adversely affect the household food security and nutritional status of its members. Thus India has become the first country to enact a legislation to improve food security of the citizens: National Food Security Act of 2013. National Food Security Act has aimed to sustained improvement of household food security by giving subsidized food grains through the PDS as a legal entitlement to over 67 percent of Indians. The estimated combination of Priority households and Eligible households (called 'Antyodaya households') is up to 75 percent of the rural population and up to 50 percent of the urban population. It has been soon understood by the authority that improvement of access to food might not be adequate in itself to improve nutritional status of the population. Therefore, the Act has called for improvement in access to safe drinking water, environmental sanitation and health care for all. Early detection and effective management of infections can prevent nutrient loss and nutritional deficiency among people of India.

Moreover, it is realized that food grains alone cannot replace balanced nutritional diet. States like Chhattisgarh and Tamil Nadu provide pulses at subsidized cost through PDS. In these States, there is also attempt to provide oil, iodized salt, iron and iodine fortified salt through PDS at subsidized cost. However it is never going to be possible by States to offer all foods at a subsidized cost to all the needy people. Therefore, there is an urgent need for a campaign for nutrition awareness with special focus on women as the target group. The nutrition awareness campaign should focus on how money can be saved by subsidized food grains (approximately Rupees 15-20/kg) and the savings can be used for purchasing other food items, vegetables, pulses, fruits, etc. to ensure balanced diet for the family.

Nutritional Status of Indians

National Nutrition Monitoring Bureau (NNMB) data suggests that there has been a slow but steady decline in the prevalence of under-nutrition in both men and women; and since 1990s there has been a slow but progressive increase in over-nutrition indicating that India has entered the 'dual nutrition burden era'. If stunting and underweight in pre-school children are used as indicators for assessment of nutritional status, nearly half of under 5 year old Indian children are under-nourished. But, if Body Mass Index (BMI) for age is used, then only 17 percent are under-nourished. More than 50 percent of the adult population and 80 percent of children below 5 years are normally nourished. However, prevalence of over-nutrition is low in India.

Cereals are the main source of energy in Indian diets. Data from NNMB surveys confirm the finding from NSSO survey that there has been a decline in cereal intake and energy intake. Over the last two decades, there has been progressive increase in mechanization of transport, occupational and household activities. Consequently, there has been reduction in physical activity and energy needs in urban and rural areas even among the poor. Average Indian's energy food intake remains inadequate due to their lack of physical activity. The reduced energy intake on the other hand balances body needs; protecting Indians from rapid rise in over-nutrition and obesity rates.

National Food Supplementation Programmes:

Ongoing nationally supported nutrition and health programmes for women and children are – the food supplementation to pregnant and lactating women (0-36 months); pre-school children (3-6 years) through Integrated Child Development Services (ICDS); and school children (6-14 years) through National Programme for Nutrition Support for Primary Education or commonly known as Mid-Day Meal Programme (MDM).

Integrated Child Development Services (ICDS)

ICDS was launched in 1975 and aimed to prevent under-nutrition in children of 0-59 months. The objectives continue to be:

- to improve health and nutrition status of children (0-6 age group) by food supplements

- to coordinate with state health departments for delivery of health inputs

- to provide early stimulation and education for psychological and social development of the pre-school children

- to provide pregnant and lactating women with nutrition supplements

- to enhance mother's child care ability through health and nutrition education

- to achieve effective coordination among the various departments for promoting policy and implementation towards child development

Data from National Family Health Survey (NFHS) indicate that coverage under food supplementation at Anganwadi is quite low.

Mid-Day Meal (MDM) Programme

To address the national concern for the lack of universal enrolment and high dropout rates in primary schools, National Programme of Nutritional Support to Primary Education (NP-NSPE) popularly known as Midday Meal programme was initiated as a centrally sponsored programme in 1995. The primary target of MDM was increasing enrolment, improving school attendance and retention of students. The programme envisaged the provision of 3kg wheat/rice per month free of cost for children studying in classes I-V in all Government, local body and Government aided primary schools who attended the school for more than 80 percent school days. However this did not address the problem of class room hunger. On November 28, 2001 the Supreme Court of India gave directive to the state governments for mandatory provision of hot cooked meals instead of 'dry rations' as given before to all children in primary schools. In October 2007, the scheme was revised to cover children in classes VI to VIII (11-14 years) also. As of 2013, more than 10.35 crore children (75 percent of the enrolled children) in 11.55 lakh schools in the country get MDM.

MDM is often used as home food substitution and not 'as additional to home food'. MDM can play a major role in reducing under-nutrition and preventing over-nutrition in school children by monitoring:

- Body Mass Index (BMI) measurements

- identifying under-nourished children and giving them double helping of MDM, if home food availability is a problem

- getting them checked by school health system for infections

- identifying over-nourished children and made to do more physical activity in play time

Optimal use of MDM and school health interventions can reduce under- and over- nutrition in school children.

Micronutrient Deficiencies

Dr. Prema also highlighted the interventions aimed at addressing micro-nutrient deficiencies. Two major national programmes aimed at improving micronutrient deficiencies are: Anemia Prevention and Control Programme and Iodine Deficiency Disorder (IDD) Control Programme.

Anemia

Majority of the 1.3 billion Indians from all age and physiological groups are anaemic. Low dietary iron intake and poor bio-availability of iron from Indian vegetarian diets are most important factors that cause anemia. Increased intake of iron and folic acid rich vegetables and vegetable rich in iron absorption enhancers and increased access to iron and iodine fortified salt are the two sustainable interventions envisaged to improve iron intake. Iron folic acid supplementation to school age children and adolescents can reduce prevalence of anemia in these groups. In pregnant women screening for anemia and appropriate management are essential to improve pregnancy outcome.

Iodine Deficiency Disorders

National Goitre Control Programme (NGCP) was launched by the Government of India in 1962 based on the results of the successful trial of iodized salt in the well-recognized sub-Himalayan 'goitre' belt - Kangra Valley of Himachal Pradesh. However availability of salt was erratic and there was no substantial reduction in IDD because of continued use of cheaper non-iodized salt and due to lack of awareness regarding need to use iodized salt. The programme generated awareness for the use of iodized salt against cheaper non-iodized salt at national level. ICMR surveys of 1980s indicated IDD problem found beyond the sub-Himalayan regions; in all the states. As a consequence, in 1992 the Central Council of Health adopted a policy to iodize edible salt available in the country. In August 1992, the NGCP was renamed as National Iodine Deficiency Disorders Control Programme (NIDDCP). The goal of universal access to iodized salt was to be achieved by 2012 or at least within the next few years.

Dr. Prema emphasized on nutrition education. According to her, it is the critical intervention for prevention of under-nutrition, which is lacking or is of poor quality under National Health Mission. Nutrition and health education can be communicated through all modes of communication. Health and nutrition services are to be covered as universal. The needed nutrition and health care can be provided by improving the content and quality of health and nutrition outreach services. It is expected that health and nutrition awareness will make population utilize gained knowledge for need-based services in order to improve their nutritional and health status. Therefore, there is a national need for a nutrition awareness campaign targeting especially women, who take decision on their ration card, on how subsidized food grains can save money (approximately Rupees 15-20/kg) which in turn can be used for purchasing vegetables, pulses, fruits, etc. - to ensure a balanced family diet. According to her, the success of nutrition education for increasing vegetable consumption in order to improve micronutrient status and reduce Non-communicable Disease (NCD) will depend on the availability of vegetables at affordable cost throughout the year. Nutrition education on appropriate *Infant and Young Child Feeding* (IYCF), like - how to prepare inexpensive balanced diet for the family, and health education on how to access needed health care - are the key interventions to reduce under-nutrition in children. However, nutrition education has been the weakest component of National Health Mission, ICDS and MDM, even though nutrition education is the critical intervention for prevention of under-nutrition in preschool and primary school children.

Health awareness and nutrition education are very important: exclusive breast feeding for first 6 months; adequate and appropriate complementary feeding of family food for 3 to 5 times a day from 6 months of age; continued breast feeding and family food feeding 4 to 5 times a day up to 24 months; feeding 2-5 year old children 4 to 6 times a day from healthy and nutritious family food consisting of cereals, pulses and vegetables; and timely immunization, safe practices to prevent infections, and care during illness and recovery process. Similarly MDM is aimed to bridge the gap between actual intake and nutrient requirements, since the gaps between the requirement and actual intake is highest among adolescent girls and boys in India. MDM therefore, has a major role to play in preventing classroom hunger, promoting school enrolment, fostering social integration and improving gender equity. And its national importance can be significantly enhanced by promotion of nutrition education.

In conclusion, Dr. Prema interestingly remarked on combating of the 'dual nutrition burden'. It is a major challenge in the Indian context, however it is in fact an opportunity for its population, since the challenge has led to policies, programmes and legislation towards national health and nutrition improvement. Thus, India should take this opportunity to cope with other major challenges in health and nutrition sectors, effectively within a short period, at an affordable cost. She also pointed out the recommendations that emerged out of the session: which concentrated around - micronutrient malnutrition - particularly anemia, under-nutrition, obesity and creation of universal nutritional awareness towards alleviation of malnutrition through a multi-pronged approach.

TECHNICAL SESSION II: Education & Dropout

The second session was on 'Gender Neutral/Sensitive Education and Dropout Prevention for Girls and Women'. The session highlighted the 'push and pull factors' of education for girls and women students in the present context. The session also addressed gender neutralization of text books, co-curricular and extra-curricular activities; as well as classroom communications for controlling the rates of dropout. The session was chaired by noted educationist Karuna Chanana, (Retired) Professor of Jawaharlal Nehru University.

Professor Ishita Mukhopadhyay, Director of Women's Studies Research Centre in the University of Calcutta presented a special lecture on *Girl's Education in Neoliberal India*. According to Prof. Mukhopadhyay, challenges for girls and women in education are already located. Female illiteracy is a major challenge. High dropout rate of girls and women is a major hindrance. Decline in attendance, relative to enrolment is also a challenge. And low mean years of schooling prevail among girl students. Moreover, girl children are more vulnerable from diverse means in society. Though the child mortality rate has fallen from 88 per 1,000 live births in 1990 to 60 in 2010, yet is insufficient for the target of 29 by 2015. 28 countries in the world represent higher child mortality rate at 100 per 1,000 live births in 2010. Between 1999 and 2010, there has been 46 percent increase of children enrolled in pre-school, but it has led to only less than half the world's children having received pre- primary education. Progress has been slowest in low income countries, which estimates only 15 percent of children completed pre-primary education in 2010. Overall, girls' participation in the pre-primary education is low and inequitable. Enrolment in pre-primary education varies widely between and within regions. For India, pre-primary Gross Enrolment Ratio (GER) [number of girls per 100 boys] has moved from 19 to 20 percent in 1999 to near to 60 percent by 2010. It is estimated that only 12 countries together represent half of the world's total number of dropout school children. For India, number of children of primary school age who are out of school has been 2.3 (millions) in 2010 or nearest years. Prof. Mukhopadhyay pointed out bottlenecks in Indian education system, being the rise in Net Enrolment Ratio (NER), on contrary to lack of retention of girls in school. There is a high rate of dropout among girls and adolescents and the reasons of dropouts being the same throughout the decade. There seems a convergence among the states in terms of social exclusion. According to Annual Status of Education Report (ASER) survey of 2011, 16.6 percent of the schools do not have drinking water supply; 37 percent of the schools do not have functional laboratories; 40 percent of the schools do not have toilets separately for girls; and for the country as a whole only 62 percent of the schools do not have a playground. In the words of many women scholars, the gender questions that need to be addressed at this juncture are the social-capital view of gender; the public-private divide; the nexus between relationships among communities, political parties, NGOs, local government agencies; and the complementarity of genders. Mainstreaming the role of the state is an important consideration to achieve gender equality in education sector. She quoted from Jeanne Vickers (1991) that new and harmonious relationship should be developed between the transnational capital, state policy, reproductive labour and gender relations to bridge public-private divide. Mainstreaming gender in policies and programmes, agency and management needed to be targeted. Amrtya Sen and Martha C. Nussbaum's (1995) 'Capability Approach' should be implemented for the empowerment of girls and women. She also quoted from Gayatri Chakravorty Spivak (1996) that it was widely believed that State policies had catered to elite women and cooption of agenda only – which needed to be critiqued and new ways of thinking and doing should be rolled out for holistic development of girl child, adolescent girls and women.

Professor Gouri Srivastava, Head of the Department of Gender Studies, National Council of Educational Research and Training (NCERT) gave a special talk on *Education as a Strategy for Addressing the Phenomenon of Dropout and Never Enrolment of Girls*. According to Prof. Srivastava, the education of girls' in contemporary India is seen as an important development input as well as an indicator for overall socio- economic progress. Educating half of the humanity is beneficial for the girl child, her family and the society at large. However, a significant concern that is discussed in all educational discourses is- should education be linked to only ensuring access and enrolment of girls, should it focus on quality dimensions or should it envelop both participation and overall quality concerns, so that the beneficiaries as well as all the stakeholders realize the intrinsic and extrinsic worth of education. Education of girls should move towards bringing equilibrium between existing supply and demand. This can happen when the beneficiaries as well as all the stakeholders involved in education realize the value and benefit of education.

The present scenario of education in India highlights that, despite existing enabling schemes conceptualized by government at the Centre and the State, like the District Primary Education Programme (DPEP-1994), Sarva Shiksha Abhiyan (SSA-2000) and Rashtriya Madhyamik Shiksha Abhiyan (RMSA-2009) - gender gaps in education continue to exist.

The educational indicator related to literacy depict that as per census 2011, the literacy rate has grown by 29.42 percent point from 1981 to 2011. Male literacy has grown by 24.51 percent and female literacy has grown by 34.88 percent. In the context of enrolment, there has been a substantial increase in enrolment of girls and boys in school, however gender disparity continues to exist. Data on enrolment by Ministry of Human Resource Development (MHRD) for the years 2010-11 indicates that there are 4.16 percentage point gender gap with boys in enrolment at the primary stage; 5.74 percentage points at the upper primary stage; 9.84 percentage points at the secondary stage; 11.74 percentage points at the higher secondary stage (GOI, 2012). Data brought out by District Information System for Education (DISE) on enrolment for primary and upper primary classes by social groups (SC, ST, OBC, Muslim minority) also indicates that though gender gaps are bridged in enrolment among children belonging to SC, ST, OBC and Muslim community, yet they still continue and increase with higher level of school stage.

The high dropout rate among girls and boys still remains a major problem in the education sector. The dropout rate for 2010-11 indicates that it stands at 28.7 percent for boys and 25.1 percent for girls between classes I to V and the same trend shows increase with the rise in educational levels. Dropout rate also draws attention to the fact that these rates are higher in case of boys at the primary level as well as at the secondary levels. Similar pattern is seen in case of children belonging to social groups. It poses a serious challenge before the planners as higher dropout rate among boys has a strong implication for girl's education.

Therefore, to address all forms of gender disparities in education and to make education an agency of transformation, there is a need to focus on emerging issues that relate to both boys and girls, more tilted in favour of girls.

Prof. Srivastava asked further- "Does education initiate the following?"

- Instil confidence and self- esteem among boys and girls
- Promote positive image of girls and women
- Develop skills related to critical thinking and negotiation
- Encourage decision making
- Enable learners to make informed choices
- Motivate children, particularly girls, to participate in all activities, unconventional and emerging fields of science and technology
- Access to information
- Exercise rights
- Awareness on legal issues

Therefore, for evolving realistic and context specific strategies for addressing the phenomenon of dropout and never enrolment of children, particularly girls, a systematic micro regional research needs to be undertaken. Also, there is a need to examine the functioning of schemes and programmes and to identify bottle necks in its implementation. Stakeholder's perspective on addressing retention and quality education needs to be elicited from time to time. School related factors that impact teaching and learning of children need to be examined from a gender lens to know the quantity, quality and its availability from the supply side, for example- teacher's availability, textbooks, attendance, scholarships and infrastructure related, etc. Quality concerns can also be realistically assessed in different school settings, for example- pedagogical practices, curriculum related, curriculum plus activities for overall personality development of children for formulating pathways for achieving the goal of Education for All.

Professor Chandrika Basu Majumder, Director of Women's Studies Centre of Tripura University talked on *Gender Sensitive Education: A Tripura Perspective*. According to her, 'gender' is not women's issue alone, it is people's issue, since both boys and men suffer from gender stereotyping that exists in any patriarchal culture. Education therefore can redress inequities of gender in society. She stressed that today Indian universities are expected to contribute directly to the pursuit and promotion of gender equality. Educational institutions can therefore facilitate in developing new values and forms of society that may enable both women and men to build their human capacities to fullest. Prof. Basu Majumder shared demographic trends in the North-Eastern State of Tripura. Tripura is predominantly a tribal state with female to male sex ratio being 961:1000; female literacy of 78.90 percent against male literacy of 89.94 percent; female to male life expectancy 74:71 years; mean age of marriage for girls is 20.2 years. As per 2001 Census, the literacy rate among tribals (47.10 percent) was much below the overall national literacy (64.84 percent). The female literacy rate among tribals remained lower (34.76 percent) to national female literacy (53.67 percent). Girls to boys dropout rate during 2012-13 in Tripura in primary level (I-V) has been 2.92:2.91 and elementary level (I-VIII) has been 8.35:8.64. Enrolment of female to male students in degree colleges during 1998-1999 has been 6341:10465 and in professional college during 2009-2010 has been 10950:13344 and in polytechnic college during 2012-2013 has been 627:648. In order to tackle this gender disparity in the State, Government of Tripura has taken some initiatives. As for example-incentives to girl child; enrolment of girl children in separate schools and separate toilet for girls; pension scheme for unmarried women above 45 years; pension scheme for widow and deserted women; implementation of Rajiv Gandhi Scheme for Empowerment of Adolescent Girls (RGSEAG) -SABLA, Integrated Child Development Services (ICDS), Integrated Child Protection Scheme (ICPS), and Indira Gandhi Matritva Sahyog Yojana (IGMSY), implementation of Gender Budgeting (in 17 Govt. departments so far); 50 percent reservation for women in the Panchayati Raj Institutional Bodies; 54 percent (20861) of Self Help Groups exclusively run by women; and 41 percent women days [4.18 crore women are benefitted under Mahatma Gandhi National Rural Employment Guarantee Act (MGNREGA, 2013)]. Prof. Basu Majumder suggested steps to be taken into account to improve enrolment status of girls and women and tackle the problem of dropout from schools and colleges. According to her, there is a need to set up more educational institutions providing educational facilities to all sections of society. There is urgent need to expand transport facilities, special incentives to poor students through scholarships, free textbook, establishing book banks, etc., vocationalise education at higher level so that it enables enhancement of girls' and women's productive capabilities in those vocations that are related to local needs and societal and market demands. In this regard, job-oriented condensed courses comprising education, skills and training must be given priority. Another need is to expand the scope of distance education so that the girls and women who are unable to receive formal education are able to access educational opportunities through various institutions such as Indira Gandhi National Open University (IGNOU), or Directorate of Distance Education. There must be provision of counsellor who is well equipped in tackling issues related to gender, caste and class in educational institutions and work organizations. A higher level of education and employable skills for girl and women are sine-qua-non for building and improving their capacity. Gender sensitization is required for both officials and non-officials so that they can work with right attitude and perspectives to meeting the special needs and problems of the disadvantaged group – women and/or men. Prof. Basu Majumder highlighted geo-political isolation of North Eastern Region in India. There are pressing regional issues like - high poverty, low per-capita income, low capital formation; inadequate infrastructure facilities, geographical isolation and communication bottlenecks; low progress in industrial field, high unemployment problem and lack of industrialisation/industry sector not being able to open-up employment opportunities. Therefore, the scope of higher education especially for women remains problematic and 'gender studies' should become compulsory subject at schools and colleges in order to tackle these issues constructively.

Chair of the education and dropout session, **Professor Karuna Chanana**, formerly with Zakir Husain Centre for Educational Studies, Jawaharlal Nehru University, New Delhi, while addressing the audience, pointed out that students receiving higher education should be regarded as national resource. They are among the fortunate ones in society because very few reach to higher education out of those who are of college-going age. A large majority of girls do not finish school, leave aside enter college. She advised students to make full use of the time available to them in the university by acquiring knowledge through textbooks, curricular and co-curricular activities. She commented on the differential treatment between boys and girls, men and women indicating societal bias towards gender equality. This is due to the reason that the socialization process leads to confirmation and adoption of gender based roles in society and by its members. In general, girls do better than boys in school education, however, choice of subjects by girls and boys differ due to differential socialization process and social practices. It does not depend on their achievement in school Board examinations which are not linked to their aspirations. Both push out and pull out factors work simultaneously to keep girls out of the education system. 'Push-out' (by the schools) and 'pull-out' (by personal-familial reasons) factors are responsible for dropout of girls and women from securing education. These 'push-out' factors for school girls are: school infrastructure, non-attendance due to distance and domestic work, language conflict (vernacular vs. medium of instruction) and academic demands. Whereas, 'pull-out' factors for female students are: social roles and obligations in family and society, safety and security of young women in public places, early marriages, poverty and fee payment difficulty, child/elder care, distance and mobility restriction. According to Prof. Chanana, 'gender-neutral education' - the objective of the symposium should be indeed a priority in the society. And gender-neutral education can be achieved by educational institutions through analysis of text/reference books and its contents; organizing extra-curricular activities for both genders; promoting awareness, communications and advocacy towards gender equality; making the educational institutions gender friendly. She further suggested alternatives to overcome gender bias and prevent dropout by undertaking following measures – i) schools should work with community, ii) availability of mentoring and tutoring of girls and women students for completion of education, iii) bridging language and communication gaps, iv) minimizing hours in school/college timing for flexibility and safety, v) offering career and technological and vocational education targeted to girls and women, vi) giving free counselling to balance life, vii) providing residential schools and safe girls'/ladies' hostel facilities, and viii) providing incentives to enter schools and colleges and to complete education by giving out scholarships to girls and women. She also urged the students in higher education to take responsibility to bring in change in the society. In a single-sex school and college, or in an all-women university, greater leadership roles are played by girl and women students. They can also take such leadership roles in co-education schools and colleges by making society women-friendly and gender equal.

The overall session pointed out the need of diagnostic research to highlight the barriers to and dropouts from education. Stress on the obligation of adopting gender inclusive and gender integrative education remains at the forefront.

In fact, 'gender studies' is to be made compulsory at schools and colleges through curricular as well as co-curricular courses. Especially, unconventional areas such as science and technology, engineering, mathematics, medicine and allied subjects need to be broadened to include 'gender studies' as part of the curriculum.

Additionally, creation and revisions of text books and preparation of teaching and learning materials towards being gender sensitive is the need of the hour. Further, students and teachers are to be gender sensitized and their training focus is to be need-based. Moreover, collaboration between scientists and social scientists will encourage gender sensitive policies in education and greater convergence of educational policies and programmes. Information dissemination and awareness on gender equality and equity need to be translated into different Indian languages for greater level of outreach to common women and men, girl and boy students, teachers and professionals.

TECHNICAL SESSION III: Skills & Vocational Training

The third session was on 'Need-based Skills Development and Vocational Training for Women'. The session emphasized on demographic changes and labour market expansion in India with greater requirement of skilled man- and woman-power. Development of skills according to vocational needs in society is gaining priority, since it is replacing traditional unskilled employment opportunities where women are involved in majority. Therefore, session focused on skills development issues and challenges among women workers, in particular the newly introduced 'Aajeevika Skills'. The session was chaired by Dr. U. Jerinabi, Dean of Commerce and Business Administration of Avinashilingam Deemed University for Women, Coimbatore, Tamil Nadu.

Mrs. Madhvi, Additional CEO of Tamil Nadu Corporation for Development of Women (TNCDW) gave a special lecture on ***Need – Based Skills Development and Vocational Training for Women***. Mrs. Madhvi introduced TNCDW which was established in 1983 under Department of Social Welfare and brought under Rural Development Department in 2006.

TNCDW started Self Help Group (SHG) Movement in 1989 and implemented major schemes - Mahalir Thittam (MaThi – Women's Development Project, fully funded by the State Government) and Swarnajayanti Gram Swarozgar Yojana (SGSY), 75 percent funded by Central Government and 25 percent by

State Government). Major activities of Mahalir Thittam are: Group Formation, SHG Formation, Capacity Building, Revolving Funds to SHGs, Credit Linkage (Direct Loan, Repeat Loan, Bulk Loan, etc.), Youth Skill Training & Placement, Enterprise Development Training for SHG Women, Formation of Panchayat Level Federations, Marketing Support and Sales Exhibition, Awards and Incentives, Economic Assistance to Rural SHGs through SGSY, Infrastructure Support (SHG building, village shandies). In Tamil Nadu, out of the total 385 blocks, Mahalir Thittam state funded scheme operates in 265 blocks and World Bank supported Pudhu Vaazhvu Project (PVP) operates in 120 blocks. Skill Development Programme in the state has commenced in the year 2006-07 and many female youth have been trained through TNCDW on various skills (cell phone service, computer skills, construction skills, garments making, industrial mechanism, leather products, light and heavy vehicle operation, medical application, other trainings). In the beginning of 2014, total number of youth covered has marked at 2,20,644, of which 2,06,317 youth completed training and 1,71,215 youth are gainfully employed in the above mentioned trades.

TNCDW is the implementing agency for the Aajeevika Skills and Placement Programme (75 percent funded by Central Government and 25 percent by State Government). Under which Tamil Nadu State Rural Livelihoods Mission (TNSRLM) is being implemented in the State since 2012-2013 onwards.

Mission of Aajeevika Skills and Placement Programme has to evolve strategies and practices, based on employment generation and time bound action plan that can be implemented. Its vision is that every youth in the targeted families of absolute poverty should have obtained skill training leading to gainful employment, reduce attrition and improve their retention in job. Key features of the programme is placement linked, market driven training for 3 to 12 months and trained youth are assured of jobs after skills training (of 80 percent in minimum). Aajeevika Skills target 1,26,100 rural youth (poor) in the age group of 18-35 years; and differently-abled, vulnerable groups (SCs, minorities, women), and tribals (STs) between 18-45 years in the 12th Plan period (2012-2017). Special focus is on Below Poverty Line (BPL) households, Persons with Disabilities (PwD), victims of trafficking, manual scavengers, transgenders, rehabilitated bonded labours, alike people. Youth who have worked as labourers in Mahatma Gandhi National Rural Employment Guarantee (MGNREG) work sites for at least 35 days in each of the previous three years will also be eligible for Aajeevika Skills and Placement Programme even if they are not from BPL. Aajeevika Skills and Placement Programme builds awareness within the community on the employment opportunities and impart knowledge, industry linked skills and attitude that enhances employability of youth in the formal sector. To achieve this aim, Aajeevika Skills and Placement Programme has adopted the strategies of skill gap analysis, skill and job 'mela', exposure visits, career guidance cell, migration support centres and alumni support. Commonly identified fields of skill training are Health/Nursing Assistants, IT Services, Textile/Apparel, Driving, Hospitality Management, Welding, Construction, Carpentry, Electrical/Electronics and Plumbing. However, new training fields are also identified like - Banking Correspondents (BC), Banking Facilitators (BF), National Bank for Agriculture and Rural Development (NABARD) promoted IIBF - Bima Mitra, Debt Recovery Agent (DRA), Rehabilitation Council of India (RCI) promoted Disability Mitigation Facilitators, Ticketing and Travelling, Solar Plant Maintenance and Repair, Accounting, Home Appliances Repair, Ship Chandlering, Stevedoring Freight (forwarding handling), Ship Building Mechanics (Maritime Unit). Moreover, Enterprise Development Training (EDT) Programme is also envisaged to bring out the latent entrepreneurial talents in SHG women in both rural and urban areas. Every Year 4000 SHG women are trained by quality skill training programme of shorter duration (3-8 weeks). A special thrust to women in the age group above 35 years is given under this programme. And majority of the women (20 percent) are placed in Garment Industry after completion of youth skills development training.

Mr. Anoop Satpathy, Fellow of V. V. Giri National Labour Institute, Noida gave a talk on ***Challenges of Skills Development in India: Recent Government Steps in Skills Space.*** He defined 'skill' as an acquired and practiced ability or to a qualification needed to perform a job or certain task competently. Skill is therefore a multidimensional concept (World Employment Report, 1998). According to him skills are two types: 'marketable skill' and 'formal skill'. Marketable skill is any skill/expertise/ability – which has potential or market value towards generating income or employment. Whereas formal skills are those developed as structured and standardized, so that it's outcomes can be measured or assessed against some objective parameters. He pointed out global trends related to skills. Skilled jobs are growing faster than unskilled employment. Knowledge-based industries are expanding rapidly and with them turning the demand for skills. Wage differentials are rising between skilled and unskilled workers in many regions, driven by skill-based technological change. Unskilled workers are increasingly more vulnerable to job loss, extended unemployment and declining real wages. There is low Labour Force Participation Rate (LFPR) for women and low share of women in the total pool of skills. Therefore, education links with labour market is predominant. In South Asia, gender gap in labour force participation rate changed from 37.8 percent (1991) to 37.5 percent (2001) to 34.1 percent (2011); while the labour force participation rate in the world changed from 16.1 percent (1991) to 16 percent (2001) to 15.6 percent (2011). Demographic data of India show that 54 percent of population is under the age of 25 years. In total workforce of 474 million, only 12-13 million per annum enters into labour force. A meager 13 percent of all university graduates are employable due to extensive shortage of skills. Only 2 percent of the youth and 6.7 percent of the total population (15-59 years) are vocationally trained in India. There is also declining female labour force participation in India. Women participation in labour force which is historically lower than men has even gone down substantially in recent years pointing at female to male percentage being 31:69 (1999-2000) to 28:72 (2009-2010). Similarly, share of female in the labour force has always been lower and in recent years and the share has gone down further (from 30-34 percent to 21 percent in rural areas and from 16-17 percent to 13 percent in urban areas). Decline is largely attributed to increase in educational participation – specially, by rural women. In 2005-2012, male employment growth has been 1.51 percent, while female employment growth has gone down to -2.04 percent.

Mr. Satpathy cautioned that the trend in differences between Employment and Gross Domestic Product (GDP) shares in agriculture and industry seemed to widen more sharply in future. Changing status of employment in India shows that there is declining share of self-employed and increase in the share of wage labour - due to regular employment being stagnant and share of casual works on the increase. According to him, formal employment is shrinking over time and nearly 46 percent of all workers in the formal sector are in informal employment. Size of informal employment is growing over time and much of the future employment will be informal in nature. However, in informal sector there is lack of 'decent work', skills and social security. Therefore, skills development is required in both formal and informal sectors. But there are challenges of skills development. Quantitative challenges of skills development are: entry into labour force (13 million/annum), training capacity (5 million/annum), skill gap (7.8 million/annum), shortage of trainers, regional imbalance and cost of skills training. Qualitative challenges of skills development are: demand-supply mismatch, quality of trainers, low industry participation, rapid change in technology, language, skilled manpower of international standards, job insecurity, recognizing prior learning and demographic dividend. There is an estimated skill gap of 347 million across 22 key sectors like- Building and Construction Industry; Infrastructure Sector; Real Estate Services; Gems and Jewellery; Leather and Leather Goods; Organized Retail; Textiles and Clothing; Electronics and IT-Hardware; Auto and Auto Components; IT and Information Technology Enabled Services; Banking, Financial Services and Insurance; Furniture and Furnishings; Tourism and Hospitality Services; Construction Material and Building Hardware; Chemicals and Pharmaceuticals; Food Processing; Healthcare; Transportation and Logistics; Media and Entertainment; Education and Skill Development Services; Selected Informal Employment Sectors (domestic help, beauticians, security guards); etc.

Mr. Satpathy argued that skill development among women workers had been a major concern and issue. Women are vulnerable and disadvantaged category in the labour market. Labour force participation of women in India is declining and it is one of the lowest in the world. Informal employment is predominant form of employment for women - mostly in low quality jobs and in invisible jobs. He pointed that out of every 100 workers only 22 are women. Therefore, skill development of women is a crucial element as skill levels of women workers are very low and acquired informally, i.e., learning by doing. Existing institutional arrangements are not suitable for women workers. Many women in the informal sector are running small businesses and cannot bear the cost of training. Women workers cannot afford full-time, long period training due to their need to earn livelihood and child care. No incentive is also given to women for acquiring new skills. Therefore, existing institutional arrangements are unsuitable for women and there is need to develop arrangements to suit the requirements of women workers as essential for any skill training programme. Hence, new innovative and flexible arrangements are required. Government should recognize work experience not education for women as entry qualification, due to high rates of dropout in school/college. Hours of training, its location and duration need to be flexible and cost of training should be free or minimum. Training of women informal workers in formal enterprises can be at public cost. There is a need to focus from basic literacy and numeracy to technical training to social networking and problems relating to balance home and workplace duties for women. Training will need to build up capabilities to shift from one profession to another or offer multi-skill abilities to women. Therefore, women's skill training is to be combined with livelihood promotion. Importantly, barriers (cultural, attitudinal, qualificatory) to skill development need to be reduced for women workers in India.

He also discussed National Skills Policy targeting 500 million skilled workers by 2022. Prime Minister's National Council for Skill Development (NCSD) is an apex body to give policy directions. National Skill Development Coordination Board (NSCB) works to harmonize government initiatives and National Skill Development Corporation (NSDC) fosters private sector participation in skills training and employment. Outcome expected from the policy and implementing agencies is to make the labour market system dynamic to match demand and supply of skills on real time so that total domestic requirement can be met and surplus may be offered to other aged and ageing economies of the world. Mr. Satpathy concluded that skilled jobs are growing faster than unskilled employment. And India needs to create 500 million skilled man- and woman-power by 2020.

Dr. K. Vasantha, Head of Department of Lifelong Learning and Extension in Avinashilingam Deemed University for Women, Coimbatore spoke on *Enhancing Women Empowerment through Skill Training*. She spread a strong message to the symposium participants. According to her, removal of gender discrimination is the key to real empowerment of women. Time has come to recognize and acknowledge women's critical contribution to national economic development. It is to be realized that unless we involve women into development process, the development will remain lopsided and incomplete. Thus, women empowerment is an essential pre-requisite for socio-economic progress of the nation. However, the human resource among women could not be utilized effectively due to illiteracy, low education and lack of skills for productive work. There is a dire need for intervention to raise the status of women by – education, skill development, vocational training, income generation activities and employment. She pointed out the advantages of imparting skill training to women: a) preparing the youth for a vocation of their choice; b) producing millions of trained people in agriculture, floriculture, horticulture, sericulture, fishery, healthcare, tourism and in the manufacturing sector; c) reducing unemployment by supplying world-class skilled people; d) reducing cost and improve the productivity of services and manufacturing by providing skilled manpower to international standards.

Dr. Vasantha continued to share the role of the Department of Life Long Learning and Extension in teaching, training, life-long learning programmes (on- and off-campus) and research related to need-based skills development for women. The department is offering vocational training (1-6 months Certificate courses) for rural and urban women of Coimbatore District in the following areas (in need and demand) – Income Generating Courses; Catering and Canteen Management; Preparation of Jam, Jelly, Squash and Pickle; Nutritious Fast Food; Bakery Techniques; Preparation of Masala Powders; Preparation of Salads and Soups; Appalam, Vathal and Vadam Making; Painting (Fabric, Glass, Nib, Pot etc.); Flower Arrangement and Bouquet Making; Preparation of Nutritious Weaning Foods; Flower Tying; Creative Gift Articles; Soft Toy Making; etc. The departmental vocational training programmes create self-employment and entrepreneurship opportunities for women, generating monthly income from Rupees 2,000-13,000. Post training women also find jobs in local areas with salary of Rupees 2,500-6,000 per month. From 2005 to 2013, about 26,307 women have been benefitted from the vocational training programmes offered by the department. According to Dr. Vasantha, schemes initiated by the Government have not been able to make any serious impact on women's development and empowerment. It is because of lack of clarity in objectives and inadequate understanding of women's multiple roles within and outside the home. There are major difficulties in identifying target groups and inability to reach the needy women and mobilize community support for women. There is widespread neglect of economic roles and training in productive skills of women in society. Lack of facilitators with proper training and orientation is also an issue in skill development for women. Finally, rigidity in design and structure of the programmes adversely affect women's interest in skills development and thereby their empowerment.

Her recommendations are to: i) place vocational education and skill training entirely under the Ministry of Human Resource Development (MHRD); ii) integrate Vocational Education Training (VET) within the mainstream education system; iii) monitor and assess the impact of vocational education and training; iv) increase allocation of resources to vocational education and training; outreach VET through innovative delivery models; v) improve training options for the unorganized and informal sector; vi) build capacities of the institutional structures; vii) enforce regulatory, accreditation, certification and proper frameworks. Dr. Vasantha stressed that education without skills training would keep the women groping in the darkness.

Chair of the skills and vocational training session, **Dr. U. Jerinabi**, Dean of Commerce and Business Administration of Avinashilingam Deemed

University for Women, Coimbatore; highlighted on the importance of vocational skills and availability of National and State Government funds for skills training, especially, for women. She pointed out that vocational training would help youth to be employable and be 'ready' for employment in industry. The vocational skills help youth to perform well at work and increases human productivity, which in turn helps to achieve higher economic growth and development for the nation. She emphasized that new generation students should be motivated to be the 'job provider' rather than 'job seeker'. She highlighted the activities undertaken by the Department of Life Long Learning and Jan Shikshan Sansthan (JSS) functioning under the Avinashilingam Education Trust and achievements in women empowerment and community development through its diverse programmes. She also suggested that skills should be given to all university students as part of their curriculum. She pointed out the importance of vocational courses for women and informed that the Avinashilingam Institute for Home Science and Higher Education for Women has been offering Bachelor of Vocational Education (B.Voc.) keeping in mind with this objective. She highlighted on the opportunities available for women in vocational training through the Ministry of Human Resource Development (MoHRD).

TECHNICAL SESSION IV: Science & Technology

The fourth session was on 'Making Science and Technology Women-friendly'. The session was oriented to motivating girls and women students to study science and work in scientific and technological professions. The session discussed issues, challenges and contributions of women doing Science, Technology, Engineering, and Medicine (STEM). It categorically addressed capacity building and mentoring of women scientists and return of women professionals after career break due to family and social responsibility. The session was chaired by Prof. Krishna Misra, Senior Scientist and Past General Secretary of National Academy of Sciences, India (NASI).

Dr. M. Vijayalakshmi, Associate Director of Indira Gandhi Centre for Atomic Research (IGCAR), Kalpakkam gave a lecture on *Gender Equality in Science: An Unfinished Dream*. In her special talk she questioned whether gender bias - a fiction or fact? Are women not empowered? Why should anyone else empower anybody else? Man or woman - both have equal hurdles and challenges, equal priorities like family and child upbringing. So why single out women? But reality in our society is different. Till 18th Century, women did not have right to vote, an unimaginable circumstance for anybody of today. Therefore, today's inequalities will be unimaginable and surprising for the future generation. There is a widespread gender disparity in terms of standard of living due to unequal wages and unemployment rate (females - 6.4 percent and males - 5.7 percent). 70 percent of world's most vulnerable population living below poverty line (BPL) are none other than women. Therefore, gender bias is unfortunately a fact at all levels in society. Thus, gender equality must be launched through transparent, merit based, unbiased system. However, she questioned whether demand of concessions for women should be withdrawn when gender equality got established. Dr. Vijayalakshmi further asked whether the possible reasons for gender difference were population distribution, inherent differences, evolutionary influences and/or biased environment. She cited *Indian National Science Academy* (INSA) Report of 2004. It agrees skewed gender distribution present in India, since about 50 percent of cases are deliberate elimination of female foeticides and infanticides. Though research points out that gray matter concentration differs from female to male (females > males) and females having higher emotional intelligence, however there are no inherent differences between male and female brains. She also recalled evolutionary influences towards women's equality from medieval to modern to postmodern period in India by Raja Ram Mohan Roy, Ishwar Chandra Vidyasagar, Swami Dayanand Saraswati and Mahatma Gandhi.

Dr. Vijayalakshmi informed the participants about a crazy experiment by Professor Ben Barres of Stanford University who chose to have a medical process to become a woman to note personal experience as both a female and male scientist and found that he was treated with more respect as a male than female scientist by society. Therefore, gender bias environment in family and society is primarily responsible for gender inequality in India. There is also gender inequality in Science and Technology (S&T) – 30 percent female doctorates in Science and 40 percent in Arts (INSA Report, 2004). Among 233 Indian universities, 50 percent enrolled women are in the age group of 20s and less than 10 percent women are in the age group of 50s. In All India Institutes of Medical Sciences (AIIMS) and Indian Institutes of Technology (IITs) women represent only 39 percent and 10 percent respectively. Employed S&T women in Council of Scientific and Industrial Research (CSIR), Department of Atomic Energy (DAE), Indian Institute of Science (IISc), etc., together constitute less than 15 percent. More women either drop out or accept low profile jobs, vacated by men due to low profitability, irrespective of holding MSc and PhD degrees in Science. Number of women is far less in the top scientific posts or science awards or as fellows of national academies of sciences. Reasons and related factors are 'Leaky Pipeline Effect' and 'Glass Ceiling Effect' due to gender discrimination, inequality, dropout due to marriage and child/elder care. Value of education and science education in particular has not reached to "poor" communities and so "girls" are taken away from school to augment family income or help parents earn more. Societal pressure, lack of perception, economic factors, access to school/colleges near home, dowry problems, etc. – lead to early marriage and dropout of female students. Percentage of women who reach professor post is 10 percent in global and only 1 percent in India. Top level posts in S&T by women is 2 percent (Indian Academy of Sciences has 28 Women Associates; Indian National Science Academy has 3 Women Fellows), while in Art, Business, Finance women represent 25 percent.

According to Dr. Vijayalakshmi, problem is not 'men versus women' or 'home maker versus bread winner'. Home making and bread winning are equally important social requirements for both men and women. The pressing need is to launch a matured society using the best characteristics of both genders portraying societal concern towards equal opportunity. However, the major problem is getting more women to study science, since those who complete their studies are unable to pursue career in science and those who pursue career in science are unable to come to the top. Attrition after higher education in science is a national waste; since, nation spends enormous resources for training scientists. When women drop out from learning and career in science, it is a 'national waste' of those resources. Possible reasons for gender inequality in science are: due to the fact that globally, gender inequality changes from region to region and time to time; and the reasons and remedies of gender inequality are also not common. In India, major problems in society are livelihood, health care, literacy; and in this backdrop, women's education, job opportunities in Science & Technology, leadership in S&T hold low priority. However, situation will definitely improve with improved economy of the country. According to her, possible remedial measures are: i) getting more women to study science by letting equal number of boys and girls to complete schools and enter colleges; ii) more women are to be motivated to finish PhDs and better job opportunities to be created so that women can pursue career in science after completing studies; iii) equal number of women as men are to be regarded as "eligible" to pursue career in science and to come up to the top positions. To encourage women in scientific profession, professional rigidity can be relaxed; social attitudes to be changed slowly in a positive direction; presence of job opportunities for both men and women as economic reforms; and support system can be introduced. Scientific profession, at the serious level, is very competitive and challenging. It demands active research and teaching life, guiding PhD students and projects, national and international collaborations, peer recognition, good visibility and good mentors. Therefore, compulsion to be established oneself as a scientist by the age of 30 is difficult to be achieved by women. Breaks or low profile in early 30s kill the forward momentum towards better later years, when family demand reduces; so can be too many concessions or leaves. Therefore, solutions for men and women are - family/professional domestic support; provision to work from home; flexi time; child/elder care facilities; 'performance' linked pay. Thus important considerations for women in S&T are: transparency in job selection; job continuity or similar opportunities in new place of transfers/displacement due to marriage; transportation, accommodation, child/elder care facilities; campus housing, infrastructure for balancing home and office; employment for eligible spouses in same organization; service sectors to tune to the concept of 'working women'. Similarly important are: gender-neutral (not 'favoured') policies; transparency in welfare policy, assignment of projects, recognition, 're-entry' opportunities based on merit; equal opportunities for networking and collaborations; mentoring and support mechanisms; schemes for display of gender equality in the organization; non-stigmatization of women for being "privileged".

Dr. Vijayalakshmi reminded about the myth of S&T Policy that no policy can fit all since there is large diversity in the nature of the problem in terms of urban/rural divide, economic status, family attitude and education. Periodic review of the policy implementation and feedback are equally necessary.

According to her, UGC, NCERT, science funding agencies and national academies together should recommend 'social and system engineering' and financial implications to the government. However, they should ensure that social engineering does not lead to 'unhappy' families but entire exercise is to launch happy society with gender equality. She concluded that recognition and acceptance of gender inequality as social evil should be the most important and identification of methods to do social engineering would be the next priority. She called for S&T to be gender sensitive by reducing female infanticide, giving compulsory education to all, improving job opportunities, increasing flexibility in jobs, improving work environment, ensuring equal wages for equal nature of jobs, giving professional recognition, enforcing women empowerment and changing social values.

She concluded with the words: "No SINGLE policy can fit all... We need to devise several policies responding to the needs of the particular group of people, depending on their background, location and other societal factors."

Dr. Jyoti Sharma, Principal Scientific Officer of Science for KIR AN & Science for Equity, Empowerment and Development (SEED) Divisions in the Department of Science and Technology (DST) spoke on *Impact of Policy Decisions and Technology Development on Women Scientists and Society*. From time immemorial and around the world, education and empowerment of women have always acted as the catalyst for rapid socio-economic growth and change. According to her, S&T is a major factor for women empowerment. Women as the specific target group is included in science to develop need-specific technologies to reduce women's drudgery on one hand and develop women entrepreneurship on the other. The relationship that Indian women and science share is about women's inclusion in science and science and technology for women. Dr. Sharma pointed out high wastage ratio of women S&T personnel due to motherhood and other family and social problems. The data reveal that in all, there are 66,302 women employed in research and Development (R&D) establishments, which is approximately 17 percent of the total workforce in the country. She mentioned that Indian Government had announced 2010-2020 as the 'decade of innovation'. Human Resource Development Minister pitched in to spell out the goal of India as an "innovation super power" by 2030. At this juncture, Dr. Sharma asked to think where did women stand in S&T and what would be women's contribution to make India 'innovation super power'?

Women constitute an important section of the workforce in S&T. But, there exists a wide gap between percentage of women studying science and percentage of women doing science. Yet, the overwhelming present situation is that due to diverse socio-personal circumstances a large number of well-educated women scientists and technologists dropout from the S&T activities, which needs to be attended immediately. DST has been making a concerted effort on-behalf of the government to give women a strong foothold into the scientific profession, help them re-enter into the mainstream and provide a launch pad for further forays into the field of S&T. During the first five year plans i.e., from 1951-1979, government adopted *Welfare Approach* however during 6th Five-Year Plan (1980-1984), government shifted its approach from *Welfare to Development*. Department of Science & Technology started the scheme 'S&T for Women' (1981) during this plan period. In the 7th Five-Year Plan (1985-1989),

Department of Women & Child Development had been setup (1985) as a part of Human Resource development and upgraded into the Ministry in 2006. In the 8th Five-Year Plan (1992-1997), National Commission for Women was setup (1992) and Women Development Corporations had been also setup in different States. In the 9th Five-Year Plan (1997-2002), Women Component Plan was adopted to ensure not less than 30 percent funds were earmarked for women related activities in all Ministries. Biotechnology Applications for Women had also been setup by the Department of Biotechnology (DBT). Year 2001 was celebrated as Women Empowerment Year and National Policy for Empowerment of Women was released by the Department of Women & Child Development (DWCD). Science & Technology aspect in National Policy for Women Empowerment in 2001 had directed to strengthen and bring about a greater involvement of women in science and technology; including awareness generation, motivation, participation, skills training, appropriate technology to reduce drudgery of women. In the 10th Five-Year Plan (2003-2007), Science & Technology(S&T) Policy 2003 was released by the Ministry of Science and Technology with the objective to promote the empowerment of women in all science and technology activities and to ensure their full and equal participation in it. During this plan period, Fellowship Scheme for Women Scientists was launched and Women Scientists Cell was setup at DST. In 2005, Scientific Advisory Council to the Prime Minister (SAC-PM) Task Force on women in science was formed. In the 11th Five-Year Plan (2007-2012), all Women Scientists/Technologists oriented schemes under DST were revamped, recast and re-energized. Biotechnology Career Advancement and Re-orientation Programme for women scientist (Bio-Care) was started in 2010-11 by DBT. In the 12th Five-Year Plan (2012-2017), all women oriented schemes have been covered under the umbrella of 'KIR AN'. It has introduced Mobility Scheme and Internship under Women Fellowship Scheme. During this plan, it is targeted to set up more Women Technology Parks to develop women friendly technologies and strengthen women entrepreneurs.

Dr. Sharma further pointed out nine issues and challenges faced by Indian women scientists as: i) lack of family support/motivation to pursue education and long term career in science; ii) lack of awareness regarding available opportunities; iii) lack of avenues for knowledge and skill enhancement leading to capacity building; iv) obstacles in re-entry in science oriented career after career-break due to various reasons; v) lack of opportunities for an alternate career path; vi) lack of mentorship; vii) lack of avenues of self-employment and entrepreneurship; viii) lack of representation in higher forums, committees, and higher decision making positions; and ix) career retention or sustainability issues due to relocation challenge. The five obstacles to women in S&T education are: (a) access or availability of science education in rural areas; (b) affordability of fees of science education; (c) patriarchal stereotyping attitude in the family and society; (d) dropout due to lack of mentoring; (e) absence of recognition by merit scholarship. Whereas, the obstacles to women in S&T career are retention of women scientists due to leaky-pipeline and glass-ceiling effects, and lack of support systems. Recruitment in S&T career is not a women friendly procedure. Re-entry in S&T career after a break due to child/elder care is not permitted. R&D participation by women is very low. Moreover, outreach of resources for skill improvement for women in S&T is not available, refresher course or training for mid-career continuation or education is also missing. Recognition of women scientists in the scientific forum or committee is not given and rewarding of women scientists by award or fellowship is insignificant in number. Unequal remuneration/wage for equal nature of job and non-availability of self-employment opportunity add to the list of above mentioned limitations for women in science in India. Government is addressing these challenges by trying to retain women in science and help re-entry of women scientists after a break into career paths within S&T sector. Government is working towards increasing the representation of women in Science, Technology, Engineering and Mathematics (STEM). It is providing avenues for capacity building, skill enhancement both at National and Global level.

Women face several problems, most significant are 'career breaks' due to motherhood and family obligations or responsibilities. Moreover, restrictions on age and qualification overburden women's option to revive their professional development at post-break in science career. Keeping this in mind, DST's 'KIR AN' Scheme has introduced a balancing approach and to enforce gender parity in science. 'KIR AN' is a scheme to address issues and challenges faced by the women S&T professionals in India, not only through the existing/on-going programmes of the DST but also by launching new initiatives in a holistic manner. Objectives of KIR AN are to utilize the potential of women scientists/technologists in S&T based empowerment process of the nation; to develop awareness of women scientists towards development in emerging areas of Science & Technology; to provide opportunity for capacity building in technology relevant areas; and to provide opportunity for women scientist/technologist for re-entry after a break. Its primary objective is to bring back the women scientists in the mainstream after 'break in their careers'.

KIR AN includes: (a) S&T for Women; (b) Women Fellowship Scheme; (c) Mobility (providing feasible employment opportunities for employed women S&T professionals whose careers are otherwise stuck or discontinued due to familial as well as social obligations on account of relocation, or to provide an alternate career path for women scientists); (d) Capacity/Orientation Building (organize leadership/mentorship programmes, science policy and general management, entrepreneurship development and management, communication and presentation skills); and (e) Institutional Development (focusing on 6 all women universities/institutions in India, including Avinashilingam Deemed University for Women). Dr. Sharma informed that there are three Women Fellowship Schemes – (i) Basic Research Fellowship – BRF (for pursuing research in basic or applied sciences in frontier areas of science and engineering); (ii) Societal Research Fellowship – SoRF (scholarship for research in S&T - based Societal Programmes); (iii) Intellectual Property Rights - (trains women with qualifications in science/engineering/medicine/ allied subjects on intellectual property rights [IPR] and its management for one year to help them generate Self-Employment in related career in S&T). Women Fellowship Scheme is especially envisioned to support women scientists in research, development and innovation in S&T applications meeting various societal issues, problems and needs. The scholarship is offered to aspiring women scientists with extended upper age limit up to 57 years, who can demonstrate S&T skills and techniques, research and design, application and adaptation in order to reduce drudgery, enhance capacity building, generate income activity for weaker sections of our society at grassroots level.

Outcome of these Women Fellowship Scheme are very much encouraging. Moreover, affiliation with DST has helped women scientists to earn not only their livelihoods but also receive higher esteem within the society by being empowered both socially and academically. DST schemes have generated among women scientists great sense of sensitivity for the grass-root women with whom they are working. These women scientists also enjoy the sense of self-dependence and increase in confidence. According to Dr. Sharma, the Government confirms its interest in S&T training for Indian women and retaining their scientific talents and encouraging them towards scientific pursuits. Government is also keen to offer flexible 'work from home', enabling them to strike a good work-life balance between professional and domestic demands of Indian women.

Chair of the science and technology session was **Professor Krishna Misra**, Senior Scientist and Past General Secretary of National Academy of Sciences, India (NASI). She is also the Honorary Professor of Indian Institute of Information Technology (IIIT), Allahabad and Centre for Biomedical Magnetic Resonance (CBMR) at Sanjay Gandhi Post Graduate Institute of Medical Sciences (SGPGIMS) campus, Lucknow. Prof. Misra put major stress on 'women power'. She quoted the words of Diane Mariechild, "a woman is the full circle, within her is the power to create, nurture, and transform". Women form 50 percent of global population and the rest 50 percent have been created by her. She believed that one woman could change many things and many women could change everything. According to Prof. Misra, women form 50 percent of human resource, play vital role in the development of societies and nations. Indian women have played crucial role in multiple challenges facing the nation in the past, example- freedom struggle and also as leaders after independence. They excel in all walks of life including corporate/business sectors, example- Kiran Mazumdar-Shaw (Managing Director, Biocon Ltd.), Chanda Kochhar (MD, ICICI Bank) and Arundhati Bhattacharya (Chairperson, State Bank of India). Out of three persons of Indian origin who went into space two were women - Kalpana Chawla and Sunita Williams. She felt the need of promoting Science and Technology for nation's progress, since no nation could achieve economic independence, cultural and social progress without S&T. Major problems of India can only be solved through technology and many of these through biotechnology. Since majority of the Indian population lives in villages, therefore, main emphasis is to be on 'rural technology. The then Prime Minister Manmohan Singh in his address at the Centenary celebration of Indian Science Congress at Kolkata confirmed that "to address the discrepancies in science in India and to free it from 'bureaucratism', it is vital to attract more women to the field of science." Prof. Misra pointed out that one of the major issues faced by India today seemed to be the facilities for science education and participation of girls and women in science education. Women are primarily regarded and designated to be the 'caregivers' for families throughout the developing world. They have to manage family budget. In some parts of the country women walk few kilometres everyday for fetching water or cooking fuel. They cook food and are responsible for nutrition and general health of the family members. They are required to be expert paramedics to manage early symptoms of diseases.

Women in developing countries comprise nearly 70 percent agriculture labour but still continue to account for over 60 percent of world's hunger. Most rural women are agricultural labourers, they grow majority food for household consumption, and are mainly involved in food processing. Despite the critical role women play in food and health security, rural women are denied of the resources, information and freedom of action for fulfilling their responsibilities. Girls in rural sector are mostly deprived of getting education. Women have less access to credit, agricultural extension services and land ownership. They do not have much power or voice in decision making. Prof. Misra therefore stated that elite women scientists did have greater responsibility to bridge disparity between women's actions and resources. She reinforced, women scientists in cities did have a crucial role to play to make their rural sisters more aware and empowered to fight for their rights. Although at Government level women empowerment has been a high priority, there is only 30 percent participation of women at District Panchayat and Municipalities. However, this tokenistic participation cannot help unless women are more aware of their rights and responsibilities. According to Prof. Misra, reservation of any kind will not help. Women are not weak, they are strong, resilient, not vulnerable. They have to learn to get out of such situations. Situation like- women's education has improved remarkably in Indian cities. Those women with personal drive, integrity and capability to manage conflicts can help change country's future. Hence, the overall objectives should be, capacity building in biotechnology and its application to agriculture specially through genetically modified (GM) products; ecological restoration of degraded forests; water harvesting; waste land utilization; crash crops and medicinal plants; self-employment through micro-credits; women empowerment through professional training; and Governmental investment in agriculture through District and State Agricultural Plans (DAP/SAP). According to Prof. Misra, major issues of India can be solved through biotechnology like- i) safe drinking water; ii) hunger/malnutrition; iii) health, hygiene and cheaper medicines; iv) agriculture (bio-fertilizers, bio-pesticides and pest resistant plants); and v) environmental safety (conservation of biodiversity, meddling with evolution, bio-remediation). Therefore, research investment should be based on the local problems. Collaborative research on national and international levels is the only solution to bring the State at par with higher national/international standards. Another important concern in the country is women related farm mechanization issues. It is important that tools or self-propelled machines (like tractors, power-tillers, transplanters, power-weeders) suiting to women workers must be designed. Intensive training programmes for rural women to impart them skills to operate these tools/ equipments are the priority. Interventions through alternate media to remove social taboo regarding operation of machines by women are the pressing needs.

Promotion of these improved tools and hand-holding of women workers using these tools are the significant steps. Proper coordination between different implementing agencies- Central/State departments, agricultural universities/institutes, Non Governmental Organizations (NGOs) – needs to be made. New or alternative income sources for poor women farmers or villagers need to be identified.

Prof. Misra also suggested that the forest department should formulate comprehensive and holistic 'Afforestation Projects' for forest dependent villagers based on Joint Forest Management (JFM) principles with financial assistance from some global sponsoring agency like World Health Organization (WHO) or Japan International Cooperation Agency (JICA). The role and responsibility of the user community living adjacent to these forests should be recognized as a crucial factor and they should be given the role of stakeholders and co-managers. The alleviation of poverty of the rural population who are mainly forest dependents is the key to ensure proper participatory management. Poverty and forest degradation invariably create a vicious circle where one leads to the other. The forest dependents and the other poorer sections may be introduced to several alternative income generation activities. The women need to be organized into Self Help Groups (SHGs) for economic development and empowerment. Capacity building of the local people (both men and women) is also one of the key indicators of development. They are to be provided with basic training in manufacturing, processing and marketing techniques.

Microcredit as seed for economic development is to be initiated widely. Microcredit is a financial innovation, which started with Grameen Bank. It is the provision and extension of financial services to the people below poverty line, so that they can themselves engage in self-employment projects generating income, gradually build wealth and exit poverty. Initially small amount of loans may be given for self-employment by skills training in embroidery, sewing, painting, textile designing, processing miscellaneous food products/consumer goods; and to farmers for seeds, fertilizers, insecticides, etc. Loans may also be given to small scale entrepreneurs for farming cash crops and medicinal or commercially important plants. Cash crops (cotton, jute, sugarcane, etc.) are grown for commercial gain and contribute to the growing economy of the country. Cultivation of medicinal plants like turmeric, aloe-vera, mentha (peppermint), poppy, isabgol, senna, cinchona, ipecac, belladonna, ergot, etc., also fetch good financial gains for women farmers. Extraction of medicinal plants at the site of their cultivation and selling the crude extracts in the form of powders or tablets can also be a good earner for women farmers and local entrepreneurs. Collection of raw material from forests can also form a part of the project, which can be further processed and sold. The organizers of these projects/programmes may help in marketing and/or selling of the produced items by local women to relevant market places. The returned loan amount may again be circulated to new women consumers and producers. Afforestation must be according to the needs of the local women and should be on sustainable basis. These socio-economic development projects/programmes can be made as an inter-sectoral linkage benefitting from the measures implemented by other Central and State Government Departments.

According to Prof. Misra, the first step of technology development for the underprivileged rural women is to identify their felt needs. This identification is best done through direct contact and 'learning from the people' as undertaken by the 'extension centres' located in rural setting. The specific felt needs thus identified have to be translated into technical changes. These technical changes must challenge technical personnel (women scientists and technologists as well) and motivate them to create appropriate solutions to the rural problems and especially in the context of rural women. The technical challenges must involve rural constraints like- low cost and ease of operation. Thus, the technical solutions that succeed are unlikely to be trivial or 'low' technology. Whether solutions are appropriate or not, must be monitored by going back 'to the people' and 'test marketing' the solutions. Prof. Misra also stated about the contributions of National Academy of Sciences, India (NASI) towards women empowerment. Through Science Communication programme NASI approaches rural masses, makes them aware of the latest developments in S&T. Development of water testing kit, food adulteration kit and distributing these kits free to rural population are major achievements of NASI. Participation of NASI in exclusively women programmes of Department of Science and Technology (DST) like 'Disha', 'Kiran' and Societal Research Fellowship (SoRF) programmes for women scientists is also significant. Educating rural population regarding clean and green technologies is the academy's future goal. Under the guidance of visionary Dr. Manju Sharma, Women Chair at NASI, it hopes the voices of women scientists will be heard by the government and people alike and common women will get justice in order to protect their rights. Prof. Misra, concluded the session urging to let gender parity prevail so that contribution from both genders could uplift the economy of the country.

TECHNICAL SESSION V: Full & Decent Employment

The fifth session was on 'Creating Equal Opportunity to Full and Decent Employment for Women'. The session questioned Equal Opportunity Law and its enforcement on women workers at large in Indian society. The session highlighted women's invisible participation in decent employment and self-employment areas. In fact, there is a larger 'push' for women to get into casual and unorganized job sectors where occupational health hazards and lack of labour/employee welfare supersede. Therefore the session raised issues like - equal work, equal pay, minimum wages, allocation of work space and resources, consideration of home as work place, flexible working time, health and safety benefits – as the integral parts of full and decent employment for women in the workforce. The session was chaired by Economist Binod Khadria, Professor of Economics of Education in Jawaharlal Nehru University, New Delhi.

Ms. Sonia George, General Secretary of Self Employed Women's Association (SEWA Kerala) shared her views on the various employment opportunities available in the informal sector and the role SEWA plays to safeguard full and decent employment for women in India. The institutional setting of SEWA creates scopes for women to negotiate terms of work regularity, decent wages, safe work conditions, social security and women welfare-development-empowerment. SEWA has unique experience with its strong political link to 'trade-union' women workforce across the nation. She pointed out that male-female bread winners were increasingly emerging due to women's financial requirement to be in the labour force for the sake of family livelihood. She highlighted that over 93 percent of workforce in the country fell under the informal sector of employment. The struggles of women workers are more discerning as they work in the most marginalized and neglected sectors within the unorganized sector. She raised the 'gap' questions like – whether women in informal sector had right to equal pay for equal work or right to minimum wage; and allocation of equal work, resource, work place/space? She stressed that in all existing work scenario of women's participation, decent work standards were lacking across India.

She further asked if employer, family or society considered 'home' as workplace for women in terms of full and decent employment? Though, domestic work is one of the growing sectors of employment generation for women due to the emerging notion of 'care economy'. Women's participation in any kind of economic sector is undervalued and poorly regulated irrespective of the skills women possess or hard work women put in to sustain their livelihoods and economic security. Moreover, commercialization of traditional sectors and cottage industries have led to men going out and the whole burden being transferred to women, turning them to workers to entrepreneurs and face economic challenges. Addressing the problems of Self Help Group (SHG), she asked if it was really improving the condition of the equality of gender. According to her, social reproduction at multi-dimensional levels is taking place at the cost of women's needs and welfare; since there are no questions asked about adequate facilities, necessary provisions, equal wages, safe working conditions, employment rights and benefits. Therefore, the pertinent question is: what is the status of the new-generation women workers?

According to Ms. George, 'decent work' can be achieved by changing the attitude of society and people, rather than by means of law or legal system. Fundamental challenge is whether women workers can achieve their most sought dignity through collective organizing, collective bargaining and collective professionalizing. She concluded her talk by asking, whether employment or self-employment was by women's own 'choice' or by family or societal 'compulsion'? Equal opportunity should be given for unequal people, especially equal opportunity should be given to women, as they hold unequal rank in every society and community. However, the question now is whether women need equal opportunity or 'special opportunity'? In other words, whether women need positive-discrimination by society, rather than non-discrimination? She suggested that more micro-studies need to correlate the various aspects for better understanding and reducing the gaps between men and women at large.

Chair of the full and decent employment session **Professor Binod Khadria**, Economics of Education, Jawaharlal Nehru University, New Delhi; continued the session by asking whether there had been equal opportunities for women at all? Whether women have decent jobs, and whether they are pushed more and more towards dirty and lower paid employment by society? According to him, in recent times, although equal opportunity is given some importance, equal employment does not receive due attention. He raised the concept of 'Decent Employment', which was not given due importance in India but debated in those very developed countries where Indian men as well as women prefer to migrate for work. He stated the example of Kerala, from where most men migrate to the Gulf countries to seek better opportunities of employment in un-skilled and semi-skilled sectors of the labour market; whereas women prefer UK, US, Canada, Australia and European Countries to take up nursing and paramedical professions. But cultural hurdles and thereby lack of participation in decision-making by girls and women going abroad make them vulnerable to temporary and indecent employment. He stressed that in general, women's decision to be the beneficiary in employment or even to avail an equal opportunity was decided upon not by themselves, but by their family members who always kept the welfare of the whole family foremost in mind, not that of the concerned individual woman. 'Gendering labour' should therefore be advocated to be practiced in both the unorganized and the organized sectors and in micro as well as macro industries.

In this context, Prof. Khadria asked whether reservation for women was justified and acceptable. He felt that even 50 percent reservation for women might not be appropriate or adequate in some cases. Judging the current status of women in India, according to him, even 75 percent of the opportunities should be targeted towards women in order to bring the two genders on equal footing. He vouched for disregarding the stereotype of the rhetoric, "there is no need for reservation for women *as women are not weak*". To him, there are many sections of society, where women are deprived in every way and every day, and they certainly need representations, extra services and differential benefits so as to enable them to struggle against odds in life and survive along with other fortunate women as well as men. Therefore girls' education, livelihood and employment should be understood in the relative perspectives and their inter-linkage must be introduced by the Government in its policies, schemes and programmes. Unless, the linkage is established across these three spheres (education, livelihood, employment), there is no point in introducing separate but segregated schemes for women.

There is need to empower girls from the very beginning so as to pre-empt their lack of skills in negotiating their strategic needs like wages, working conditions, job satisfaction and so on. Women also lack legal awareness and fail to exercise their legal rights or demand fairness and justice for themselves. It is also important not to overlook intra-gender discrimination in those sectors, where both the owners and the employees are women and exploitation of women by women is prevalent. In short, there is an urgent need to revisit Indian laws and regulations and introduce enough flexibility to adapt to the special situations and contexts specific to girls and women in work in Indian society and culture. Prof. Khadria called for industry and academia to come together to undertake further research on such issues. It must turn the former's human resource management practices from being decided mechanically to innovative and imaginative processes, which but incorporate appropriate gender concerns and discretions.

RECOMMENDATIONS

The conclusive recommendations made by the distinguished panel chairs at the end of the two day symposium on national empowerment of girls and women are as following:

- ❖ Nutrition, under-nutrition and micronutrient deficiency especially among adolescent girls' and elderly should be given priority;

- ❖ Gender study should be included in the school and college education as curricular and co-curricular courses;

- ❖ Vocational skills training provide employment and self-employment opportunities for women, whereby their productive contributions are recognized in human resource development and economic growth of India;

- ❖ Science, Technology and Engineering education for girls and women should be encouraged at community levels so that national progress is equally benefitted by women's innovations and contributions;

- ❖ Decent employment should consider flexi-time and flexi-place, occupational health and safety for women workers; since requirements of women labour force is not the same as for men.

It was agreed by the dignitaries that the recommendations would not only benefit micro-studies and long-term research, but perhaps contribute to the overall government initiatives in order to bring 'women empowerment' a reality.

<u>**Recommendations emerging from Technical Session I**</u>

STRATEGY FOR REDUCING MALNUTRITION AND IMPROVING HEALTH OF GIRLS AND WOMEN

Experts emphasized on the need to focus on national nutrition priorities such as under nutrition, over nutrition and micronutrient deficiencies such as Anemia, Vitamin A deficiency (VAD), Vitamin D deficiency (VDD) and iodine deficiency disorders (IDD).

▶ There is a need to focus on nutritional concerns of the elderly.

▶ There should be emphasis on social behaviour change communication.

▶ Focus on women from adolescence. Further focus on 1st 1000 days from conception to first 2 years of life.

▶ Diagnose anemia at least among pregnant women before treating anemia.

▶ Find out the most appropriate intervention based on the level of anemia:

• Whether iron should be given along with Folic acid alone or with vitamin B12 alone or with B12 and Folic acid.

• De-worming to be introduced based on the type of worm infestation.

▶ Research can focus on government policies and nutrition programme implementation.

▶ Identify situation specific or local problems and provide solutions for improved programme management.

<u>Recommendations emerging from Technical Session II</u>

GENDER NEUTRAL/SENSITIVE EDUCATION AND DROPOUT PREVENTION FOR GIRLS AND WOMEN

The recommendations are based on some ground realities such as: unavailability of reliable, transparent and exhaustive statistics on access, participation and outcomes of girls' and women's education in India. While some data are available at school level, not much is available on higher education; even the school statistics from different government sources do not tally.

▶ Ensure equal access and participation to schooling by reducing dropout and non-enrolment especially, of girls from the disadvantaged homes and marginal groups. In order to achieve that:

- Provide a safe, fearless, and healthy environment for girls to attend school.

- Location of schools should not be too far and if necessary, transport may be made available.

- Provision of drinking water and toilets should be mandatory.

- Ways to prevent sexual harassment at school or in transport should be strictly enforced.

▶ Make education relevant, qualitative and women-friendly.

▶ Improve the economic returns of education by introducing skills-oriented education and making it more relevant to the labour market.

▶ Reservations and scholarships for girls and women.

▶ Recruitment, training and professional development of women teachers.

▶ After-school tutoring and mentoring programmes in both primary and secondary schools.

▶ Gender sensitization training programme for teaching and non-teaching staffs to promote gender equality by identifying where the gender disparities are widest, what factors contribute disparities, and which interventions are most likely to be effective for gender equality and equity.

▶ Gender glossary of terms and operational procedures should be made public.

<u>**Recommendations emerging from Technical Session III**</u>

NEED BASED SKILLS DEVELOPMENT AND VOCATIONAL TRAINING FOR WOMEN

▶ Skill training is very important.

▶ There should be more and more skills training in the curriculum. Example - introduction of Bachelor of Vocational Education (B.Voc.) Degrees.

▶ It is not always important to go for regular degrees. Vocational and skill training programmes offer abundant opportunities for women to start self-employment or own entrepreneurship/business.

▶ Human Resource Management relevant to industry to be taught in colleges and universities and on completion they can be taken back to the industry.

<u>Recommendations emerging from Technical Session IV</u>

MAKING SCIENCE AND TECHNOLOGY WOMEN FRIENDLY

▶ Girls and women should take up science, which leads to the field of technology.

▶ When technically qualified women do not work, it becomes a national loss. Therefore, it is important to pursue some profession. If compelled to discontinue studies, women should go for distance learning.

▶ Aspiration should not be limited to teaching posts. Aspire for higher research and development (R&D) positions.

▶ National Sample Survey (NSS) data should be updated on women in science and technology. Comparative data on graduation to research in Science and Technology (S&T) by women should be generated.

▶ All programmes should focus on women empowerment.

▶ Skills Training is important for self-employment and entrepreneurship.

▶ It is important to introduce machinery for women's drudgery reduction.

▶ Research projects should focus on local problems, identify local solutions through indigenous technology. Research should have an impact on the life of rural people. Examples include:

- Soil fertility, post-harvest technology especially for fruits and vegetables, biodiversity, water purification, water harvesting, wasteland utilization, recycling, treatment of waste, oil extraction, awareness creation, sanitary napkins, etc.

- The models should be sustainable.

- Interface with technical institutions is essential.

▶ Department of Science & Technology (DST) made intervention for flexibility of pursuing S&T by women and return of women in S&T after career-break due to family and social responsibility.

▶ Under the 12th Plan, KIRAN by DST has been introduced to address the problems of women scientists.

▶ DST Curie supports internship for persons interested in self-employment.

▶ Women's Technology Parks (WTPs) are encouraged since it is a source of information and income generation for local women.

<u>**Recommendations emerging from Technical Session V**</u>

CREATING EQUAL OPPORTUNITY TO FULL AND DECENT EMPLOYMENT FOR WOMEN

► Traditional recommendation of equal opportunity for women needs to be reviewed, since requirements of women labour force are not being the same.

► There should be equal opportunity and equal pay for equal work.

► Flexi-time could be considered for both women and men.

► Globalized labour market - domestic and neighbouring country markets should be studied for moving from a narrow to global perspective.

► Since dirty and lower paid jobs go to women, there is a need for women to move to higher levels through education and skills training.

► Long term focus should be: attitudinal change of society and government.

► Micro-level studies and research undertaken should be contributory to larger or macro-level studies.

► Raising of time-bound points for political manifesto which can be translated into policy.

NATIONAL GENDER CAUCUS

for equality in nutrition, health, education,
training, science and technology

At the end of the National Symposium, 'National Gender Caucus' was formed by the eminent dignitaries to facilitate taking up *'burning agenda'* and initiate a gender-based movement across scholars, professionals, industrialists, entrepreneurs, policy makers, activists and individuals; in order to impact on the national women empowerment agenda from the grassroots.

'National Gender Caucus' was formed to address the need for concerted efforts to move the recommended agenda of the National Symposium way forward. National Gender Caucus is primarily exchange of ideas, meeting and discussion platform for members and supporters to raise 'one voice' for a nationwide gender movement in order to challenge and lobby for change in social policy process. It is a group of thinkers coming together with shared concerns and interested in acting on gender-equality and women-empowerment in India. Since members are spread out in different parts of the country, the caucus primarily exchanges ideas through the web. The caucus has chosen 'recommendations' as its first set of 'objectives' in consensus. National Gender Caucus hopes to make a difference in the real-life of girls and women and to society at large by its transforming action-research approach. The caucus engages in collective advocacy and greater public awareness through meetings, press releases and press interviews. Lobbying and undertaking diagnostic-multidisciplinary research for women-friendly policies are to remain the caucus' shared concern and determined action.

'National Gender Caucus' hopes to make a difference in the real-life of girls and women and to society at large by its transforming action-research approach. It begins by taking up critical issues reflected in the "recommendations" from different sessions and extends to other emerging issues in societies across regions. It commits to move women's issues and gender concerns in different levels from academic to political to communal. Gradually, it is widening its scope of research, study and community mobilization towards women empowerment from micro analytic levels to pan-India level. 'National Gender Caucus' is therefore a research and advocacy body reaching out to gender and women scholars from national and international institutions who are committed to the cause of women empowerment for community development and national progress.

PART II

Research Papers & Micro Studies

Edited by Dr. Minnie Mathew

SYMPOSIUM CONTRIBUTIONS TO EXISTING BODY OF RESEARCH

Sayani Das

National Symposium on *"Access and Participation of Women and Girls to Nutrition & Health, Education & raining, Science & Technology"* organized by Women's Studies Centre; has contributed to the substantial need-areas for girls' and women's development in India. Women's Studies Centre (WSC) grounded on interdisciplinary framework that draws from different bodies of knowledge whether sciences, social sciences and humanities; focuses on respective women's concerns within the disciplines and influences application of disciplinary knowledge to women's development and empowerment. WSC extended its social responsibility through the international women's week national symposium by bringing together fifteen nationally distinguished scholars and professionals to share their varied experiences and critical opinions in order to impact girls and women empowerment in five key areas: *nutrition, education, training, science/technology, and employment.* The national symposium was a multi-disciplinary approach to transform the 'life-cycle of women' by addressing girl's basic needs of nutrition and education to women's pertinent need of skills training, drudgery removal and employment. This symposium traced debates on gender equality and equity from inter-disciplinary and multi-disciplinary perspectives. It highlighted 1) how women can transform her family health through awareness of nutrition; 2) how women can help themselves, their daughters and other women through knowledge and skills, science and technology; and 3) how women can address their economic needs and security and rise up from job-seekers to job-givers. Thus, the national symposium was an important initiative to the holistic understanding and realistic resolution of multi-faceted problems encountered daily by girls and women in Indian society. Importantly it stressed that national growth-development would be impossible to achieve without ensuring women's equality and equity.

Another significant contribution of the International Women's Week National Symposium was the formation of 'National Gender Caucus' in order to continue the debate and discussions on gender equality and equity that evolved during the two day meeting; to develop the plan of action for symposium recommendations in order to be productive; to undertake action research that can create social impact; to broaden network of gender scholars committed to girls' and women's issues and solutions; to increase the visibility of the pressure group in influencing women-friendly policies and services in India.

PARALLEL SESSIONS: Research Papers & Micro Studies Presentation

Diverse papers were presented by the participants of international women's week national symposium under all thematic areas. Session Chairs and Panelists have provided in-depth inputs on each paper based on research work and micro studies undertaken by the participants on adolescent girls' and women's nutrition, education, vocational training, technology transfer, self-employment and entrepreneurship. In the health and nutrition session, a wide range of papers were presented on adolescent girls' and women's health in the age group of 10-59 years covering the topics like – overweight and obesity, anemia, cardiovascular health, bone mineral health risk factors, mental health and autism, dietary habits and lifestyle, consumption pattern of micronutrient rich foods, impact of industrial pollution and role of homemakers in health at national/regional/district levels. The education and dropout session included papers on the status of girl child in India, empowerment of women and special needs children through education. In the skills and vocational training session, the research papers focused on vocational training education and skills development for girl students, women and homemakers - from awareness level to self-employment and entrepreneurial levels. The science and technology session discussed the micro studies on solar cooker for household use and green technology for rural women. The full and decent employment session concentrated on various issues like micro insurance and micro seed entrepreneurship; women's role in textile, handicrafts and IT industries in Tamil Nadu; and work-life balance.

PRENATAL AND POSTNATAL FACTORS IN AUTISM – NEED FOR SENSITIZATION

M.V. Alli[1] and S. Premakumari[2]

[1]Dr. M.V. Alli, Assistant Professor, Seethalakshmi Ramaswami College, Tiruchirapalli, Tamil Nadu. Email: alli.m.v@gmail.com

[2]Dr. S. Premakumari, Dean, Faculty of Community Education and Entrepreneurship Development, Avinashilingam Institute for Home Science and Higher Education for Women, Coimbatore, Tamil Nadu. Email: premakumari2001@rediffmail.com

ABSTRACT

Autism is a pervasive developmental disability increasing in epidemic proportion among the children with a male predominance characterized by impairments in socialization, communication and imagination. These children exhibit classical atypical behaviours that are difficult to manage increasing the rate of divorce, separation and broken homes, with women bearing the brunt of this burden in the families with autistic children. The above study was conducted to examine the prenatal and postnatal risk factors that increased the incidence of autism among 400 mothers with autistic children. Prenatal events such as the low weight gain during pregnancy (2.2 percent), premature birth (2.5 percent) and consanguinity (27 percent) were the factors that commonly increased the risk of autism. Environmental exposure of pregnant women to chemicals (0.5 percent) and pesticides (2.3 percent) and birth complications were found to increase the incidence of autism. Postnatal factor such as instrumental delivery was correlated to autism. Infant factors such as, hypoxia (10.2 percent) and 'Rh' incompatibility (6.5 percent) also contributed to autism. The identification of this abnormality had been as late as 4 years in about 53 percent of the samples and 2 years in about 47 percent. Many of the above factors are controllable and sensitization on the causes, risks and management of autism could help in alleviating and mitigating this problem.

Keywords: low weight gain, consanguinity, hypoxia

INTRODUCTION

Autism is a neuro-behavioural and cognitive disorder that is characterized by impaired development of interpersonal and communication skills, limited interests and repetitive behaviours. Autism is one of the most severe childhood disorders, affecting nearly one out of every 500 children. Autism is complex and involves a spectrum of challenging behaviours. Symptoms of autism occurs as early as age of three years, and the autistic individuals family and professionals care throughout their life (Kolevzon, *et.al.,* 2007:326) because these children display abnormal behaviours that cause stress to the affected child and their family. The autistic children usually have abnormal eating habits, disturbed sleep patterns, temper tantrums and aggression behaviour to self and to others are the most common abnormal behaviours (Dominick, *et.al.,* 2007:145).

Need for the Study

Families reported high levels of burden following their child's diagnosis as they are confronted with extraordinary demands on their time, energy, and financial resources (Barbaresi *et.al.,* 2006:1167). Each individual with autism is unique and this makes the experience of raising a child with autism a difficult task for each family (Gupta and Singhal 2005:62-63), and it was found that divorced parents are a common side effect of autism. Divorce rates in autism community is high ranging from 80-85 percent, autistic child care being result in marital hardships and broken families (www.blisstree.com) since the parents have limited exposure in handling this disability.

Studies reveal that three parental features and two obstetric conditions occur as potential risk factors for autism viz., father's paternal age, mother's maternal age, non-residents, growth restriction and new born hypoxia. However, low Apgar score, prenatal or perinatal fetal distress, caesarean delivery, hypertension and hemorrhage during pregnancy could also be the cause (Kolevzon *et.al.,* 2007:326). Other possible causes include chemical exposures prior to conception and prenatal or intrapartum use of medications (Tendon, 2004:239) but the findings are inconclusive.

The objective of the present study was to find out the prenatal and postnatal risk factors that were involved in the aetiology of autism and the influence of the demographic factors on such events.

METHODOLOGY

Selection of the Area and Sample

Four hundred autistic children belonging to 20 different centres catering to the needs of the autistic children in Tamil Nadu were selected for conducting the study.

Schedule to Collect Background Details

An interview schedule was specially designed to elicit information on the prenatal and postnatal events of the mothers with autistic children. Data on the age of identification of the problem, specific problems of the child, treatment modalities, immunizations pattern were collected to ascertain their awareness on their child's disability. Details on the prenatal history of the mother including the pattern of weight gain, type of delivery, complications during pregnancy and delivery, maternal and paternal age at conception, gestational period, birth weight of the child, period of breast feeding, environmental exposures during pregnancy, consanguinity, immunization during pregnancy and 'Rh' incompatibility were collected to find the impact of these factors in the aetiology of autism.

RESULTS AND DISCUSSION

Table I presents the age at which the disorder was identified and the symptoms leading to the identification of the disorder.

Table I
IDENTIFICATION OF AUTISM

(N=400)

Details	Number	Percentage
Age of identification		
<2 years	188	47.0
2-4 years	171	42.7
>4 years	41	10.3
Total	**400**	**100.0**
Abnormalities leading to identification		
Lack of Speech	126	31.5
Hyperactivity	42	10.5
Inappropriate Behavior	33	8.3
Developmental Delay	139	34.7
Fits	28	7.0
Not Responding to Environment	19	4.8
Irritability	1	0.2
Lack of Eye Contact	12	3.0
Total	**400**	**100.0**

The age of identifying the disorder was below 2 years in 47 percent of the children, between 2- 4 years in 42.7 percent of the children and above 4 years in 10.3 percent of the children. The age of identification is very vital in the autistic children since early intervention is essential to initiate corrective measures. The study conducted by Rapin (1991:751) found that, many children with autism are first diagnosed between the ages of 2 and 4 years which correlate with the present study.

The problem leading to identification of autism in children varied among the different samples, 34.7 percent of the mothers reported developmental delays in their children since the various milestones of development were either prolonged or delayed. There was lack of speech amongst 31.5 percent of the children; this however was ignored by some parents in the initial stages assuming that the speech development in the boys was delayed when compared to the girls. Around 10.5 percent of the parents found their child to be uncontrollable and hyperactive. Inappropriate behaviours, such as improper emotional response was found among 8.3 percent of the children. There were certain episodes of seizures among 7.0 percent of the children which was present since infancy in some children and it continued in childhood. Around 4.8 percent of the children did not respond to the environment appropriately such as a loud noise and three percent of the mothers were able to say that their children did not make eye contact, which was a specific indicator of autism. One of the mothers stated that her child was highly irritable.

Most of the mothers understood the problem of their child only when the child was enrolled in the school which showed the ignorance of the parents. On identification of the problem 73 percent of the children received medical therapies and most of them were unaware of the other therapeutic options. A variety of drugs were given to their children for hyperactivity, fits, aggression, sleeplessness, memory and for the control of temper tantrums. Twenty seven percent of the children did not receive medical treatment due to inaccessibility or they believed that the medicines would cause side effects.

Prenatal and Postnatal Factors Leading to Autism

1. Prenatal Factors

A. Prenatal Events Based on the Level of Income and Place of Living

The following Table II elucidates the prenatal events based on the level of income and living.

Table II
PRENATAL EVENTS BASED ON THE LEVEL
OF INCOME AND PLACE OF LIVING

(N = 400)

Details		Level of income (₹/Month)						Location				
		<4500		4501-7500		>7501		Chi-square	Rural		Urban		Chi-square
		No.	%	No.	%	No.	%		No.	%	No.	%	
Weight Gain	Normal	51	12.8	71	17.8	269	67.3		34	8.5	357	89.3	
	Low	3	0.8	1	0.2	5	1.2	3.151^{NS}	2	0.5	7	1.8	
	Total	54	13.5	72	18.0	274	68.5		36	9.0	364	91.0	
Duration of Gestation	37–40 weeks	50	12.5	71	17.8	269	67.3		36	9.0	354	88.5	1.965^{NS}
	< 37 weeks	4	1.0	1	0.2	5	1.3	6.370^{NS}	0	0.0	10	2.5	
	Total	54	13.5	72	18.0	274	68.5		36	9.0	364	91.0	

Consan - guinity	Present	12	3.0	26	6.5	70	17.5		11	2.8	97	24.3	
	Absent	42	10.5	46	11.5	204	51.0	3.951[NS]	25	6.3	267	66.8	0.254[NS]
	Total	54	13.5	72	18.0	274	68.5		36	9.0	364	91.0	

NS - Not Significant

i. Weight Gain and Family Income

Prenatal events that were a risk factor in the occurrence of autism were analysed corresponding to the level of income and the locality in which the mothers resided. The body weight and nutritional status of the woman before pregnancy, coupled with the weight gain during pregnancy are important indicators for the future events. Out of the 400 mothers surveyed 391 mothers had a normal weight gain and nine mothers had an abnormal weight gain pattern during their pregnancy. Low gestational weight gain was recorded in 1.2 percent of the HIG, 0.2 percent of the MIG and 0.8 percent of the LIG mothers indicating that the income of the families alone does not determine the weight gain during pregnancy.

Abeysena and Jayawardana (2011:374) stated that the risk factors for low prenatal weight gain were due to low per-capita monthly income and multiparity and the findings of the National Natality Survey revealed that the risk of low weight gain (less than 7.3 kg) increased nearly twice as the annual household income fell.

ii. Duration of Gestation and Family Income

The infants born before the end of the gestational period are exposed to perinatal and environmental risks. Out of the 400 mothers 390 mothers had delivered between 37-40 weeks and ten mothers had delivered before 37 weeks. Children who were born before 37 weeks of gestation were found to be 1.3 percent in the HIG, 0.2 percent in the MIG and 1.0 percent in the LIG families, indicating that the number of premature births were more in the HIG when compared to the LIG mothers. About 12.5 percent, 17.8 percent and 67.3 percent of the mothers belonging to the LIG, MIG and HIG respectively delivered their babies between 37- 40 weeks.

Premature births were expected to be low among the HIG mothers, since the prenatal care received during their gestational period and their health seeking behaviour is expected to be better than the other income groups, but the above findings elucidate that the duration of gestation was independent of the level of income of the family. Viswanathan *et.al.* (2008:23) stated that women who have reduced gestational weight gains were found to be at risk of preterm birth who would subsequently deliver a Lower Birth Weight (LBW) infant.

iii. **Consanguinity and Family Income**

Although consanguineous marriages have been thought to be out dated and out of practice in many populations as a result of social change and migration, 108 parents had consanguineous marriages. About 17.5 percent of the consanguineous marriages had occurred among the high income group, which was almost an unexpected finding. Around 6.5 percent of marriages in the MIG and 3.0 percent in the LIG were consanguineous. Intra familial marriages or consanguineous marriages had been cited as reasons for the occurrence of autism due to genetic reasons. Research results from a population with more consanguineous marriages highlighted the importance of autosomal recessive genes linked to autism mutations. (http://www.sciencemag.org/content/321/5886/172.3.full.pdf).

iv. **Weight Gain and Location of Families**

The access to health care facilities, good nutritious food and other utilities are some of the determinants for the successful completion of pregnancy. The availability of these is usually different in the rural and the urban settings. The prenatal events of the mother were analyzed based on the living place of the families in order to explore the influence of the environment on the prenatal events and the occurrence of autism.

Low gestational weight gain was recorded among 1.8 percent of the urban mothers whereas it was only 0.5 percent among the rural mothers. Maddah and Nikooyeh (2008:783) stated that the rural women with normal as well as low preconcepteral weight, gained lesser weight than the urban counterparts. However in the present study the gestational weight gain was not associated with the locale in which the mother lived. The main reason behind the non- association might be due to very less number of rural subjects (36) when compared to the number belonging to urban areas (364) in this study.

v. **Duration of Gestation and Location of Families**

Infants who were born before 37 weeks of gestation were 2.5 percent in the urban mothers and 0 percent in the rural mothers. The infants with a gestational age of 37-40 weeks were 88.5 percent in the urban mothers and 9 percent in the rural mothers. The above findings reveal that the infants born, short of gestational age was more in urban mothers when compared to the rural mothers indicating that the duration of gestation was independent of the residence of the mother. Infants born before 35 weeks of gestation were about 2.5 times as likely as infants born between 37 and 42 weeks of gestation to be diagnosed with an autism spectrum disorder (http://www.medicalnewstoday.com), also small for date children, low birth weight or slow growth was associated with a 2-fold increase in the risk for autism.

vi. **Consanguinity and Location of Families**

Consanguineous marriage is common where individuals prefer to marry within their clan. In villages people belonging to the same community and related by blood live as clusters and the probability of consanguineous marriages were expected to be more. But in the present study the consanguineous marriages were 24.3 percent in the urban mothers and only 2.8 percent in the rural mothers; this again could be because the number of urban samples was more than that of the rural samples.

Nath *et.al.* (2004:41) reported that foetal losses occurred in 18.8 percent of consanguineous group and congenital malformations were also very common in these families. The occurrence of consanguineous marriages in the present investigation did not seem to have an association with the residence of the mother. In general, in this study, a considerable number of autism children were from low or middle income families, born prematurely, born out of consanguineous marriages and belonging to rural areas under inadequate care. However association could not be established may be due to unequal distribution of subjects present in the study.

B. **Environmental Exposure Based on the Locality**

Exposure to environmental toxins based on the locality of families is given in Table III.

Table III
ENVIRONMENTAL EXPOSURE BASED ON THE LOCALITY

(N=400)

Locality	Exposure								Chi-square
	Pesticides		Chemicals		Nil		Total		
	No	%	No	%	No	%	No	%	
Rural	0	0.0	3	0.8	33	8.3	36	9.0	
Urban	2	0.5	6	1.5	356	89.0	364	91.0	6.831*
Total	2	0.5	9	2.3	389	97.3	400	100	

* Significant at five percent level

Exposure to chemicals and pesticides has been associated with the prevalence of autism. Prenatal exposure to chemicals was found among 1.5 percent of the mothers with autism children who resided in urban areas. These mothers had resided in industrialized area and 0.5 percent of the urban mothers had been exposed to pesticides during their pregnancy. About 0.8 percent of the rural mothers had also been exposed to chemicals in their work places. The locality in which the mother lived and the environment to which they were exposed was found to be significantly associated in the present investigation (p<0.05). Several environmental factors have been positively associated with the occurrence of autism. Women living near farm fields with frequent use of organochlorine pesticides, dicolfol and endosulphan in the first eight weeks of pregnancy increased the risk of autism (Roberts *et.al.*, 2007:1482).

C. **Complications of Pregnancy Associated with the Demography of the Mother**

The effect of demography of the mother associated with the pregnancy complications are depicted in Table IV.

Table IV
COMPLICATIONS OF PREGNANCY ASSOCIATED
WITH AGE AND LOCALITY

(N=400)

Complication*	Locality			Maternal age (Yrs)			
	Rural	Urban	Total	<20	21-30	>31	Total
Multiple Birth	2	4	6	2	4	NIL	6
Anemia	2	24	26	NIL	24	2	26

Hypertension	3	21	24	NIL	22	2	24
Fits	1	4	5	NIL	4	1	5
Respiratory Problem	NIL	5	5	NIL	3	2	5
Allergy	NIL	13	13	1	12	NIL	13
Fungal Infection	NIL	2	2	NIL	2	NIL	2
Diabetes	NIL	6	6	NIL	3	3	6
Arthritis	1	8	9	2	6	1	9
Hypothyroidism	1	7	8	1	5	2	8
Total	10	94	104	6	85	13	104

*Multiple responses

i. Multiple Birth

Out of the 400 mothers surveyed 104 mothers had certain complications during pregnancy and it included multiple birth (6), anemia (26), hypertension (24), fits (5), respiratory infection (5), allergy (13), fungal infection (2), diabetes (6), arthritis (9) and hypothyroidism (8). Despite research efforts into the potential role of gestation and birth complications in the occurrence of autism the casual nature of these associations is still uncertain. The number of multiple births was highest in urban mothers (4). Two teen aged mothers, four mothers belonging to the ideal age group had multiple births. Most of the autism research institutes agree that autism is caused due to genetic reasons.

ii. Anemia

Similarly out of 364 urban women 24 were found to be anaemic and two rural mothers out of 36 were found to be anaemic. Anemia was the highest among mothers 21-30 years of age. Anemia increases the risk of premature delivery and LBW (htpp://paa2006.princeton.edu download aspx submission).

iii. Hypertension

The blood pressure of the pregnant woman alters due to the physiological and hormonal changes that occur during this period. Urban mothers (24) were more prone to hypertension indicating the presence of stressors. About 22 mothers of the ideal age group were hypertensive Gardener, *et.al.* (2009:7) reported that high blood pressure and edema of gestating women may cause poor placental perfusion and damage fetal growth and development through hypoxia and prenatal and perinatal conditions associated with foetal hypoxia.

iv. Fits

Four mothers each belonging to urban area and ideal age group had eclampsia during their pregnancy. Eclampsia and preeclampsia in the pregnant woman may cause complications to the mother as well as the foetus.

v. Respiratory Problem

Allergic rhinitis is a frequent problem during pregnancy (Demoly *et.al.,* 2003:1813). Respiratory infections were more common among the urban mothers (5), three mothers who were of ideal age also suffered from problems such as running nose, wheezing and tonsillitis. Studies show that in women with asthma, immune response is dysregulated, this can result in transferring certain crucial factors to the foetus during critical periods of gestation.

vi. Allergy

Maximum number of allergic respondents belonged to the urban area (13), and the ideal age group (12). They had experienced a few episodes of allergy with the allergic manifestations in the skin or the respiratory system in the form of rashes, itching or wheezing during pregnancy. The findings of the present study are in line with the reports of Croen *et.al.* (2005:151), allergies were reported in mothers of ASD-affected children. TH2 cytokine profile is altered during acute allergic episode histamine is released through mast cells.

vii. Fungal Infection

Infection-associated immunological events during pregnancy may affect neural development when compared with infections in late pregnancy (Meyer *et.al.,* 2007:241). Fungal infection in the skin had occurred in two mothers each who were urban residents and were of the ideal age group. According to maternal antibody theory hypothesizes immunoglobulin G present in the pregnant woman's blood can cross the placenta, enter the foetal brain, react against foetal brain proteins and cause autism (Dalton *et.al.,* 2003:533).

viii. Diabetes Mellitus

Gestational diabetes has a two-fold risk of autism (news.bbc.co.uk). Diabetes mellitus was found to be more among urban mothers (6), mothers of the ideal age group (3) and older mothers (3). Atladottir, *et.al.* (2009:687) observed that associations between familial auto-immunity and infantile autism are probably attributable to a combination of a common genetic background and a possible prenatal antibody exposure or alteration in fetal environment during pregnancy.

ix. **Arthritis**

Eight mothers living in urban areas and six mothers who were of the ideal age group also suffered from arthritis. Mothers who had autoimmune diseases such as rheumatoid Arthritis is nearly 1.5 times reported (Atladottir *et.al.* 2009, :687) he also hypothesized that the cause of autism may be due to exposure to maternal antibodies produced during pregnancy or other changes during pregnancy.

x. **Hypothyroidism**

Thyroid problems cause thyroxine deficiency in the mother between 8-12 weeks of pregnancy have been hypothesized to produce changes in the foetal brain leading to autism (Roman 2007). Seven mothers in urban living had hypothyroidism. Five mothers who were of the ideal age group also suffered from hypothyroidism. Studies show that maternal hypothyroidism resulting in low T3 in the foetal brain during the period of neuronal cell migration may produce changes in the brain morphology leading to autism (Roman 2007:15).

Out of the 400 mothers surveyed, 14 mothers had two complications, four mothers had three complications and one mother had four complications during their pregnancy. Studies suggest that exposure to pregnancy complications may increase the risk of autism.

2. **Postnatal Factors**

A. **Mothers Age and Mode of Delivery**

The influence of the mothers' age on the mode of delivery is presented in Table V.

Table V
MATERNAL AGE AND MODE OF DELIVERY

(N= 400)

Mothers' Age (yrs)	Mode of Delivery								Chi-square
	Normal		Caesarean		Instrument		Total		
	No.	%	No.	%	No.	%	No.	%	
<20	26	6.5	14	3.5	3	0.8	43	10.8	
21-30	192	48	95	23.7	28	7	315	78.7	11.965[NS]
>31	22	5.5	18	4.5	2	0.5	42	10.5	
Total	240	60	127	31.7	33	8.3	400	100	

NS -Not Significant

About 3.5 percent of younger mothers (<20 years), and 4.5 percent of older mothers (>31 years) did not have a normal delivery and had undergone a caesarean delivery which showed that the age of the mother influenced the mode of delivery but 23.7 percent of ideal age group mothers of autistic children also had undergone caesarean delivery due to certain complications. Around 0.8 percent of younger mothers, 7 percent of ideal age group mothers and 0.5 percent of older mothers had undergone, instrumental delivery. Instrumental delivery is always associated with certain risks. This increases the chance for the occurrence of autism. Since a majority (40 percent) of mothers with autistic children in the ideal age group (21-30 years) had undergone assisted methods of delivery, the age of the mother was not found to be associated with the mode of delivery in the present investigation. However studies relating to the maternal age, the mode of delivery and the complications during the birth process reveal that older mothers had an increased risk of obstetric complications due to uterine muscle dysfunction and reduced blood supply with age (Mason-Brothers *et.al.,* 1990: 514). Several obstetric variables such as fetal distress, caesarean delivery, including a low Apgar score remained a classical risk factor in the occurrence of autism. In this study out of 400 mothers 160 had caesarean or instrument delivery. This finding supports the statement that there are a number of birth injuries that can cause brain damage which leads to autism.

B. **Birth Weight and Demographic Profile**

Influence of socioeconomic factors of mother corresponding to child's birth weight is shown.

Table VI
BIRTH WEIGHT OF THE CHILD IN ASSOCIATION WITH
SOCIO-ECONOMIC FACTORS

(N=400)

Details		Low (wt) No.	%	Normal (wt) No.	%	High (wt) No.	%	Total No.	%	Chi-square
Mothers' Education	Elementary	4	1	11	2.5	1	0.2	16	3.7	82.903*
	Higher Sec	25	6.3	138	34.6	41	10.3	204	51.2	
	Higher Edu	12	3	113	28.3	55	13.8	180	45.1	
	Total	41	10.3	261	65.4	97	24.3	400	100	
Monthly Income (₹)	<4500	13	3.3	34	8.5	7	1.7	54	13.5	21.425*
	4501-7500	7	1.8	50	12.5	15	3.7	72	18	
	>7501	21	5.3	178	44.5	75	18.7	274	68.5	
	Total	41	10.3	262	65.5	97	24	400	100	
Mothers' Weight Gain	Normal	37	9.1	258	64.5	96	24	391	97.6	14.414*
	Low	5	1.2	4	1	1	0.2	9	2.4	
	Total	41	10.3	262	65.5	97	24.2	400	100	
Mothers' Age (Years)	< 20	9	2.3	29	7.2	5	1.2	43	10.7	34.306[NS]
	21-30	30	7.5	206	51.5	79	19.7	315	78.8	
	> 31	2	0.5	27	6.7	13	3.3	42	10.5	
	Total	41	10.3	262	65.5	97	24.2	400	100	
Fathers' Age (Years)	21-30	28	7	137	34.2	35	8.7	200	50	27.681[NS]
	31-40	13	3.3	121	30.3	59	14.7	193	48.2	
	>41	0	0	4	1	3	0.8	7	1.8	
	Total	41	10.3	262	65.5	97	24.2	400	100	

* Significant at five per cent level; NS- Not Significant

i.   **Mother's Education and Birth Weight of the Child**

Around 6.3 percent of the mothers educated upto higher secondary level and 3.0 percent educated upto higher education had given birth to low weight babies. High birth weight babies were born to 13.8 percent of graduate mothers and 10.3 percent of the mothers who had received higher secondary education. About 34.6 percent of the mothers with higher secondary education and 28.3 percent of the graduate mothers had given birth to infants with normal weight. Among the mothers of autistic children, their educational status and the birth weight of the child were found to be significantly associated (p<0.05).

It was also found that the educational status of a woman increased their health consciousness especially during pregnancy and parent education was significantly related to fetal outcome. Hickey (2000: 1364S) supported that weight gain increased with educational attainment and lesser weight gains are common for women with less than an elementary school education.

ii. Family Income and Birth Weight of the Child

Around 5.3 percent of the mothers of autistic children belonging to the high income group gave birth to LBW babies whereas 3.3 percent of the mothers who were from low income group delivered LBW babies. Similarly 18.7 percent of the mothers who were from the HIG and 3.7 percent of the mothers from the MIG had given birth to HBW babies as against only 1.7 percent of LIG mothers. Children with a normal birth weight were the highest in the high income group (44.5 percent), followed by the middle income group (12.5 percent). As in the case of normal population groups, the family income and the birth weight of the infant were significantly associated in case of autism children also. Studies indicate that the children born to poorly nourished women of low income groups have a low birth weight as found in the present study.

iii. Mother's Weight Gain and Birth Weight of the Child

The prenatal history of the mothers of autistic children revealed that though they had normal weight gain during their pregnancy, 9.1 percent of the mothers delivered babies whose weight was less than 2.5 kg and 1.2 percent of the mothers who gained lesser weight also delivered LBW babies. A major segment of the mothers (88.5 percent) with normal weight gain had given birth to babies of optimal weight and 24 percent of the mothers with normal weight gain during pregnancy had given birth to children of higher birth weight. The weight gain during the gestational period and the birth weight of the child were therefore found to be associated (P<0.05). The findings are in line with Wilcox (2001: 1233) who reported that infants with low weight are often an indicator of earlier intra uterine effects.

iv. Mother's Age and Birth Weight of the Child

In the present study 2.3 percent of the mothers of autistic children below the age of 20 years and 0.5 percent of the mothers above the age of 31 years had given birth to LBW infants. Around 7.5 percent of the mothers of ideal age

(21-30 years) had also delivered small for weight babies. It was also found that 7.2 percent of the younger mothers and 6.7 percent of the older mothers had delivered normal weight babies. The maternal age and the birth weight of the infant did not have an association in the present study.

v.   **Father's Age and Birth Weight of the Child**

From the Table VI, it is clear that about 3.3 percent of the fathers of 30-40 years and 7 percent of the fathers of 21-30 years had LBW babies. Around 15.5 percent of the older fathers and 8.5 percent of ideal aged fathers had HBW babies. It was also found that 35 percent of the younger fathers and 59 percent of the ideal aged fathers had babies with a normal birth weight. Hence birth weight was found to be independent of the paternal age in the present study.

C.   **Mode of Delivery and Duration of Breast Feeding**

The association between the mode of delivery and the period of breast feeding is shown in Table VII.

Table VII
MODE OF DELIVERY AND DURATION OF BREAST FEEDING

(N=400)

Mode of Delivery	Duration of Breast-feeding (months)												Chi-square
	0-6		7-12		13-18		>18		Nil		Total		
	No.	%	No.	%	No.	%	No.	%	No.	%	No.	%	
Normal	46	11.5	73	18.2	42	10.5	64	16.0	15	3.8	240	60.0	
Caesarean	37	9.2	40	10.0	22	5.5	19	4.8	9	2.3	127	31.8	10.435[NS]
Instrument	10	2.5	10	2.5	6	1.5	6	1.5	1	0.2	33	8.2	
Total	93	23.2	123	30.7	70	17.5	89	22.3	25	6.3	400	100	

NS- Not Significant

Though exclusive breast feeding for six months had been widely campaigned, it was not successful in various segments of the population. Around 16 percent of the mothers who had normal delivery had breast fed their infants for the longest period of 18 months as against 4.8 and 1.5 percent of mothers who had caesarean and instrumental delivery respectively. According to Leung *et.al.*, (2002: 785) instrumental delivery, although not associated with breast feeding initiation was a significant risk against breast- feeding duration. Obstetric procedures that were associated with poorer breastfeeding, outcomes included instrumental delivery. About 9.2 percent of the mothers who underwent caesarean delivery and 2.5 percent of the mothers who underwent instrumental delivery had breast fed their infant for the shortest period of less than six months. However it was encouraging to find that 30.7 percent of the mothers comprising all the three categories had breast fed their infant upto 1 year. Breast fed infants are healthier, have fewer illness, strengthens the infant mother bond, and improves cognitive development among low birth weight infants.

D. Infant Factors in Autism Development

Infant factors leading to autism are given in the Table VIII.

Table VIII
INFANT FACTORS IN
AUTISM DEVELOPMENT

(N=400)

Details	Number present	Percentage
Immunization Done	397	99.2
Hypoxia Present	41	10.2
'Rh' Incompatibility	26	6.5

Immunization of the child against the contagious diseases was a prerequisite for the healthy childhood. Out of the 400 children 397 (99.3 percent) were immunized, however 0.9 percent had skipped certain vaccinations in the immunization schedule due to illness. Although there is no proof that autism is caused by vaccines or any preservative or additive used in their preparation, many parents are concerned about the risks of vaccination due to various theories related to vaccines and many parents delay or avoid immunizing their child (Hilton *et.al.,* 2006:4321).

Several investigations have hypothesized that certain perinatal conditions that lead to prolonged or acute oxygen deprivation (hypoxia) to the foetus may be a causative factor for neuropsychological and neuropsychiatric disturbances (Msall *et.al.,* 1998:52). In the present study 10.3 percent of the autistic children had experienced hypoxia at birth while 89.7 percent were normal.

Foetal hypoxia is associated with a low Apgar score, hypoxia-related obstetric complications and foetal hypoxia may possibly increase the risk of autism.

'Rh' incompatibility was found in 6.5 percent of the subjects where the mother and foetus had different 'Rh' factors.

Need for Sensitization

Autism is a devastating condition with no cure. The rising prevalence, coupled with the severe emotional and financial impact on the families has led to distress and marital conflicts. While there is increasing awareness of autism in the industrialized world, this is not the case in the developing countries. A lack of understanding of autism can lead to a variety of problems, from inappropriate responses to poor services and provisions. Developing an awareness of autism is therefore vital in building a better future for the people with autism. There is a need for sensitization and capacity building of the parents with autistic children. Raising public awareness for autism is the need of the hour, formation of parent groups with autistic children would facilitate them to share their experiences to fill up the lacuna in training their children.

The parents, guardians and caretakers should be exposed to the various avenues of autism management which is multidisciplinary, including educational therapy, psychotherapy, physiotherapy, occupational therapy, behaviour therapy, nutrition therapy, and alternate therapies with drug treatment. Autism management should aim at lessening the difficulties and deficits and to improve the quality of life and functional independence. The parents must appreciate that no single treatment is best and management needs to be tailored to the child's needs.

Prenatal counseling on the characteristics of children with special needs and particularly autism would help in early identification and subsequent specialty treatment for the disorder which can help in rectifying most of the complications associated with autism.

CONCLUSION

The study on the prenatal and postnatal events revealed that most of the autistic children were born to mothers' who were of ideal age group, had a normal weight gain during pregnancy, were full term, underwent a normal delivery and had a normal birth weight breaking the misconceptions surrounding the aetiology of autism. About one- third of the marriages were consanguineous and about five percent of the mothers had 'Rh' incompatibility. Very few mothers were exposed to chemicals and pesticides during their gestational period. Some of the mothers had suffered from pregnancy related complications. The findings reveal that many of the prenatal and postnatal factors are modifiable and appropriate interventions and effective sensitization on issues related to autism would help in safeguarding the future of these children.

REFERENCES

Abeysena, C. and Jayawardana, P. (2011) Sleep deprivation, physical activity and low income are risk factors for inadequate weight gain during pregnancy: A cohort study. *Journal of Obstetrics and Gynaecology Research,* Vol. 37(7), p. 734.

Atladottir, H. O., Pedersen, M. G., Thorsen, P., Mortensen, P. B., Deleuran, B., Eaton, W. W. and Parner, E. T. (2009) Association of family history of autoimmune diseases and autism spectrum disorders. *Pediatrics*, Vol.124 (2), p. 687.

Barbaresi, W. J., Katusic, S. K. and Voigt, R. G. (2006) A review of the state of the science for pediatric primary health care clinicians. *Archives of Pediatrics and Adolescent Medicine*, Vol. 160, p. 1167.

Croen, L.A., Grether, J.K., Yoshida, C.K., Odouli, R. and Van de Water, J. (2005) Maternal autoimmune diseases, asthma and allergies, and childhood autism spectrum disorders - A case-control study. *Archives of Pediatrics and Adolescent Medicine*, Vol. 159, p. 151.

Dalton, P., Deacon, R. and Blamire, A. (2003) Maternal neuronal antibodies associated with autism and a language disorder. *Annals of Neurology*, Vol. 53(4), p. 533.

Demoly, P., Piette, V. and Daures, J.P. (2003) Treatment of allergic rhinitis during pregnancy. *Drugs*, Vol. 63, p. 1813.

Dominick, K.C., Davis, N.O., Lainhart, J., Tager-Flusberg, H. and Folstein, S. (2007) Atypical behaviours in children with autism and children with a history of language impairment. *Research in Developmental Disabilities*, Vol. 28(2) p. 145.

Gardener, H., Spiegelman, D. and Buka, S.L. (2009) Prenatal risk factors for autism: comprehensive meta-analysis. *British Journal of Psychiatry*, Vol. 195 (1), p. 7.

Gupta, A. and Singhal, N. (2005) Psychosocial support for families of children with autism. *Asia Pacific Disability Rehabilitation Journal*, Vol.62 (2), p.62.

Hickey, C. A. (2000) Sociocultural and behavioural influences on weight gain during pregnancy. *American Journal of Clinical Nutrition*, Vol. 71(5), p.13-64.

Hilton, S., Petticrew, M. and Hunt, K. (2006) Combined vaccines are like a sudden onslaught to the body's immune system: parental concerns about vaccine 'overload' and 'immune-vulnerability'. *Vaccine*, Vol. 24(20), p. 4321.

Hultman, C. M., Spare'n, P. and Cnattingius, S (2002) Perinatal risk factors for infantile autism. *Epidemiology*, Vol. 13, p. 417.

Kolevzon, A., Gross, R. and Reichenberg, A. (2007) Prenatal and perinatal risk factors for autism. *Archives of Pediatrics and Adolescent Medicine*, Vol. 161 (4), p. 326.

Leung, G. M., Lam, T. H. and Ho, L. M. (2002) Breast-feeding and its relation to smoking and mode of delivery. *Obstetrics & Gynecology*, Vol. 99(5), p. 785.

Maddah, M. and Nikooyeh, B. (2008) Urban and rural differences in pregnancy weight gain in Guilan, Northern Iran. *Maternal and Child Health Journal*, Vol.12 (6), p.783.

Mason-Brothers, A., Ritvo, E.R. and Pingree, C. (1990) The UCLA University of Utah epidemiologic survey of autism: prenatal, perinatal, and postnatal factors. *Pediatrics*, Vol.86 (9), p.514.

Meyer, U., Yee, B.K. and Feldon, J. (2007) The neurodevelopmental impact of prenatal infections at different times of pregnancy: the earlier the worse? *Neuroscientist*, Vol. 13 (3), p. 241.

Msall, M.E., Bier, J.A., LaGasse, L., Tremont, M. and Lester, B. (1998) The vulnerable preschool child: the impact of biomedical and social risks on neurodevelopmental function. *Seminars* in *Pediatric Neurology,* Vol. 5, p.52.

Nath, A., Patil, C. and Naik, V.A. (2004) Prevalence of consanguineous marriages in a rural community and its effect on pregnancy outcome. *Indian Journal of Community Medicine,* Vol.29 (1), p.41. News- bbc.co.uk

Rapin, I. (1991) Autistic children: diagnosis and clinical features. *Pediatrics,* Vol. 87(5), p. 751.

Roberts, E. M., English, P. B., Grether, J. K., Windham, G. C., Somberg, L. and Wolff, C. (2007) Maternal residence near agricultural pesticide applications and autism spectrum disorders among children in the California Central Valley. *Environmental Health Perspectives,* Vol. 115(10), p. 1482.

Roman, G. C. (2007) Autism: transient in-utero hypothyroxinemia related to maternal flavonoid ingestion during pregnancy and to other environmental antithyroid agents. *Journal of the Neurological Sciences,* Vol. 262 (1–2), p. 15.

Tendon, R. K. (2004) Child Psychology, A. P. H. Publishing Corporation, New Delhi, p. 239.

Viswanathan, M., Siega-Riz, A. M., Moos, M. K., Deierlein, A., Mumford, S., Knaack, J., Thieda, P., Lux, L. J. and Lohr, K. N. (2008) Outcomes of maternal weight gain. Evidence Report/ Technology Assessment, Vol.168, p. 23.

Wilcox, A. J. (2001) On the importance—and the unimportance—of birthweight. *International Journal of Epidemiology,* Vol.30 (6), p. 1233.

http://www.blisstree.com

htpp://paa2006.princeton.edu download.aspx.submission

http://www.medicalnewstoday.com

http://www.sciencemag.org/content/321/5886/172.3.full.pdf

BODY COMPOSITION MEASURES OF OVERWEIGHT AND OBESE ADULT FEMALES OF 20 – 24 YEARS AGE

S. Kowsalya[1] and Avanthi Amara[2]

[1]Dr. S. Kowsalya, Professor, Department of Food Science and Nutrition (FSN), Avinashilingam Institute for Home Science and Higher Education for Women, Coimbatore, Tamil Nadu. Email: kowsiskk@gmail.com

[2]Avanthi Amara, Research Scholar, FSN, Avinashilingam Institute for Home Science and Higher Education for Women, Coimbatore, Tamil Nadu. Email: avanthiamara@gmail.com

ABSTRACT

In urban areas of India, Obesity is becoming an important public health problem. The rising prevalence of obesity and overweight is also related to the associated disorders like dyslipdemia, hypertension, type II diabetes mellitus and cardiovascular diseases. Not many studies are available on the association between body composition measures and anthropometry among overweight and obese young adult females. Hence was the need for the present study. The study aimed at assessing the incidence of overweight and obesity among young adult females (20 – 24 years), determining the body composition and finding the association between body composition measures, anthropometry and energy balance. Around 400 young adults (20-24 years) from Coimbatore district were screened for overweight; obesity and underweight based on body mass index and forty five subjects, fifteen from each BMI category were chosen for the study. Their background information and life style pattern was recorded by an interview schedule and nutritional status was assessed using the biochemical profile (blood profile, glucose, and lipid profile), clinical examination and diet survey. Body composition measures were done using Biospace Inbody – 720 - body composition analyzer using BIA principle. Results showed that all the body composition parameters were found to be higher in obese subjects when compared to that of normal and overweight individuals. Visceral fat area was above normal in obese and fat free mass, total body water and protein were deficit in normal subjects. The study showed association between body composition, biochemical parameters, energy balance and anthropometry.

Keywords: body composition, visceral fat area, fat free mass, total body water

INTRODUCTION

Adults are individuals who have completed their growth and are ready to assume their status and responsibilities in society. Psychologists generally consider early adulthood to begin around age 20 and last until about age 40 to 45, and middle adulthood to last from about age 40 to 45 to around 65 (Bhatt, 2007). Adults include a broader age range and all those in 20 to 64 yr (WHO, 1998). Individuals in the age group of 20 - 24 year are also referred to as young adults (Jekielek and Brown, 2002). As per WHO, Obesity leads to changes in physical, psychological and social implications and thereby cause a risk in morbid mortality rates and exposing individuals to chronic life style related disorders.

The prevalence of obesity in India is 16.0 percent in women and 12.1 percent in men (NFHS, 2006). In Tamil Nadu, the prevalence of obesity among the age group 20- 29 years is 19.4 percent in women and 9.5 percent in men (NFHS, 2007). The major determinants of epidemiology responsible for obesity are dietary fat intake, exercise and energy expenditure, smoking and alcoholism. The measurement of BMI based on height does not differentiate fat and lean body mass. Further the distribution of fat in the body is not assessed. Whereas in the determination of body composition, the total body weight contributed by bone, muscle, fat and other tissues are considered. The recent methods introduced are dual X-ray Absorptiometry (DEX A), Magnetic Resonance Imaging (MRI) or Computed Tomography (CT), Bio Electrical Impedance (BIA) distinguish fat depots from nonfat body mass (Visser, 2009). Body composition is a key element in determining energy expenditure (Insel *et.al.*, 2003). Body composition gains importance in term of correlating the adipocity with degenerative disorders. In India, data on body composition measures among different age groups of population are not available. Hence, there is an urgent need to collect data on measures of body composition of different age groups of Indians. Towards achieving this goal, the present study was an effort to measure body composition among adults especially to compare the body composition of normal, overweight and obese adult females (20 – 24 years). The specific objectives of the study were to:

- Assess the incidence of overweight and obesity among adults aged 20 – 24 years

- Assess the nutritional status of the selected adults

- Assess the body composition measures of the selected adults

- Find the association between anthropometric measures, energy balance and body composition

MATERIALS AND METHODS

1. Selection of the Study Area and Subjects

The area chosen for the study was Coimbatore district. For the conduct of the study, 400 female subjects in the age group of 20-24 years were selected from different taluks of Coimbatore. Based on their willingness to participate in the study, informed consent was obtained from the subjects before the conduct of the in-depth body composition studies.

2. Formulation of Interview Schedule for Data Collection

The interview method of collecting data involves presentation of oral – verbal stimuli and reply in terms of oral – verbal responses (Kothari, 2011). A specially designed interview schedule was used by the investigator to collect information on socio – economic background, health history, life style pattern and dietary pattern of selected individuals.

3. Assessment of Nutritional Status of Selected Subjects

Nutritional assessment involves interpretation of data from the nutritional screen and incorporates additional information. The nutrition assessment organizes and evaluates the information gathered to make a professional judgment about nutritional status (ASPEN, 2002). In the present study, the nutritional status of the subjects was from anthropometric measurements, biochemical estimation, dietary recall method, and body composition measures.

3. a. Anthropometric Measurements

To evaluate the nutritional status of children and adults, it is important to determine the measurements of anthropometry. Anthropometric measurements have become an indispensable approach for the evaluation of nutritional status of children and adults. It is a simple, inexpensive and safe method. Height, Weight and Body Mass Index of all the 400 subjects was determined.

3.a.i. Height: The subject was allowed to stand in stadiometer with his/her back and heel against the height scale, the head being in horizontal plane and person stand erect in position.

3.a.ii. Weight: Body weight is the most widely used and the simplest reproducible anthropometric measurement used to assess the nutritional status. This actually is one of the indicators of one's individual's health. A digital platform weighing scale was used for the measurement of the weight. The balance was adjusted to zero and the reading noted when the subject was standing barefoot and erect on the machine to the nearest 0.1 kg. The balance was checked for accuracy against standard weights.

3.a.iii. Body Mass Index (BMI): Body Mass Index (BMI) also called Quetlet Index. The body composition may be estimated by measuring one's weight to height to lean body mass that correlates an individual's weight and height to lean body mass obtained by dividing weight in kilograms by height in metres squared.

$$BMI = \frac{Weight\ (kg)}{Height\ in\ m^2}$$

Forty five girls were selected for the conduct of the study based on their body mass indices. They were selected in such a way that one group consisted of fifteen girls with BMI normal (BMI – 18.5 – 23.0, according to WHO standard for Asian – Pacific Population), second group of fifteen girls whose BMI was overweight (BMI – 23.1 – 26.9, according to WHO standard for Asian – Pacific Population) and the last group of fifteen girls whose BMI was obese (BMI - ≥ 27, according to WHO standard for Asian – Pacific Population).

3.b. Biochemical Tests

Biochemical tests are the most objective and sensitive measures of nutritional status. The hematological parameters namely hemoglobin (Cyanmethemoglobin method), blood glucose (GOD – PAP method), total cholesterol (CHOD – PAP enzymatic colorimetric method), serum triglycerides (GPO – PAP method) and HDL cholesterol (Direct enzymatic colorimetric method) were analyzed. The VLDL cholesterol and LDL cholesterol were calculated using the desired formulae.

3.c. Clinical Assessment

Careful observations of physical signs of nutritional status provide an important added dimension to the overall assessment of the individuals (Robert and Williams, 2000). Using ICMR (1989) clinical assessment proforma, clinical examination was done with the help of a medical practitioner and the deficiency signs and symptoms of the selected adolescents were recorded.

3.d. Food and Nutrient Intake

24 hour recall method was used to obtain details regarding the food intake of the selected individuals. The nutrient intake was calculated for individuals using the 'Nutritive Value of Indian Foods' (ICMR) and compared with Recommended Dietary Allowances (ICMR, 2010).

3.e. Body Composition Measures

Nutritional assessment using anthropometry is now increasingly augmented through additional measurement of BIA. The technique of BIA is based on properties of electrical conductivity using sensors to predict body composition (Shils *et.al.*, 2006). In terms of health risk, body composition is more important than body weight (Insel, 2003). Body composition was determined using Bioelectrical Impedance Analysis (BIA) with Inbody – 720 (USA), a four compartment model.

BIA is based on the concept that electrical f low is facilitated through hydrated fat free body tissues and extracellular water compared to fat tissue because of the greater electrolyte content (and, thus, lower electrical resistance) of the fat – free component. Once the resistance exists, the current f low is measured which is directly related to the amount of fat in the body. (Mcardle *et.al.*, 2007). BIA is recorded at five segments namely left arm, right arm., trunk, right leg and left leg and measured at six different frequencies namely *1 kHz,115 kHz, 50 kHz, 250 kHz, 500 kHz, 1000 kHz.* It was ensured that the subjects were well hydrated and had not carried out any physical exercise in the previous four to six hours. The subjects were asked to present themselves early daylight without food and water consumption for measuring their body composition. The subject was then asked to stand on the analyzer by adjusting her foot in such a way that they are placed correctly on the two electrodes provided near the feet and the weight was recorded. The subjects name, age, height and gender were entered by the user. Two electrodes were provided for the left and the right arm. The subject was asked to hold the electrodes by placing the thumb and the four fingers in the space provided and the subject was asked to stand motionless till the test is done. The four main body components measured in the analyser are total body water, protein, fat and mineral mass. Other parameters measured include skeletal muscle mass, percent body fat, waist hip ratio, lean balance, visceral fat area, arm circumference, arm muscle circumference, Degree of obesity, mineral content in bone, body cell mass, basal metabolic rate ratio to ECF to TBF.

4.a. Computation of Energy Balance

A balance exists between nutrient intake which regulates body weight and in the energy balance maintenance, the intake of nutrients and energy expenditure are regulated and related in the formula:

$$\Delta E = Ein - Eout \text{ (Eastwood, 2003)}$$

4.b. Total Energy Expenditure (TEE)

For arriving at the factorial calculations to estimate total energy expenditure, the time line of activities followed by an individual in a day should be recorded. A BMR multiple is used to calculate the energy cost of activities followed by the individual in a day. BMR multiple per minute is also referred to 24 hour energy requirements using physical activity level:

PAR = Energy cost of an individual activity per minute
= Energy cost of BMR per minute
PAL (for the day) = Total PAR hours / Total time
TEE (24 hr) = Predicted BMR × PAL

The PAL values proposed by ICMR expert group (2010) was used for calculation of PAL of individuals, sedentary or light activity lifestyle - 1.53, active or moderately active lifestyle - 1.8, vigorous or vigorously active lifestyle - 2.3.

5. Statistical Analysis and Interpretation of Data

The data was consolidated and tabulated in which mean, standard deviation and percentage were computed. The data was analyzed using the software SPSS version 16.0. Comparisons were made between various parameters of three groups using Student's t-test. Correlation between anthropometric measurements, body composition parameters, and biochemical parameters were derived using Karl Pearson's co–efficient of correlation. Probability at both 0.05 and 0.01 levels of significance was considered to draw conclusions.

RESULTS

1. Incidence of Overweight and Obesity

A total of 400 girls in the age group of 20 to 24 years were screened for the prevalence of overweight and obesity using anthropometric measures like height, weight and BMI as parameters. The results are presented Figure 1.

Figure 1
INCIDENCE OF OVERWEIGHT AND OBESITY IN ADULT FEMALES

(N=400)

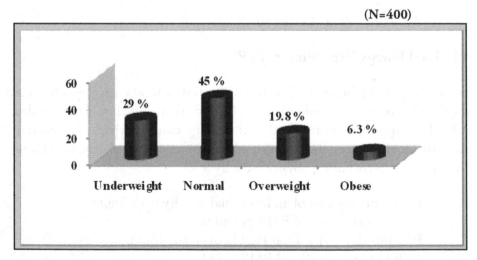

2. Health History of the Subjects

Table I provides the health history of the selected adults.

Table I
HEALTH HISTORY OF THE SELECTED ADULTS

(N=45)

Details	Normal (n = 15)	Overweight (n = 15)	Obese (n = 15)	Total (n = 45)
	No.	No.	No.	No.
Recent Illness*				
Diarrhoea	2	0	1	3
Fever	4	2	4	10
Dysentery	1	0	1	2
Jaundice	1	0	0	1
Common Cold	12	7	9	28
Typhoid	2	0	0	2
Food Poisoning	1	0	2	3
No Recent Illness	4	2	3	9
Age Of Menarche				
12 Years	5	2	9	16
13 Years	4	11	3	18
14 Years	1	1	2	4
15 Years	5	1	1	7
Problems In Menstrual Cycle*				
Excessive Bleeding	3	1	2	6
Irregularities	6	3	7	16
Physical Discomfort	6	3	3	12
Other Problem	0	1	4	5

*Multiple responses

Common cold was more common among overweight (46.7 percent) and obese (60 percent) subjects, whereas fever was seen in all the three groups.

Among the forty five selected adult females, a majority of them were in the age of 13 years at the start of their menstrual cycle. The onset of puberty for nine of the obese subjects was at the age of 12 years. Three of forty five girls said they had excessive bleeding. Sixteen subjects from all the three groups complained about irregularities in menstruation. Twelve subjects said that they had physical discomfort during menstrual cycle. Problems like poly cystic ovarian syndrome (PCOS), thyroid hormone level changes were seen among 26.7 percent of obese subjects.

3. Lifestyle Pattern of the Selected Subjects

Data on lifestyle pattern adopted by the selected subjects is shown in Table II.

Table II
LIFESTYLE PATTERN ADOPTED BY THE SELECTED SUBJECTS

(N = 45)

Details	Normal (n = 15)	Overweight (n = 15)	Obese (n = 15)	Total (n = 45)
	No.	No.	No.	No.
Mode of Travel				
By Walk	13	10	3	26
By Bus	0	0	5	5
Others	2	5	7	14
Hours of Sleep Per Day				
< 6 Hours	2	1	2	5
6 – 8 Hours	11	13	13	37
>8 Hours	2	1	0	3
Habit of Snacking				
Yes	14	12	12	38
No	1	3	3	7
Television Viewing, Hours/ Day				
1 Hour	8	10	8	26
2 Hours	3	2	0	5
>2 Hours	4	3	7	14
Regular Exercise				
Yes	2	2	5	9
No	13	13	10	36

From the above Table, it is seen that 26 of them travelled to college / work by walk, 5 of them by bus and 14 of them by other means of travel. Around five subjects slept less than six hours a day, 37 subjects slept for 6-8 hours a day and three of them slept for more than eight hours a day. Thirty eight of the selected individuals had the habit of snacking. This included junk foods, carbonated beverages and healthy foods.

Fourteen subjects watch television more than two hours, five subjects for two hours a day and twenty six subjects for one hour a day. The results showed physical activities did influence change in BMI. It is seen that among the obese subjects only 10 subjects exercise regularly whereas the rest five subjects do not exercise at all.

4. Dietary Pattern of the Selected Subjects

Table III provides the dietary pattern data of the selected adult females.

Table III
DIETARY PATTERN OF ADULT FEMALES

(N=45)

Details	Normal (n = 15)	Overweight (n = 15)	Obese (n = 15)	Total (n = 45)
	No.	No.	No.	No.
Vegetarian	2	1	6	9
Non-vegetarian	12	14	7	33
Ova-vegetarian	1	0	2	3

From the above table, it is seen that 33 subjects were non – vegetarians, 9 subjects were vegetarians and 3 subjects were ova vegetarians.

5. Assessment of Anthropometric Parameters

Data on mean and standard deviation of body measurements of subjects based on their BMI categories is shown in Table IV.

Table IV
ANTHROPOMETRIC PARAMETERS OF THE SELECTED NORMAL, OVERWEIGHT AND OBESE SUBJECTS

Parameters	Standard*	Normal (18.5 – 22.9) (n=15)	Overweight (23 – 26.9) (n=15)	Obese (≥ 27) (n=15)
Height (cm)	160.7	158.35 ± 2.77	157.65 ± 7.05	157.78 ± 6.66
Weight (kg)	56.7	53.05 ± 3.86	64.63 ± 6.12	78.69 ± 7.96
BMI (kg/m^2)	21.2	21.12 ± 1.09	25.93 ± 1.19	31.64 ± 3.15
Waist Hip Ratio	0.70 – 0.80	0.80 ± 0.01	0.85 ± 0.02	0.88 ± 0.04

AC (cm)	22.6	27.08 ± 1.01	31.05 ± 0.91	34.85 ± 2.32
AMC (cm)	18.8	20.93 ± 0.65	22.89 ± 0.82	25.03 ± 1.07

*NNMB standards, 2002

The standard height for the age group 18 – 24 years was found to be 160.7 cm. The mean height of normal (158.4cm), overweight (157.7 cm) and obese (157.8 cm) was found to be lesser than that of the standard. Mean weight of the normal was found to be 53.05kg, that of overweight was 64.63kg and that of obese was 78.69kg.

The BMI is an indicator of overweight and obesity. The BMI of overweight and obese subjects was greater than the standard BMI whereas the normal subjects lie within the normal value. Arm circumference and arm muscle circumference were also seen to be higher with obese when compared to normal or overweight.

6. Assessment of Biochemical Parameters

The various biochemical profiles of the subjects are shown in Table V.

Table V
BIOCHEMICAL PARAMETERS OF THE SELECTED NORMAL, OVERWEIGHT AND OBESE SUBJECTS

(N=45)

Parameters	Standard	Normal (n = 15)	Overweight (n = 15)	Obese (n = 15)
Blood Hemoglobin (g/dl)	12 – 13	13.33 ± 1.09	12.98 ± 0.58	12.31 ± 1.15
Glucose (mg/dl)	74 – 105	83.87 ± 15.65	84.66 ± 13.33	88.02 ± 5.58
Total Cholesterol (mg/dl)	<200	149.47 ±12.27	165.73 ± 21.04	170 ± 13.89
Triglycerides (mg/dl)	50 -150	74.4 ± 19.43	82.8 ± 16.96	94.53 ± 30.64
High – Density lipoprotein(mg/dl)	>45	42.6 ± 9.81	42.07 ±9.32	41.93 ± 11.43
Very Low – Density Lipoprotein (mg/dl)	<40	14.87 ± 3.86-	16.07 ± 3.60	19 ± 6.25
Low – Density Lipoprotein (mg/dl)	<100	90.67 ± 14.52	107.6 ± 23.97	100.93 ± 18.98

The mean blood hemoglobin level was found to be higher in normal subjects and the least in obese girls. The normal hemoglobin level for adult female is 12 – 13 g/dl. Most of the girls had normal hemoglobin levels and were not anemic, the range being 12.24 – 14.42 g/dl. The overweight subjects were within the range of 12.4 – 13.56g/dl and obese subjects were within the range 11.16 -13.46 g/dl. Few girls were found to be mildly anemic among the obese group. The levels were high in obese subjects when compared to those of normal or overweight. All the forty five subjects including the obese fall under the normal range in both lipid profile and glucose level.

Figure 2
BIOCHEMICAL PARAMETERS OF THE SELECTED SUBJECTS

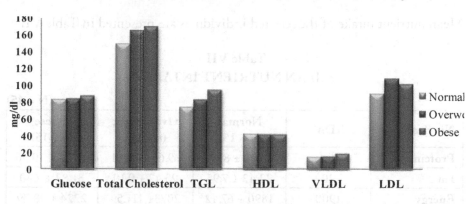

7. Clinical Assessment of the Selected Subjects

Table VI presents the data on clinical signs and symptoms of the selected individuals.

Table VI
CLINICAL SIGNS AND SYMPTOMS OF THE SELECTED SUBJECTS

(N=45)

Symptoms	Normal	Overweight	Obese
Healthy	6	5	5
Easily Plucked Hair	2	1	1
Rough and Dry Skin	0	1	2
Edema	0	0	2
Lethargy	0	0	3
Mild Anemia	4	2	7

Six girls from normal and five girls from both obese and overweight were free from all deficiency symptoms. Four girls from the forty five subjects had easily pluck - able hair. Three girls had rough and dry skin. Edema was not seen among normal or overweight subjects but 2 obese subjects had edema. Similarly no normal or overweight showed signs of lethargy but three obese subjects showed lethargy. Thirteen subjects showed symptoms of mild anemia. No signs of dental carries were seen.

8. Dietary Pattern of the Selected Individuals

a. Mean Nutrient Intake of the Selected Subjects

Mean nutrient intake of the selected individuals are presented in Table VII.

Table VII
MEAN NUTRIENT INTAKE

(N = 45)

Nutrient	RDA*	Normal (n = 15)	Overweight (n = 15)	Obese (n = 15)
Protein	55	29.02 ± 8.62	39.65 ± 14.91	42.98 ± 10.96
Fat	20	22.42 ± 7.95	25.42 ± 9.18	31.82 ± 7.40
Energy	1900	1890 ± 67.42	2073± 111.59	2224 ± 98.79
Calcium	600	331.47 ± 76.91	382.32 ± 140.54	355.10 ± 150.25
Iron	21	7.11 ± 4.18	9.84 ± 5.66	7.17 ± 4.27

*RDA, ICMR, 2010

From the above table it is seen that the obese subjects consumed protein and fat at a higher level when compared to the normal or overweight subjects and therefore the mean energy intake by obese subjects was higher compared to the rest.

9. Body Composition Measures of the Selected Subjects

The mean of the various body composition measures are given in Table VIII.

Table VIII
BODY COMPOSITION PARAMETERS OF THE SELECTED
NORMAL, OVERWEIGHT AND OBESE SUBJECTS

(N=45)

Parameters	Standard'	Normal (n=15)	Overweight (n=15)	Obese (n=15)
Body Fat Mass (kg)	10.5 – 16.8	18.13 ± 2.87	26.89 ± 3.59	36.89 ± 6.02
Percent Body Fat (%)	18 – 28	34.05 ± 8.78	41.69 ± 4.78	46.68 ± 4.08
Fat Free Mass (kg)	36.2 – 44.5	34.90 ± 2.24	37.73 ± 5.17	41.81 ± 4.01

Total Body Water (l)	26.5 – 32.7	25.51 ± 1.66	27.55 ± 3.76	30.59 ± 2.90
Intra Cellular Water (l)	16.3 – 20.3	15.81 ± 1.02	17.09 ± 2.32	18.96 ± 1.78
Extra Cellular Water(l)	10.2 – 12.4	9.7 ± 0.66	10.48 ± 1.44	11.63 ± 1.15
Protein (kg)	7.2 – 8.8	6.85 ± 0.43	7.4 ± 0.10	8.21 ± 0.77
SMM (kg)	19.9 – 24.3	18.64 ± 1.32	20.29 ± 3.03	22.71 ± 2.34
Mineral (kg)	2.5 – 3.0	2.55 ± 0.17	2.79 ± 0.42	3.02 ± 0.36
BMC (kg)	2.0 – 2.5	2.13 ± 0.14	2.34 ± 0.36	2.52 ± 0.31
Body Cell Mass (kg)	23.8 – 29.1	22.67 ± 1.45	24.48 ± 3.35	27.15 ± 2.55
Visceral Fat Area(cm^2)	<100	54.35 ± 9.32	87.87 ± 12.30	119.1 ± 22.56
ECF/TBF	0.36 – 0.39	0.333 ± 0.004	0.333 ± 0.003	0.334 ± 0.006
ECW/TBW	0.31 – 0.34	0.380 ± 0.004	0.380 ± 0.003	0.380 ± 0.006

*Reference range as per In Body composition analyzes data for normal subjects.

The normal range for total body fat content is said to be 10.5 to 16.8 kg for adult females. From the findings, it is seen that the body fat mass of normal (18.13 kg), overweight (26.89kg) and obese (36.89kg) vary largely. The normal subjects were close to the reference value, whereas the overweight and obese subjects had a fat content way beyond the reference value. Normal, overweight and obese subjects were found to have a total body water of 25.51, 27.55 and 30.59 respectively. The water content of normal subjects was found to be less than the normal range (26.5 – 32.7 l) whereas the obese and overweight subjects were within this range. The protein content of overweight and obese subjects were found to be within the normal range but the normal subjects had a mean protein level less than the normal range which directly reflected on the skeletal muscle mass which showed similar results. Minerals were found to be within the normal range in all the forty five adult females likewise the bone mineral content was also found to be within the normal range. The body cell mass was found to be below the normal range in normal subjects and was found to be normal in overweight and obese subject.

Figure 3 shows the body composition parameters such as body fat mass, total body water, protein, mineral of the selected individuals.

Figure 3
BODY COMPOSITION PARAMETERS OF
THE SELECTED INDIVIDUALS

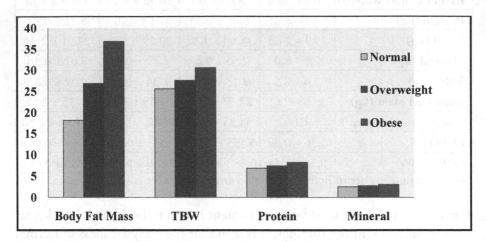

The association between anthropometric and body composition parameters of normal overweight and obese subjects are given in Table IX.

Table IX
CORRELATION BETWEEN ANTHROPOMETRIC AND
BODY COMPOSITION PARAMETERS OF NORMAL
OVERWEIGHT AND OBESE SUBJECTS

Parameters	BMI Category		
	18.5 – 23.0 Normal (n=15)	23.0 - 26.9 Overweight (n=15)	≥ 27.0 Obese (n=15)
Weight vs. BFM	0.816**	0.533*	0.871**
Weight vs. %BF	0.551*	-0.180[NS]	0.468[NS]
Weight vs. FFM	0.673**	0.811**	0.681**
Weight vs. TBW	0.674**	0.810**	0.683**
Weight vs. Protein	0.654**	0.799**	0.652**
Weight vs. SMM	0.654**	0.803**	0.656**
Weight vs. Mineral	0.717**	0.833**	0.686**
Weight vs. VFA	0.763**	0.536*	0.828**
Weight vs. BCM	0.658**	0.804**	0.654**

BMI vs. BFM	0.915**	0.799**	0.845**
BMI vs. %BF	0.767**	0.621*	0.821**
BMI vs. FFM	0.366**	0.088^{NS}	0.004 ^{NS}
BMI vs. TBW	0.365**	-0.086^{NS}	0.015 ^{NS}
BMI vs. VFA	0.909**	0.793**	0.893**
BMI vs. Protein	0.365**	-0.084^{NS}	0.006 ^{NS}
BMI vs. Mineral	0.415^{NS}	-0.103^{NS}	-0.067 ^{NS}
BMI vs. BCM	0.362^{NS}	-0.085^{NS}	0.006 ^{NS}
WHR vs. BFM	0.607*	0.408^{NS}	0.503 ^{NS}
WHR vs. %BF	0.523*	0.709**	0.680**
WHR vs. FFM	0.235^{NS}	-0.639*	-0.328 ^{NS}
WHR vs. VFA	0.747**	0.464^{NS}	0.625*
WHR vs. Protein	0.270^{NS}	-0.633*	-0.298 ^{NS}
AC vs. Protein	0.449 ^{NS}	0.236^{NS}	0.141 ^{NS}
AC vs. SMM	0.435 ^{NS}	0.237^{NS}	0.136 ^{NS}
AC vs. FFM	0.423 ^{NS}	0.228^{NS}	0.091 ^{NS}
AC vs. BFM	0.767**	0.670**	0.677**
AC vs. Mineral	0.412^{NS}	0.217^{NS}	-0.073 ^{NS}
AMC vs. Protein	0.792**	0.791**	0.477 ^{NS}
AMC vs. SMM	0.784**	0.790**	0.473 ^{NS}
AMC vs. FFM	0.774**	0.790**	0.437 ^{NS}
AMC vs. BFM	0.522*	0.329^{NS}	0.573*
AMC vs. Mineral	0.704**	0.738**	0.242 ^{NS}

** Significant at 1 percent level * Significant at 5 percent level NS Not Significant

a) Weight and Body Composition Parameters

Weight when correlated with body composition parameters like FFM, TBW, protein, SMM, mineral and BCM showed a one percent significance an all the three groups. This shows that weight is directly proportional to FFM, TBW, protein, SMM, mineral and BCM. When correlated with BFM weight showed one percent significance in normal (r = 0.81) and obese (r =0.87) subjects and five percent significance in overweight (r = 0.53) subjects. Percent body fat and weight when correlated showed five percent significance in normal subjects and no significance was found in overweight and obese subjects. With VFA one percent significance is seen in normal (r = 0.76) and obese (r = 0.83) subjects, and a five percent significance is seen in overweight (r = 0.54) subjects.

b) BMI and Body Composition Parameters

BMI correlated with BFM and VFA was found to have one percent significance in all the three groups. The body fat mass and visceral fat area had a positive correlation with BMI. As the degree of obesity increases the body fat content is found to increase greatly. BMI with PBF was found to have one percent significance in normal (r = 0.77) and obese (r = 0.82) subjects and five percent significance in overweight (r = 0.62) subjects. FFM was not significant in overweight and obese subjects when correlated with BMI, but significance at one percent level was seen in normal subjects. Similar results were seen with TBW and protein with BMI. BMI correlated with minerals was not found to be significant in all the three groups.

c) WHR and Body Composition Parameters

WHR correlated with BFM showed five percent significance in normal (r = 0.61) subjects and no significance was seen in overweight and obese subjects. With percent body fat, WHR ration showed a high positive correlation (p<0.01) in overweight and obese and five percent significant in normal subjects. FFM and protein when correlated with WHR was not found to be significant in normal and obese subjects but a negative correlation at five percent level is seen in overweight subjects. WHR with VFA correlation was not found to be significant in overweight subjects but had significant correlation with normal (p<0.01; r = 0.75) and obese (p<0.05; r = 0.63) subjects.

d) AC and Body Composition Parameters

AC when correlated with protein, SMM, FFM and mineral was not found to be significant in all the three groups. AC correlated with BFM showed a high positive significance (p<0.01) in normal (r = 0.77), overweight (r = 0.67) and obese (r = 0.68) subjects.

e) AMC and Body Composition Parameters

AMC when correlated with protein, SMM and FFM showed a high positive correlation in normal (p<0.01) and overweight (p<0.01) subjects and was not found to be significant in obese subjects. AMC and BFM was not found to be significant in overweight subjects where as one percent significance is seen in normal (r = 0.52) and obese (r = 0.57) subjects. AMC with minerals showed one percent significance in normal (r = 0.70) and overweight subjects (r = 0.78) and was not found to be significant in obese subjects.

Table X shows the data on correlation within body composition parameters in the selected subjects.

Table X
CORRELATION WITHIN BODY COMPOSITION PARAMETERS
AMONG NORMAL, OVERWEIGHT AND OBESE SUBJECTS

Parameters	BMI Category		
	18.5 – 23.0 Normal (n=15)	23.0 - 26.9 Overweight (n=15)	≥ 27.0 Obese (n=15)
BFM vs. %BF	0.931**	0.734**	0.839**
BFM vs. FFM	0.122 NS	-0.063 NS	0.234 NS
BFM vs. TBW	0.123 NS	-0.064 NS	0.236 NS
BFM vs. Protein	0.103 NS	-0.082 NS	0.200 NS
BFM vs. Mineral	0.208NS	-0.040 NS	0.270 NS
BFM vs. VFA	0.908**	0.946**	0.976**
FFM vs. Protein	0.990**	0.998**	0.993**
FFM vs. TBW	1.000**	1.000**	1.000**
FFM vs. SMM	0.995**	0.999**	0.994**
FFM vs. Mineral	0.964**	0.985**	0.995**
TBW vs. ICW	0.995**	0.999**	0.994**
TBW vs. ECW	0.987**	0.998**	0.989**
Protein vs. SMM	0.998**	1.000**	1.000**
Mineral vs. BMC	0.999**	0.999**	0.999**

** Significant at 1 percent level NS Not Significant

Body fat mass was found to be highly correlated with percent body fat ($r = 0.93$ for normal; $r = 0.73$ for overweight and $r = 0.84$ for obese) in all the three groups. No significant correlation was seen between BFM and FFM, TBW, protein, mineral in all the three groups. The BFM when correlated with VFA showed a high positive significance ($p<0.01$). FFM was correlated with protein, TBW, SMM and mineral which showed a high positive significance ($p<0.01$) in normal, overweight and obese subjects. TBW when correlated with ICW and ECW showed one percent significance in all the three groups. Protein correlated with SMM and mineral correlated with BMC showed one percent significance in the three groups.

10. Energy Balance of the Selected Adults

From the data collected, BMR was calculated using the prediction equation and the mean BMR for normal, overweight and obese was found to be 1214, 1376 and 1573 respectively. The total energy expenditure was calculated using their physical activity expenditure and BMR Table XI presents the energy balance data of the selected individuals.

Table XI
MEAN ENERGY BALANCE OF THE SELECTED INDIVIDUALS

(N=45)

BMI Category	Energy Intake (kcal)	Energy expenditure (kcal)	Energy balance (Kcal)
Normal	1867 ± 59	1809 ± 38	57 ± 68
Overweight	2038 ± 70	1830 ± 60	209 ± 90
Obese	2214 ± 69	1691 ± 68	523 ± 109

Positive energy balance was seen among the overweight and the obese subjects which indicate that their energy intake is greater than their energy expenditure.

DISCUSSIONS

The results were similar to a study conducted by Chhabra *et. al.* (2007) in New Delhi which showed the prevalence to be 24.8 percent among underweight, 19.4 percent among overweight, and 6.1 percent among obese. The remaining 45 percent were normal. The incidence of overweight and obesity was found to be more among 400 subjects.

The onset of puberty for 60 percent of the obese subjects was at the age of 12 years. Girls who reach sexual maturation early are more likely to become overweight or obese than girls who do not mature until later. Age and stage of sexual maturation are associated with body fat and overall weight (Staci, 2009). In the present study, body weight was found to be directly proportional to BMI. Also, greater variations in body weight were noticed in subjects with normal BMI and the other two groups. There is significant difference between the overweight and obesity. Similar findings were shown in a study conducted by Nande *et.al.* (2009) in adult women.

The normal range for total body fat content is said to be 10.5 to 16.8 kg for adult females. From the findings, it is seen that the body fat mass of normal (18.13 kg), overweight (26.89kg) and obese (36.89kg) vary largely. The normal subjects were close to the reference value, whereas the overweight and obese subjects had a fat content way beyond the reference value. This indicates that a major portion of weight for the obese subjects was their fat content. The body fat mass, percent body fat, visceral fat area was found to increase with increase in the degree of obesity. Similar result was given by Nande *et. al.* (2009) with a study on body composition of adult women. These results indicated that each group differed significantly from each other for BF content.

From the foregoing results and discussion, it is evident that the incidence of overweight and obesity among the selected adult female subjects were 19.7 percent and 6.3 percent respectively. The anthropometric measurements and body composition measures showed significantly higher values among the overweight and obese adult female subjects when compared to their normal counterparts. Though the normal subjects had a normal BMI, their body composition measures especially percentage body fat and WHR were above the standard. Similarly the biochemical values though within normal levels in all the three groups, the values were higher in overweight and obese groups. Thus there existed an association between energy balance, body composition and anthropometry.

SUMMARY AND CONCLUSION

The study shows that the incidence of obesity to be around 6 percent. With regard to anthropometric measurements the obese subjects had a greater WHR, arm circumference and arm muscle circumference (25.03 cm) than the overweight and normal subjects. On comparing all the 45 subjects, mild anemia was found to be observed among the obese subjects. Oedema was found in few of the obese subjects. The mean nutrient intake of the obese subjects showed that they had a deficit intake of protein, calcium and iron, but excess intake of fat and energy was noted. All the body composition parameters were found to be higher in obese subjects when compared to that of the normal and overweight. The VFA was found to be normal in both overweight and normal subjects, but was found to go beyond the normal value in obese subjects. Fat free mass, TBW, protein and mineral content were found to be deficit in normal subjects but considerably normal in overweight subjects and normal in obese subjects. Weight showed a positive and significant difference with FFM, TBW, Protein, SMM, Mineral, VFA, and BCM in all the three subjects. BMI showed a high significance with all the measures in normal subjects but a less significant data with overweight and obese. All the biochemical parameters when correlated with the body composition measures was not found to be significant. The energy intake of three group of subjects showed significant difference. A high positive and significant difference (p<0.01) was seen among all the three groups for energy intake, energy expenditure and energy balance. The highest difference was seen between the normal and obese (t = 14.317) energy intake, expenditure (t = 5.726) and energy balance (t = 13.465). The study showed that there was a positive energy balance in overweight and obese subjects and there existed a significant difference in the energy balance among the three groups. Further studies on larger sample size are recommended.

REFERENCES

American Society for Parenteral and Enteral Nutrition (A.S.P.E.N.), (2002), Board of Directors and Clinical Practice Committee. *Definition of terms, style, and conventions used in A.S.P.E.N. Board of Directors—approved documents*. American Society for Parenteral and Enteral Nutrition. http://www.nutritioncare.org/Library.aspx. Published July, 2010. Accessed July 8, 2010.

Bhatt, N. (2007), *Human Development - A Lifespan Perspective*, Aavishkar Publishers, Jaipur, Pp: 268- 272.

Eastwood, M., (2003), Principles of Human Nutrition, 2nd Edition, Blackwell, United Kingdom Pp: 133 – 135

Indian Council for Medical Research, (2010), *Nutrient Requirement and Recommended Dietary Allowances for Indians*, National Institute of Nutrition, Hyderabad. Pp: 40, 41

Insel, P., Turner, R. E., and Ross, D., ADA, (2003), *Discovering Nutrition*, Jones and Bertlett Publishers, Pp: 256

Jekielek, S. and Brown, B. The Transition to Adulthood: 4. Characteristics of Young Adults Ages 18 to 24 in America. Kids count/PR b /Child Trends Report on Census 2000. The Annie Casey Foundation, Population reference bureau, and Child trends, Washington DC; 2005 May. Available from: http://www.prb.org/pdf05/transitiontoadulthood.pdf, accessed on June 20, 2012

Kothari, (2011), *Research Methodology – Methods and Techniques;* 3rd edition, Wishwaprakasan Publishers, New Delhi, Pp: 120 – 121

Mcardle, D.W., Katch, I. F., and L. Katch, V.L., (2007), Exercise Physiology: Energy, Nutrition and Human Performance, (7th edition), Lea & Febiger, Philadelphia, 850p.

Nande, P., Hussain, M. and Vali, S., (2009), Inf luence of Obesity on Body Measurements and Composition in Adult Women Belonging to Minority Community, *Indian Journal of Nutrition and Dietetics*, 47, 137 – 151.

National Family Health Survey – 3 (2007), National Family Health Survey (NFHS – 3), 2005 – 06, India, Volume 1, Pp:26

National Nutrition Monitoring Bureau, (2002), National Institute of Nutrition, Hyderabad

Robert, T., Williams, S. (2000). http://blog.360.yahoo.com/blog-qEKK9K8er93iv.cq&p=4117

Shils, M.E., Shike, M., Ross, A.C., Caballero, B. and Cousins, J.R., (2006), *Modern Nutrition in Health and Disease*, Lippincott Williams and Wilkins, Pp: 751 – 768.

Staci, N., (2009), *William's – Basic Nutrition and Diet Therapy*, 13th Edition, Mosby – an imprint of Elsevier. Pp: 269 – 275.

Visser, M., (2009), Changes in body composition with aging: results from longitudinal studies. *VU University and VU University Medical Center.*

World Health Organization. (1998) Health across the life span. In: The World Health Report 1998. Life in the 1st Century. A vision for all. Report of the Director - General. Geneva: World Health Organization; 1998 p. 66-111. Available from: http://www.who.int/whr/1998/en/whr98en.pdf, Last accessed on January 8, 2013.

http://www.ahrq.gov/

http://www.icmr.nic.in/icmrsql/reportpub.asp?expno=00011393

IMPROVEMENT OF HEMOGLOBIN LEVELS OF SELECTED TRIBAL ANAEMIC ADOLESCENTS THROUGH NUTRITION EDUCATION

C. Padmavathi

Mrs. C. Padmavathi, Associate Professor, Dept. of Food Service Management and Dietetics (FSMD), Avinashilingam Institute for Home Science and Higher Education for Women, Coimbatore, Tamil Nadu. Email: padmajayu@gmail.com

ABSTRACT

Anemia is a major health problem primarily caused by inadequate intake of iron rich foods and deficient consumption of vitamin C rich foods which is essential for the absorption of iron. Subsequently the poor health parameters interfere in social and economic development in developing and developed countries. In India prevalence of anemia is as high as 79 percent among children 6-35 months. Prevalence among women in the age group 15-59 years ranges from 56-58 percent. (NFHS 3 (2005-06). The incidence of maternal anemia continues to be high (over 70 percent) in India in spite of a major nationwide intervention programme. Several research studies have revealed that anemia is more common among Indian children. A study was therefore initiated in one of the Indian states to see if nutrition education could make a difference in prevalence of anemia. Total of 300 families at Pasighat, situated in East Siang District of Arunachal Pradesh were selected randomly and interviewed by using a well-structured interview schedule which was formulated to elicit information on socio-economic background of the subjects, like sex, age, type of family, educational status, occupational status and income status of the family, dietary pattern, life style practices and health problems of the tribal adolescents. Irrespective of the gender there was an improvement of knowledge on nutrition after nutrition education and it was statistically significant at t< 0.05. The impact of nutrition education showed improvement in the hemoglobin levels, which was significant at one percent level and five percent level among girls and boys respectively. It can be inferred that the nutrition education given to the adolescents proved to be beneficial with the increment of hemoglobin level among the selected tribal anaemic adolescents. Nutrition education has proved its potential as one of the powerful tools to educate and alleviate iron deficiency anemia among the adolescents. The research is based on the fieldwork of Ms. Manisha Teronpi, past research student of FSMD.

Keywords: tribal, adolescent, iron deficiency, anemia, hemoglobin, nutrition education

INTRODUCTION

Adolescence is considered to start with the onset of puberty. Puberty is a period of transformation from a stage of reproductive immaturity to a stage of full reproductive committence. Adolescence is a period of greatly enhanced awareness of and attention to physical status and well-being (Vulkenburg and Peter, 2009). The physical growth of adolescents is mainly influenced by the nutrition factor. But the nutritional needs of adolescents are not adequate due to the constraints of socio-economic, environment and dietary factors. This in turn will have complications during reproductive years. The main nutritional problems affecting adolescents include under-nutrition in terms of stunting, thinness, catch up growth, iron deficiency anemia, iodine, vitamin A and calcium deficiencies, and deficiencies of zinc and folate (Hart *et.al.*, 2003). Adolescent girls and boys often suffer from anemia which is detrimental to growth and perpetuates the vicious cycle of malnutrition (Jolly *et.al.*, 2000). Iron requirements peak during adolescence due to rapid growth with sharp increase in lean body mass, blood volume and red cell mass which increases iron needs for myoglobin in muscles and hemoglobin in blood (Beard, 2000). Prevalence of anemia in South Asian countries are among the highest in the world. WHO estimates that even among the South Asian countries, India has the highest prevalence of anemia (Demayer, 2008). National Family Health Survey (NFHS-3) reveals the prevalence of any anemia to be 55.3 percent (IIPS, 2006). The World Health Organization (WHO) estimates anemia as a major public health problem with almost 2 billion people having anemia below normal values (WHO, 2005 and de Benoist *et.al.*, 2008).

Prevalence of anemia in South Asia is among the highest in the world, mirroring overall high rates of malnutrition (WHO, 2000). Africa has the highest prevalence of anemia for all groups of population, but the greatest numbers of people affected are in Asia, where 58 56 and 68 percent of the anemia burden in pre-school aged children, pregnant women and non-pregnant women respectively exists.

Census Report of 2011 revealed that prevalence is very high in Jharkhand, the eastern India. The maximum of female adolescent tribal groups in the age range between 15 and 19 years especially the illiterates, married and belonging to low standard of living were anaemic. According to the 2011 census, the tribal population groups form 11.3 percent of the nation's total population in rural (9,38,19,162) and in urban 2.8 percent (1,04,61,872). This population lives in concentrations in various parts of the country. The 39 million people of Northeast India constitute only about 3.8 percent of the total population of the country. Over 68 percent of this population (26.64 million) lives in the state of Assam alone. Mizoram has the lowest population of less than a million. The density of population varies from 13 per sq. kilometre in Arunachal Pradesh to 340 per sq. kilometre in Assam.

The adolescent population in Arunachal Pradesh (Pasighat) is unaware of the significance of nutrition and health. It is imperative to safeguard and protect the adolescent population from malnutrition. So the research in this line will provide information needed to study the tribal anaemic adolescents and improve their nutritional status by nutrition education.

Hence the present study is undertaken with the objective of imparting nutrition education and find out its effect among selected anaemic adolescents. The study focused with the following specific objectives:

- Study the prevalence of anemia among the tribal adolescent girls

- Understand the socio-economic, dietary behavior and nutritional knowledge of adolescent boys and girls

- Assess the hemoglobin level among the selected adolescent subjects

- Conduct nutrition intervention programme and assess its impact on the selected subjects

METHODOLOGY

A. Selection of the Area

The study was conducted in two schools situated in Pasighat area (East Siang District) Arunachal Pradesh. These schools were selected based on convenience, easy access and cooperation extended by the subjects. Moreover the tribal population hailing from these areas, mostly the adolescents lacked nutritional knowledge and were under developed in many aspects.

B. Selection of Subjects

A total of 300 sample of tribal adolescents both boys and girls were selected from the chosen schools by random sampling method. From these, 266 subjects belonging to the age group of 13-15 were selected and a sub-sample of 30 adolescents, after clinical examination with anaemic status were selected by purposive sampling method for conducting Hemoglobin estimation.

"Purposive sampling was selected because there is good evidence that it is very representative of the total population" (Taylor *et.al.*, 2007).

C. Formulation of Interview Schedule and Conduct of the Study

Selected adolescent groups are shown in Table II. In order to fulfill the objectives of the study it is essential to use suitable tools and techniques to elicit information from the samples. An appropriate interview schedule was formulated. Using this well-structured interview schedule data was collected by personal interview method from 300 subjects.

D. Clinical Examination

The Clinical Examination of 266 selected subjects was carried out with the help of a physician using a clinical schedule to observe the signs and symptoms of anemia among the selected adolescents.

E. Hemoglobin Estimation

To observe the effect of nutrition education, hemoglobin was estimated for 30 selected sub samples before and after nutrition education, who were identified as anaemic through cyanmethemoglobin method for which the blood sample was collected by finger prick.

F. Weighment Survey

Weighment survey was carried out for three consecutive days for the selected 30 sub samples. The weight of the cooked foods was measured using standard measuring devices. The raw equivalents of the cooked foods were computed and the day's mean nutrient intake of the adolescent girls was calculated using the Nutritive value of Indian Foods by ICMR. This was compared with the recommended Dietary Allowances (RDA) (ICMR, 2010) in order to identify the Nutrient adequacy.

G. Nutrition Education

Nutrition Education was given to the adolescents through the distribution of pamphlets, recipe book, lecture with demonstration and charts. Audio-visual aids were also used in order to improve the nutritional knowledge of the samples regarding anemia.

H. Impact of Nutrition Education

The impact of the nutrition education was assessed by finding out the nutritional knowledge before and after nutrition education using a checklist. The hemoglobin level of the selected subjects was estimated before and after imparting nutrition education. The duration between the hemoglobin estimation was 30 days.

I. Analysis of Data

The collected data was edited, tabulated, analyzed and interpreted using appropriate statistical methods.

RESULTS & DISCUSSION

A. Food Expenditure Pattern

The percent of income spent on food is given in Figure 1.

Figure 1

FOOD EXPENDITURE PATTERN

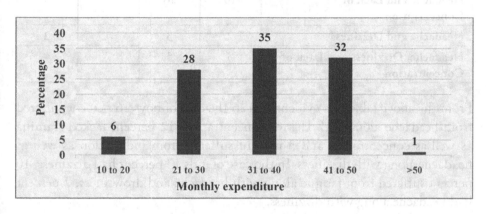

Figure 1 shows that 35 percent of the families spent 31-40 percent of the income on food. 32 percent and 28 percent of the family spent 41-50 and 21-30 percent on food respectively. And only one percent of family spent more than 50 percent on food.

B. Problems experienced by the adolescents

The problems faced by the subjects are given in Table I.

Table I
PROBLEMS AT PRESENT

(No. of subject: 266)

Problems	Boys		Girls	
	Number	Percent	Number	Percent
Fatigue	5	8	19	9
Lack of Stamina	8	12	12	6
Weakness	3	4	7	4
Shortness of Breath	4	6	19	9

115

Lack of Concentration	8	12	12	6
Drowsiness	3	5	21	10
Dizziness	3	5	26	13
Indigestion	2	3	18	9
Headache	5	8	16	8
Fatigue and Headache	3	5	21	10
Failure and Lack of Concentration	5	8	11	5
Headache and Lack of Concentration	10	16	9	5
Headache and Dizziness	2	3	4	2
Headache, Dizziness and Lack of Concentration	3	5	7	4

From the above table it is evident that in the case of boys 16 percent suffered from headache along with lack of concentration, 12 percent lacked stamina as well as concentration and 3 percent suffered from indigestion as well as headache along with dizziness. In the case of girls 13 percent had dizziness, 10 percent suffered from fatigue along with headache and drowsiness, 2 percent had headache along with dizziness.

C. Clinical Signs and Symptoms of Anemia among the Subjects

The clinical signs and symptoms of anemia among the subjects were tabulated and categorized in Table II.

Table II
CLINICAL SIGNS AND SYMPTOMS

(No. of subject: 266)

Problems	Boys		Girls	
	Number	Percent	Number	Percent
Pale Skin	8	13	17	8
Pale Eye	11	17	12	6
Brittle Nail and Scanty Hair	4	6	20	10
Cracks in Sides of Mouth	3	5	7	4
Loss of Hair	5	8	29	15
Glossitis (Soreness of Tongue)	2	3	4	1
Pale Eyes and Skin	6	9	19	9

Pale Eyes and Brittle Nails and Hair	6	9	24	12
Pale Eyes and Loss of Hair	10	16	36	18
Pale Eyes and Cracks in Mouth	5	8	24	12
None	4	6	10	5

Table II shows that 17 percent of boys had pale eyes, 16 percent had loss of hair and pale eyes, 13 percent had the symptoms of pale skin. Nine percent showed the signs of pale eyes along with brittle hair and scanty hair. Five percent had cracks in sides of mouth. Only 6 percent did not have any problems. In case of girls, 18 percent had pale eyes with hair loss. Twelve percent of girls had pale eyes with brittle nails and scanty hair; 5 percent showed no clinical signs and only one percent had soreness of tongue.

D. Mean Nutrient Intake

From the three day dietary survey, energy, protein, fat, carbohydrate, iron, vitamin-C, calcium, fibre, thiamine and vitamin B12 content of the diet was calculated and presented in Figure 2.

Figure 2
MEAN NUTRIENT INTAKE

(N=30)

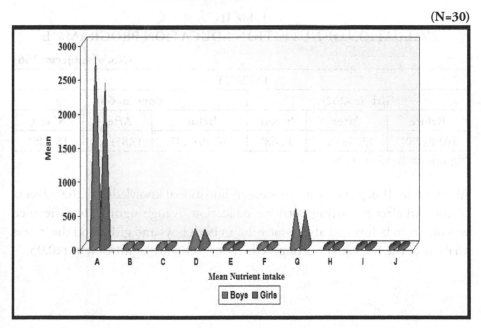

It is seen that the mean energy intake were 2778±125 kcal and 2391±329 kcal for boys and girls respectively, which was higher than the RDA. In the case of fat, it was high for both boys and girls. The mean intake of iron was less than the RDA for both boys and girls. The mean values of calcium, fibre and thiamine were also less than the RDA. Intake of protein was higher than the RDA for both the sexes. Intake of vitamin-C was adequate for both boys and girls.

E. Impact of Nutrition Intervention Programme

The effectiveness of the intervention programme was observed rendering a knowledge checklist to the selected subjects before and after nutrition education programme. Hemoglobin levels were also estimated for the selected anaemic subjects.

1. Evaluation of Nutrition Education Programme

Using a knowledge checklist, to check the knowledge of the selected subjects before and after the nutrition education programme, 't' score on the evaluation of the education programme was statistically analyzed and interpreted in Table III.

Table III
EVALUATION OF NUTRITION EDUCATION PROGRAMME

(No. of subjects: 266)

IMPACT					
Girls (n=202)			Boys (n=64)		
Before	After	't' test	Before	After	't' test
10.98±2.01	17.22±1.12	32.68*	10.90±1.87	17.85±2.0	18.325*

*significant at 5% (t<0.05)

Above table III depicts the mean score in nutritional knowledge of the subjects before and after imparting nutrition education. A high significant difference was observed before and after education in both boys and girls. And the 't' test analysis of the impact of nutrition education is highly significant at t<0.05.

2. Hemoglobin Levels of the Subjects Before and After Nutrition Education

Based on the WHO (2007) criteria below 12g/dl of hemoglobin level for anemia was chosen as the 'cut-off' to identify the moderate (8-10.9g/dl) and mild anaemic (11-11.9g/dl) tribal adolescents.

The hemoglobin levels of the selected subjects were estimated before and after imparting nutrition education and they are presented in Table IV and Figure 3.

Table IV
HEMOGLOBIN LEVELS OF THE SUBJECTS BEFORE AND AFTER NUTRITION EDUCATION

(No. of subjects: 30)

Reference value (g/dl)	Boys			Girls		
	Before	After	't' Value	Before	After	't' Value
Normal (≥12)	8	12	't' Value	3	11	't' Value
Mild (10-11.9)	4	-	7.49*	9	4	5.35**
Moderate (8-9.9)	-	-		6	3	
Severe (<8)	-	-		-	-	

(WHO-2005); *- significant at 5 percent; **- significant at 1 percent

Figure 3
HEMOGLOBIN LEVELS OF THE SUBJECTS BEFORE AND AFTER NUTRITION EDUCATION

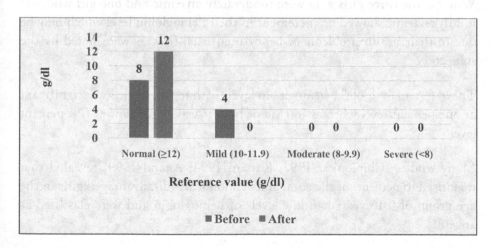

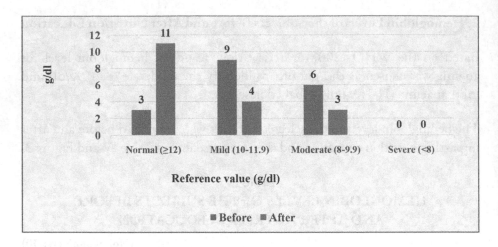

Reference value (g/dl)

■ Before ■ After

Table IV projects the difference in the hemoglobin levels of the selected subjects before and after nutrition education programme. It reflects that the impact of the nutrition education was positive. In the case of boys all the subjects showed increment in their hemoglobin level after imparting nutrition education. Before education, four subjects who were mildly anaemic showed normal hemoglobin level after education and the remaining eight subjects were already at normal level ≥12g/dl.

With regard to girls there was an increment in their hemoglobin levels after the education. The hemoglobin levels of the 11 subjects were ≥12g/dl and the moderately anaemic three subjects were mildly anaemic after the education. Whereas the three girls who were moderately anaemic and one girl who was mildly anaemic showed no increment in their hemoglobin level which may be due to their health problems or heavy menstrual flow as were stated by the subjects.

The 't' test analysis of the hemoglobin levels with regard to girls was significant at one percent level whereas in case of boys it was significant at five percent level.

Many studies (Chiplonkar 1992; Kanani 1994; Anand 1999) revealed that majority (46 percent) of the rural and economically disadvantaged girls in the age group of 9-16 years had low levels of hemoglobin and were classified as anaemic.

CONCLUSION

The prevalence of iron deficiency anemia among adolescents is rising and the knowledge pertaining to anemia and proper dietary pattern is extremely poor in adolescents. Therefore in order to improve the existing situation, imparting nutrition education regarding iron deficiency anemia can play a vital role in prevention. It can be inferred that the nutrition education given to the adolescents proved to be beneficial with regard to their hemoglobin levels. Nutrition education has proved its potential as one of the powerful tools to alleviate iron deficiency anemia among the adolescents. Dietary habits were modified and low cost iron rich foods were included in their diets.

REFERENCES

Anand K, Kant S, Kapoor SK 1999. Nutritional status of adolescent school children in rural North India. Indian Pediatrics, 36(8): 810-815.

Beard J.L. (2000). Iron requirements in adolescent females. Journal of Nutrition, 130:440S-442S.

Census (2011), Primary Census Abstract for Total population, Scheduled Castes and Scheduled Tribes, 2011, Office of the Registrar General & Census Commissioner, India.

Chiplonkar S, Joshi S, Kanade A, Veena C, Rao S 1992. Physical work performance and nutritional status of rural adolescent Indian children. In S Rao, AKanade (Eds.): Proceedings of National Workshop on Adolescence: Need for Critical Appraisal. Pune Maharashtra, India: Department of Biometry and Nutrition, Agharkar Research Institute, pp. 58-65.

De Benoist (2008), Worldwide prevalence of anemia 1993-2005. WHO Global Database on Anemia, Geneva, World Health Organisation.

DeMayer, E.M. and Tegman, A. (2008), Prevalence of anemia in the World. *World Health Organization Quarterly Newsletter, 38*: 302-16.

Hart, K.H., Herriot, A, Bishop, J.A. and Truby, H. (2003) Promoting healthy diet and exercise patterns amongst primary school children: a qualitative investigation of parental perspectives. *Journal of Human Nutrition and Dietetics*, 16, 89–96.

Indian Council of Medical Research (ICMR) (2010), *Micronutrient Profile of Indian Population*. New Delhi.

International Institute for Population Sciences (IIPS, 2006), NFHS-3 Report – Chapter Nutrition and Anemia.

Jolly L, McCoin M, Kris-Etherton PM, (2000). The evidence for dietary prevention and treatment of cardiovascular disease. Journal of the American Dietetic Association 2004; 108:287.

Kanani S (1994). Combating anemia in adolescent girls: A report from India. Mothers and Children, 13(1): 1-8.

Mclean, A.F., James, M.W., McIntyre, A.S. and Scott, B.B. (2008), Guidelines for the management of iron deficiency anemia. *Gut*. (Oct 2008);60(10):1309-16. Valkenburg, P.M., and Peter, J. (2009). Social consequences of the Internet for adolescents: A decade of research. Current directions In Psychological Science, 18, 1-5.

World Health Organization (2001), Iron deficiency anemia: Assessment, prevention, and control. WHO/NHD/01.3.

WHO (2005), Assessing iron status of populations, Report of Joint World Health Organization / Centers for Disease Control and Prevention Technical Consultation on the assessment of iron status at the population level, WHO Publications.

WHO (2007), Hemoglobin concentrations for the diagnosis of anemia and assessment of anemia and assessment of severity, Vitamin and Mineral Nutrition Information System.

PROMOTION OF CARDIOVASCULAR HEALTH THROUGH DIET AND LIFESTYLE INTERVENTIONS AMONG YOUNG ADULT WOMEN

S. Thilagamani[1] and Uma Mageshwari[2]

[1]Dr. S. Thilagamani, Assistant Professor (SS), Department of Food Service Management and Dietetics, Avinashilingam Institute for Home Science and Higher Education for women, Coimbatore, Tamil Nadu. Email: sthilagamanifsmd@gmail.com

[2]Dr. Uma Mageshwari, Associate Professor, Department of Food Service Management and Dietetics, Avinashilingam Institute for Home Science and Higher Education for women. Email: magikrish@rediffmail.com

ABSTRACT

The epidemic of infectious diseases is rapidly being overtaken by non-communicable diseases. A lifestyle associated with poor diet, lack of exercise and depression, increase the risk of lifestyle diseases such as heart disease. The control of risk factors of the lifestyle disorders can delay or even halt the progression of heart disease. Hence the study was undertaken to study the role of diet, lifestyle interventions such as physical activity and yoga among the young women with risk of cardiovascular disease. A total of 1000 women in the age group of 20 to 40 years were selected as the target group to assess the heart health risk. Women with high risk of cardiovascular disease (n= 198) were given interventions with diet, physical activity and yoga for a period of four months. A fibre rich supplement in the form of cookies was developed for the diet intervention with ingredients such as whole grains and millets, carrots, curry leaves and spices. Aerobic exercises for 30 minutes every day for physical activity along with yoga and positive therapy formed the components of lifestyle intervention. The results showed that the parameters such as weight, Body Mass Index and Waist to Hip ratio, lipid profile had significance at one percent level revealing the positive impact of improving the cardiovascular health.

Keywords: health risk, therapeutic, lifestyle, lipoproteins

INTRODUCTION

Non-communicable diseases reduce Gross Domestic Product (GDP) between one and five percent in developing countries as a result of productivity loss, due to morbidity and mortality in the most productive years of population groups stated Alwan *et.al.* (2009). The prevalence of cardiovascular disease in India has risen four-fold in the past four decades stated Rissam *et.al.* (2010). Indians are succumbing to heart disease and stroke in the most productive age of their lives and about a decade earlier than their western counterparts. The primary prevention of cardiovascular disease involves the assessment and management of risk factors in an asymptomatic person. Persons with multiple risk factors are the largest population for primary prevention (National Cholesterol Education Programme, 2002). In order to reverse the tide of rising cardiovascular disease epidemic in Indians, the implementation of preventive strategies is vital. The principle strategy must include interventions not only to detect and treat cardiovascular disease aggressively but control the risk factors that have already developed and prevent the development of risk factors in the first place (primordial prevention). Given the burgeoning epidemic lifestyle disorders in the growing population, it is vital to identify the risk factors that can be modified which may form the basis of preventive programmes. Being aware of the risk factors, taking proactive measures to tide over them or keep an existing disease under control and screen for high risk cases to catch the disease early is important. Young women are highly prone to risk of developing cardiovascular disease in this modern day lifestyle. Hence this study was undertaken with the objective to study the role of diet, lifestyle interventions such as physical activity and yoga among the young women with risk of cardiovascular disease.

METHODOLOGY

Women in the age group of 20 to 40 years were selected as the target group to assess the heart health using Heart Health Risk Assessment Index (HHR

AI). This age group was selected because this is the prime age and women get affected by various physical and psychological problems. A total of one thousand women, 500 employed and 500 unemployed in the age group of 21 to 40 years who had no known history of cardiovascular disease were selected using stratified sampling. One thousand women both employed and unemployed were assessed for risk of cardiovascular disease with Heart Health Risk Assessment Index.

Figure 1

RISK FOR CARDIOVASCULAR DISEASE AMONG YOUNG WOMEN

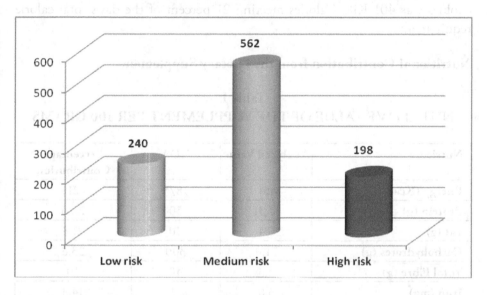

The risk for cardiovascular disease among the selected women showed that 198 women (19.8 percent) were at high risk for cardiovascular disease. Twenty four percent (n=240) were at low risk maintaining desirable heart healthy habits such as diet, physical activity and stress management. It was observed that 31.2 percent at low risk were in the employed category and 16.8 percent were in the unemployed category.

Women with low risk (n=240) and medium risk (n=562) were given individual counseling based on the diet and lifestyle modifications. All the women (n=198) with scores above 81 categorized as high risk were selected for the therapeutic lifestyle intervention with the role of diet, physical activity and yoga. Therapeutic Lifestyle Changes (TLC) are the first and possibly the most important therapy to treat many chronic health problems. Therapeutic

Lifestyle changes are recommended as the first line of therapy for reducing the risk of serious health conditions, such as heart disease, stroke, diabetes, arthritis, osteoporosis and obesity (Gordon *et.al.*, 2004).

Diet and lifestyle interventions for the women with high risk for cardiovascular disease were administered for four months. Cookies with Italian millet flour, wheat flour, and soya flour in the ratio of 1:1:0.5 obtained the highest overall acceptability and hence was selected for supplementation. Four Cookies weighing 25 grams each was given for a period of four months, two as midmorning and two as evening snack. The nutritional contribution of the cookies was 401 Kilo Calories meeting 21 percent of the day's total calorie requirement.

Nutritional Contribution from the Dietary Supplement

Table I
NUTRITIVE VALUE OF THE SUPPLEMENT PER 100 GRAMS

Nutrients	Analyzed Value	RDA	Percentage Contribution
Energy (Kcal)	401	1875	21
Protein (g)	11.31	50	22.6
Fat (g)	6.4	30	21.3
Carbohydrates (g)	71.0	300	23.6
Total Fibre (g)	4.3	40	10
Iron (mg)	3.0	21	14.3
Sodium (mg)	515	2400	21.5
Potassium (mg)	448	4700	9.5
Calcium (mg)	168	600	74.7
Beta Carotene (mcg)	2158.6	2400	89.9

The protein content was 11.31 grams meeting 22.6 percent of the total requirement for a day. Ten percent of the RDA for fibre was noted. A high calcium and beta carotene content with 74.7 and 89.9 percent of RDA respectively was present as it contained carrots and curry leaves. The total antioxidant activity was 0.52 percent. The nutritive value of the cookies proved to be effective to be given as a nutritional supplement.

They were also exposed to two modules on therapeutic lifestyle changes. Aerobic exercises for 30 minutes every day was given for weight management. Aerobic exercise is any form of exercise that can be sustained for few minutes while the heart, lungs, and muscles work higher. The women were advised to maintain food and activity diary. Module I comprising yoga classes were conducted by a yoga expert. Women performed yoga for 30 minutes every day for four months. Module II, was conducted twice a month with the components of positive therapy including deep breathing exercises, auto suggestions for positive thoughts, counseling, tension releasing exercises including smile therapy and laughter therapy. The impact of the therapeutic lifestyle changes were evaluated by testing for changes in risk scores of Heart Health Risk Assessment Index, blood pressure and lipid profile at pre and post intervention for the 198 women categorized as high risk

RESULTS AND DISCUSSION

Results of the comparison of parameters for women with diet, weight and stress management at pre and post intervention are given below.

Table II
DIET, WEIGHT AND STRESS MANAGEMENT
(PRE AND POST INTERVENTION)

Parameters	Pre Intervention (n=24)	Post Intervention (n=24)	't' value	Significance
	Mean ± S.D	Mean ± S.D		
BMI	28.16 ± 4.7	26.11 ± 2.98	7.274	**
WHR	1.05 ± 0.08	0.93 ± 0.09	3.256	**
BP – Systolic	138.5 ± 26.50	121.0 ± 23.20	2.350	**
BP – Diastolic	87.25 ± 10.10	84.50 ± 09.56	2.190	**
Triglycerides	116.46 ± 35.82	113.34 ± 30.45	0.688	**
Total Cholesterol	192.71 ± 20.56	184.67 ± 11.57	6.236	**
HDL	43.42 ± 4.001	44.54 ± 0.88	-1.446	NS
LDL	125.0 4 ± 16.35	116.04 ± 10.17	6.845	**
VLDL	24.16 ± 9.15	24.12 ± 7.35	0.017	NS
Risk Scores	118.67 ± 27.80	67.00 ± 13.42	6.27	**

** - Significant at one percent level,* - Significant at five percent, NS - Not Significant

The intervention group of women with strategies namely diet, weight and stress management showed a positive impact for parameters such as Body Mass Index, Waist to Hip Ratio, Blood Pressure, Total Cholesterol, Triglycerides and Low Density Lipoproteins. The lipoproteins namely high density lipoproteins, very low density lipoproteins did not show any significant difference at pre and post intervention but there was a mean difference noted between pre and post intervention for the women in this group. The mean reduction of weight of the women was five kilograms during the intervention period.

CONCLUSION

Simple intervention strategies like a combined approach of diet, weight and stress management by the young age groups will help in controlling the risk factors contributing to cardiovascular disease. Simple dietary and lifestyle changes are highly important in today's modern lifestyle and adoption of these will help to keep young women healthy.

REFERENCES

Alwan, A., Alleyne, S.G and Silink, M.(2009), Non communicable disease gap in the development agenda, Indian Heart Journal, 61:175 – 179.

Gordon, N.F., Salmon, R.D. and Franklin, B.A. (2004), Effectiveness of therapeutic lifestyle changes in patients with hypertension, hyperlipidemia, and/or hyperglycemia. American Journal of Cardiology; 94(12):1558-61.

National Cholesterol Education Program (2002), "Expert panel on Detection, Evaluation and Treatment of High Blood Cholesterol in Adults (Adult Treatment Panel III)", Final Report, 106:3143.

Rissam, H.S., Kishore, S. and Trehan, N. (2010), Coronary Artery Disease in young Indians – The missing link, Journal of Indian Academy of Clinical Nutrition, 83:1265 – 1271.

COOPERATIVE LEARNING AS AN INSTRUCTIONAL METHOD IN INCLUSIVE CLASSROOMS

G. Victoria Naomi

G. Victoria Naomi, Professor, Department of Special Education, Avinashilingam Institute for Home Science and Higher Education for Women, Coimbatore, Tamil Nadu. Email: gvnaomi@gmail.com

ABSTRACT

Today's system of Education is Inclusive Education wherein differences are welcome. The challenge in education is to effectively teach students of diverse ability and differing rates of learning. Teachers are expected to teach in a way that enables pupils to learn science and mathematics concepts while acquiring process skills, positive attitudes, values and problem solving skills. A variety of teaching strategies have been advocated for use in science and mathematics classroom, ranging from teacher-centered approach to more students-centered ones (Zakaria and Iksan, 2007). Recently cooperative learning has been advocated as a technique that promotes positive relationship between disabled students and non-disabled students and assists in the disabled student's academic achievement.

Keywords: cooperative learning, inclusive schools, special needs students, academic achievement, work habit

Sarva Shiksha Abhiyan (SSA) is a massive attempt of the Government of India and the State Governments to address the objectives made in the Dakar Framework for Action, which was implemented in the year 2002, towards achieving 'Education for All (EFA)'. Without the inclusion of children with disabilities EFA is not a reality and hence the SSA Scheme has made special provision for serving children with disabilities.

A. Cooperative Learning as an Instructional Method in Inclusive Classrooms

Cooperative learning among students is also an essential element of inclusive classrooms. As with interactive learning, students may take on various roles as a facilitator or an assistant working with, or in providing help to other students in a particular subject or even become a learner who benefits from the knowledge or skills of another student (Jorgenson, 1992).

Cooperative learning's effects on attitudes are evidenced by increases in self-esteem, social acceptance, and teacher ratings of students with disabilities (Putnam, Markovchick, Johnson and Johnson, 1996). Cooperative learning also improves the social acceptance of mainstreamed academically handicapped students by their classmates (Madden and Slavin 1983, Johnson *et.al.*, 1983).

Cooperative learning has received increased attention in recent years due to the movement to educate students with disabilities in the least restrictive environment. The use of classroom Cooperative learning, peer groups with cooperative goal structures is a promising alternative to better serve students with disabilities.

Cooperative learning in real sense emphasizes on academic leaning success for each individual and all members of the group which is the one feature that separates cooperative learning groups from the other group tasks. Kagan (1994) propounded that cooperative learning promotes higher achievement than competitive and individualistic learning. In the last decade, there is a vast amount of research done on cooperative learning in science and mathematics. Cooperative learning is grounded in the belief that learning is most effective when students are actively involved in sharing ideas and work cooperatively to complete academic tasks. Cooperative learning has been used both as an instructional method and as a learning tool at various levels of education and in various subject areas (Zakaria and Iysan, 2007). Although a great deal of work has explored active learning pedagogy in a variety of disciplines, this study specifically explores the effect of cooperative learning in science subject in Grade VIII. Literature survey has revealed that the effect of cooperative learning for students with disabilities has hardly been studied. Hence a study was planned with the following objectives.

Objectives

1. Compare the academic achievement of students before and after cooperative learning
2. Compare the academic achievement of students with special needs before and after cooperative learning
3. Study the attitude of students towards cooperative learning
4. Examine the level of work habit of students after cooperative learning

Hypothesis

1. There is no significant difference between pre-test and post-test of students with special needs on academic achievement.

METHOD

Participants

Three hundred and sixty participants in Grade VIII distributed in 12 inclusive schools in Coimbatore and Pollachi Educational Districts of Tamil Nadu were involved and among them 30 were children with special needs. The 30 special needs children were assessed for their nature of disability viz., visual impairment *(7)*, hearing impairment *(8)*, movement impairment *(7)* and cognitive impairment *(8)*.

Research Design

Quasi-experimental design was adopted for the Research study. The design is as follows:

$$Q1 \times Q2$$

The Q1 and Q2 denote pre-test and post-test respectively. Here x means treatment.

Tools

The researcher developed three tools to assess the academic and social skills of children in inclusive schools. Details of the tools are given below:

Curriculum Based Assessment: This was used for the academic achievement of both special needs children and non-disabled peers involved in Cooperative Learning. Academic mark statement before and after implementation of Cooperative Learning was compared. The scores were taken in terms of the children's performance in objective type and short answer questions.

Work Habit Scale: This scale included components such as completion of work on time, persistent attitude towards work, accepting responsibility, asking for help, participating in discussions and following school rules. The Work Habit Rating scale contains 15 items. The scoring was based on a four point rating scale: Always *(3)*, Very Often *(2)*, Sometimes *(1)* and Never *(0)*.

Attitude of Children towards Cooperative Learning Scale: This scale included 10 items of attitude components such as interest in the method, learning behaviour, group learning, sharing of knowledge and learning experience etc. The scoring of these items was *2, 1* and *0* in the rating of Strongly Agree, Agree, Strongly Disagree respectively.

Grouping

Grouping was the initial step in implementing cooperative learning. Heterogeneous grouping was done with 4 to 5 children in a group. For instance, in a class of 20 children, there were 6 groups. A group consisted of high achiever, low achiever, a disruptive child, a special need child and an average child. Roles were assigned as leader, reporter, checker, materials in-charge and safety officer.

Pre-testing

Pre-testing was done in the lesson "Body Movements", immediately after the lesson was completed by the teacher. The academic performance of the subject was assessed using a questionnaire which consisted of Objective type

(15 Marks) and Short answer type (10 Marks), thus making a total score of (25 marks) for each child. The questionnaire had:

>Part I – Fill in the blanks for 10 marks (1x1=10)
>
>Part II – Match the following type question for 5 marks (5x1=5)
>
>Part III - Short answers for 10 marks (5x2=10)

B. Implementation of Cooperative Learning: Steps Involved in the Implementation

The topic selected for cooperative learning was *"Type of Circuits"*

Step 1: Introducing the topic. For example: "Type of Circuits" for 5 minutes.

Step 2: The investigator demonstrated each experiment viz., Simple circuit, Series circuit and Parallel circuit for 10 minutes.

Step 3: Groups were asked to do the Experiment on "Simple Circuit, Series Circuit and Parallel Circuit" on their own with the supervision of the researcher and the classroom teacher. Each group would follow the instructions given by the teacher. Then the children did the activities for example connecting the Series Circuit - i) connecting the bulb on the holder, ii) linking the wires to the switch, iii) connecting the wire with the battery, iv) switch on for glow of all the three lights v) removing one bulb to check how series circuit is affected. vi) dismantle the experiment items. The students were asked to interact with each other in the group and share the concept and ensure that everyone in the group learnt the concept and acquired necessary skills. This exercise would take 25 minutes.

Step 4: Discussion on the topic quietly and sharing the learning among peers for 5 minutes.

Step 5: Brainstorming on a question given. The following were some of the question posed:

1. How is a simple Circuit made?
2. What kind of a path is required by a f low of current?
3. How will be the series circuit if a bulb gets diffused?

133

4. What happens when one of the bulbs in the parallel circuit is removed or fused off?

5. Explain the difference between series and parallel circuit?

This session would be for 15 minutes.

Step 6: Supply of worksheet to each group. All in a group discuss and write the answer in the worksheet given to the whole group. This would take 10 minutes.

Step 7: Written answer were shared to the whole group for another 10 minutes. This teaching method would take 2 periods with 40 minutes for each period.

Depending on the lesson, time will vary but will not exceed 2 periods or 1 hour 20 minutes.

The similar procedure was followed to complete the lesson. Classroom teacher was monitoring and helping students as and when assistance was required.

Post-testing

After intervention using cooperative learning method, post-test was administered adopting the same method as in the pre-test. The academic achievement of students was assessed using questionnaire consisting of Objective Type (15 Marks) and Short Answer Type (10 Marks) and a total score of 25 marks for each student.

RESULTS

Result 1: Academic Achievement

The results of this aspect of the study are further discussed as follows:

Comparison of Mean Scores Before and After Introduction of Cooperative Learning- School-wide Population

Table I
ACADEMIC ACHIEVEMENT WITH RESPECT
TO PRE AND POST-TEST

S. No.	Name of the School	Test	Mean	SD	df	't' value
1.	School 1	Pre	18.42	3.68	48	2.1*
		Post	19.14	3.42		
2.	School 2	Pre	15.71	2.80	17	3.6**
		Post	16.96	2.60		
3.	School 3	Pre	11.96	4.04	44	9.8**
		Post	14.33	3.93		
4.	School 4	Pre	12.43	3.80	37	9.9**
		Post	15.71	4.29		
5.	School 5	Pre	13.32	2.31	6	2.3*
		Post	14.71	2.87		
6.	School 6	Pre	14.40	2.82	24	2.6*
		Post	15.00	2.83		
7.	School 7	Pre	18.27	3.31	25	3.3**
		Post	19.26	3.28		
8.	School 8	Pre	16.14	4.11	25	6.9**
		Post	17.46	4.17		
9.	School 9	Pre	15.70	2.68	20	2.4*
		Post	16.62	3.02		
10.	School 10	Pre	16.30	2.87	39	5.2**
		Post	16.91	2.98		
11.	School 11	Pre	15.54	3.45	26	3.9**
		Post	16.27	3.35		
12.	School 12	Pre	12.87	4.07	37	10.1**
		Post	15.34	4.05		

*Significant at 0.01 level ** Significant at 0.05 level NS-Non significant*

An analysis was made to compare the mean scores before and after cooperative learning.

It is evident from the above table that the 't' value for pre and post mean score for the 12 schools is significant either at 0.01 level or 0.05 level. This indicates that there is significant difference between pre-test and post-test mean scores of students in all schools. Hence it may be concluded that Cooperative Learning enhances learning among students.

Result 2: Comparison of Mean Scores of CWSN Before and After

Introduction of Cooperative Learning

Table II
ACADEMIC ACHIEVEMENT OF CHILDREN WITH SPECIAL NEEDS

Variable	Test	N	Mean	SD	't' value
Academic	Pre	30	14.02	4.50	
Achievement	Post	30	16.32	4.06	4.1**

**Significant at 0.01 level

From Table II, it is evident that the 't' value for the Academic Achievement of students with special needs before and after introduction of Cooperative Learning is 4.1 which is significant at 0.01 level. It indicates that there is significant difference between pre-test and post-test of students with special needs on Academic Achievement. Hence, the hypothesis stated that ***there is no significant difference between pre-test and post-test of students with special needs on academic achievement is rejected.*** It is concluded that Cooperative Learning strategies were efficacious in enhancing learning of students with special needs (Figure 1).

Figure 1
ACADEMIC ACHIEVEMENT OF CHILDREN WITH SPECIAL NEEDS

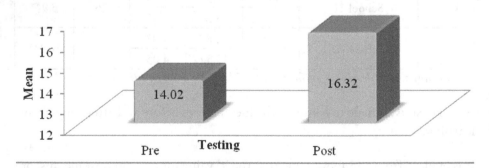

When the mean scores of each category of disability was compared with respect to their pre and post scores, the visually impaired students secured higher scores followed by the hearing impaired, movement impaired and then cognitive impaired (Figure 2).

Figure 2

COMPARISON OF A ACADEMIC ACHIEVEMENT AMONG CHILDREN WITH SPECIAL NEEDS

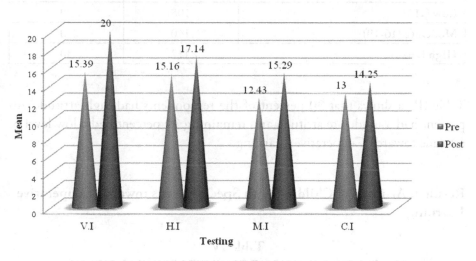

Result 3: Attitude of Students towards Cooperative Learning

Table III

ATTITUDE OF STUDENTS TOWARDS COOPERATIVE LEARNING

No.	Minimum	Maximum	Mean	SD
360	10.00	20.00	17.25	2.62

A descriptive analysis was made to find out the attitude towards cooperative learning among students. The respondents were grouped as low, moderate and high. Table III reveals that attitude ranged from a minimum of 10 to a maximum of 20 and the average score was 17.25 with SD 26.2.

The respondents whose attitude score was between 0.5 SD value were classified as low attitude score and the respondents whose attitude score was above + 0.5

SD were classified as higher attitude score. The respondents whose attitude score was between mean -0.5SD and Mean +0.5 SD were classified as moderate attitude group. The distribution of respondents as per the classification is given in Table III. a.

Table III. a
ATTITUDE SCORES OF RESPONDENTS

Level	No.	Percent
Low (<15)	108	30
Moderate (16-19)	140	40
High (>=20)	112	30

Table III. a shows that 30 percent of the respondents had high attitude, 40 percent had a moderate attitude and remaining 30 percent had a low level of attitude towards Cooperative Learning.

Result 4: Attitude of Children with Special Needs towards Cooperative Learning

Table IV
ATTITUDE OF CHILDREN WITH SPECIAL NEEDS
TOWARDS COOPERATIVE LEARNING

No.	Minimum	Maximum	Mean	SD
30	14.00	20.00	18.0	2.14

A descriptive analysis was made to find out the level of attitude towards cooperative learning among students with special needs. The respondents were grouped into low, moderate and high. Table IV reveals that attitude ranged from a minimum of 14 to a maximum of 20 and the average score was 18 with SD 2.14.

The respondents whose attitude score was between 0.5 SD value were classified into low attitude score, the respondents with attitude score above + 0.5 SD were classified into higher attitude group. The respondents whose attitude scores fall between mean -0.5 SD and Mean +0.5 SD were classified as moderate attitude group. The distribution of respondents by classification is given in Table IV. a.

Table IV. a

Level	No.	Percent
Low (<16)	8	27
Moderate (17-19)	9	30
High (>=20)	13	43

Table IV. a shows that 43 percent of the respondents showed high attitude towards Cooperative Learning, 30 percent showed moderate attitude and 27 percent presented low level of attitude towards Cooperative Learning.

Result 5: Work Habit of Children from Selected Sample

Table V

WORK HABIT OF CHILDREN

No.	Minimum	Maximum	Mean	SD
360	17.00	45.00	35.0	6.3

A descriptive analysis was made to find out the level of work habit among students after cooperative learning. The respondents were grouped into low, moderate and high. Table V reveals that work habit varied ranging from a minimum of 17 to a maximum of 45 and the average score was 35.0 with SD 6.3.

The respondents whose work habit score was between 0.5 SD values were classified into low level of work habit, the respondents whose work habit score was above + 0.5 SD were classified into higher level of work habit group. The respondents whose score was between mean -0.5 SD and Mean +0.5 SD were classified as moderate level of work habit respondents. The distribution of respondents based on this classification is given in Table V. a.

Table V. a
STUDENTS CLASSIFIED UNDER WORK HABIT SCORE

Level	No.	Percent
Low (<31)	92	26
Moderate (32-38)	145	40
High (>=39)	123	34

Table V. a shows that 40 percent of the respondents reflected moderate level of Work Habit Score 34 percent of students reflected higher level of Work Habit Score after Cooperative Learning and the remaining 26 percent presented low level of Work Habit Score.

Result 6: Work Habit of Children with Special Needs

Table VI
WORK HABIT OF CHILDREN WITH SPECIAL NEEDS

No.	Minimum	Maximum	Mean	SD
30	22.00	45.00	36.3	5.7

A descriptive analysis was made to find out the level of work habit among children after cooperative learning. The respondents were grouping into low, moderate and high. Table VI reveals that work habit varied from a minimum of 17 to a maximum of 45 and the average score was 36.3 with SD 5.7.

The respondents whose Work Habit Score was between 0.5 SD values were classified as persons with low work habit group, respondents whose Work Habit Score was above + 0.5 SD were classified into higher level of work habit group. The respondents whose score was between mean -0.5SD and mean +0.5 SD were classified as moderate level of work habit respondents. The distribution of respondents based on this classification is given in Table VI. a.

Table VI. a
RESPONDENTS CLASSIFIED BY WORK HABIT SCORE

Level	No.	Percent
Low (<32)	7	23
Moderate (33-39)	12	40
High (>=40)	11	37

Table VI. a shows that 40 percent of children had moderate Work Habit Score, 37 percent of children had high score of work habits after Cooperative Learning and only 23 percent had low level of Work Habit Score.

MAJOR FINDINGS

The findings emerged out this study are:

1. In general Cooperative Learning strategies enhanced the learning of most of the students in a classroom. The mean score of pre-test was 14 whereas it was 16.32 in the post-test indicating that cooperative learning improved the students' learning behaviour.
2. Cooperative Learning enhanced the learning of students with special needs (Visually Impaired - pre mean: 15.39 & post mean: 20.00; Hearing Impaired - pre mean: 15.16 & post mean: 17.44; Movement Impaired - pre mean: 12.5 & post mean: 15.29; Cognitive Impaired – pre mean: 15.39 & post mean: 14.25).
3. Descriptive statistics reflected that a majority 70 percent (High: 30 percent and Moderate 40 percent) showed greater positive attitude towards cooperative learning.
4. Among students with special needs, 73 percent (High: 43 percent, Moderate: 30 percent) presented positive attitude towards cooperative learning.
5. Pertaining to the work habit of students, 74 percent respondents had better Work Habit Scores.
6. Regarding the work habit of students with special needs, 77 percent (High: 37 percent and Moderate: 40 percent) acquired better work habit indicating the impact of cooperative learning.

REFERENCES

Kagan, S. Dr. (1994). *Cooperative Learning* San Clemente, CA: Kagan.

Madden, N.A., & Slavin, R.E. (1983). "Effects of CL on the social acceptance of mainstreamed academically impaired students", *Journal of Special Education*, Vol.17, Pp.171-82.

Putnam J, Markovchick K, Johnson DW, Johnson RT. (1996). Cooperative learning and peer acceptance of students with learning disabilities. The Journal of Social Psychology, Dec; 136 (6):741-52. Retrieved from http://www.ncbi.nlm.nih.gov/pubmed/9043203.

Zakaria, E., & Iksan, Z. (2007). Promoting cooperative learning in science and mathematics education: A Malaysia perspective. *Eurasia Journal of Mathematics, Science & Technology Education, 3*, 35-39.

CAN WOMEN'S STUDIES REDUCE DROPOUT? SURVEY RESPONSES FROM TERTIARY-LEVEL FEMALE STUDENTS

Sayani Das

Sayani Das, Assistant Professor, Women's Studies Centre, Avinashilingam Institute for Home Science and Higher Education for Women, Coimbatore, Tamil Nadu. Email: sayanidas.wgs@gmail.com

ABSTRACT

The study puts and tests the subject matter of 'Women's Studies' into practice. It is a diagnostic and impact assessment study to highlight the barriers to and reasons for dropout from education for college/university going 'women' and the role of Women's Studies in their personal lives. The study is based on analysis of the responses gathered through survey and conversation from undergraduate female students across disciplines (Arts, Humanities, Education, Social Sciences, Sciences and Technology) enrolled in an all-women university setting, who have chosen to study 'Women's Studies' as a co-curricular credit course. The study finding is path-breaking as it explains that even a short certificate course on 'Women's Studies' can influence mindset of female students coming from rural backgrounds and raised in traditional patriarchal culture and practices. The study substantiates the need and scope of Women's Studies as a compulsory course in higher education, which can have positive impact on their mindset to reduce their dropout against the highly prioritized age factor among female students – 'early marriage and pregnancy'. Women's Studies Course also encourages supportive communal environment for more female students to complete their undergraduate studies without gender bias and social restriction.

Keywords: Women's Studies, female students, higher education, dropout, marriage and pregnancy

INTRODUCTION

Women's Studies is the inter- and multi-disciplinary study of the social position and contribution of women – their roles, experiences and achievements in society; their relationships with gender, power and hierarchy; their struggles against history and injustice and for voices. Thus, Women's Studies subject matter is not theoretical only, but connected to grassroots pragmatism. Women's Studies explores our gendered existence and attitude, which is again constructed by our own society. Women's Studies is therefore multi-cultural and questions the very patterns of 'patriarchy' (male-dominance) and its effect on women folks. Patriarchy is a prevalent social system accepted by every section of Indian society, whereby male members perform important roles, hold primary power and position, lead socio-cultural-economic-political life, possess moral authority, enjoy social privilege and higher status, control wealth and property, dominate family (women and children). Women's Studies scholars unanimously have supported the social fact that 'gender' is not biological identity but socially constructed stereotypes. Gender stereotypes are created by the social norms, mores, folkways, etc., in order to control deviant individuals and maintain social harmony. As such, men and women are separated by their division of labour in society – whereby men are the productive bread-earners spending time outside home for long hours; whereas women are the reproductive agents spending lifetime inside four walls of house for home-care, child-care, adult-care and old-care. It is the social dominance of masculine-mastery over feminine-nurturing that creates deep impression in an individual's mindset from childhood to old-age. Hence, boys or girls, men or women act or play gender-appropriate roles, conforming and strengthening 'gender stereotypes' in society. Breaking gender stereotypes then becomes even more difficult and individuals become slaves to their own traditional mindset, believing in the physical and social difference of power and authority between superior men and inferior women.

What matters more at this juncture is the identification of gender stereotypes and breaking of gender stereotypes. No subject other than the Women's Studies - whose fundamental aim and scope is to identify blatant gender stereotypes present in society, explore socially hidden myths of gender stereotypes; and critique social construction of gender stereotypes as the root-cause for gender inequality in cultural beliefs, social norms and individual actions. Importance of Women's Studies lies in its success to sensitize students for equality between sexes, nurture egalitarianism among men and women, promote complementary than supplementary gender roles. Women's Studies has been struggling to achieve its goal since 1960s and has achieved to quite an extent. The present study was aimed to prove or disprove the achievement of Women's Studies in a pragmatic context, whereby a sample of 168 women under-graduate students from various disciplines (Arts, Humanities, Education, Social Sciences, Sciences and Technology) having studied Women's Studies as co-curricular course, were surveyed to assess their mindset towards enrolment and dropout among women in higher education.

Recent Trends in Higher Education of Women

The issue of women entering in higher education came firmly from the global political agenda in 1998 under the leadership of UNESCO, which prepared *The Higher Education and Women: Issues and Perspectives* for the 1998 World Conference on Higher Education, specifically focused on the issues related to women. However in India, it was much earlier by the Kothari Commission (1964-66) that had emphasized on equal educational opportunities for women and had also suggested effective steps to achieve it. As pointed out by Karuna Chanana, the first two Five Year Plans (1951-56 and 1956-61) acknowledged the problems related to women's education and tried to link education with employment. It was after the publication of the Report of the Committee on the Education of Women in 1959 that led to a more focused attention, which later got sharpened with the Report of the Committee on the Status of Women in 1974 and women's education was placed within the broader framework of developmental issues. The National Policy of Education (1986), broadening the vision further underscored the role of education in empowering women that would overcome inequalities and disparities (Chanana, 2005).

Subsequent Five Year Plans and various committees including the National Perspective Plan (1988-2000) have stressed the need for greater participation of women in higher education. These efforts have resulted in increase in women accessing higher education. According to Educational Statistics published by Ministry of Human Resource Development (2014), the enrolment in education in India has witnessed a Compounded Annual Growth Rate (CAGR) of about 25.7 percent, in Secondary to Higher Secondary Education (Standards IX-X and XI-XII respectively). The Dropout Rates between school education have fallen to 18.3 percent from 2000 to 2014. The enrolment in Higher Education has grown at a CAGR of about 44.5 percent with total enrolment in different years of study in Higher Education in India with about 29.6 million students by 2013. According to All India Survey on Higher Education (2012-13) the Gross Enrolment Ratio (GER) [ie., total enrolment of students in a given level of education] among age group (18-23 years) in higher education in India is 21.1 (Male - 22.3 and Female - 19.8; Gender Gap is 2.5) and in Tamil Nadu is 38.2 (Male - 41.1 and Female - 35.2; Gender Gap is 5.9). Gender Parity Index (GPI) [ie., the ratio of girls to boys in a given level of education] for the same age group among all categories of students in higher education in India is 0.89 (SC - 0.89 and ST - 0.79) and in Tamil Nadu is 0.86 (SC - 0.89 and ST - 0.82). Number of girls per hundred boys enrolled in Higher Education in India in 2012-13 is 81, which is a steep rise from 13 in 1950-51. Dropout Rate [ie., the percentage of students who dropout from a given level of education] among age group (18-23 years) in higher education in India is not available and it may be estimated from the available data (AISHE, 2012-13) as given below.

Table I
ESTIMATED DROPOUT RATE AMONG AGE GROUP
(18-23 YEARS) IN HIGHER EDUCATION

Higher Education	Male (in million)	Female (in million)	Total (in million)	Ratio (in %)	Gender Gap (in %)
Estimated Population	73.2	67.5	140	52:48	4.1
Enrolled Population	16.3	13.3	29.6	55:45	10.2
Dropout Population	56.9	54.2	110.4	52:49	2.4

Among dropout population 51.5 percent are male and 49.1 percent are female students. Gender Gap in dropout population is 2.4 percent only. This is due to the fact that male students in the age group of (18-23 years) dropout to meet the societal or gender stereotypic demand for being 'bread-winner' in the family. While female students in the same age group dropout to meet the societal or gender stereotypic demand for 'marriage'. We have to notice here that there is a large gender gap of 10.2 percent between the male and female students enrolled in higher education than the population demography and dropout statistics. The above table can explain the social discrimination on women in the age group of (18-23 years) to not enroll in higher education due to priority given on marriage, child-bearing and family care. According to Gandhi Kingdon (2010), the gender gap in educational attainment in India can be potentially explained by differential treatment of sons and daughters by parents. The gender difference in educational attainment is decomposed into the part that is explained by men and women's differential characteristics and the part that is not so well explained (the conventional 'discrimination' component). Girls face significantly different treatment in the intra-household allocation and expenses on education and there is a large unexplained component in the gender gap in education attainment.

According to National Sample Survey Organisation (NSSO), more students choose higher education, but dropout even more. Survey comparing data from 1991-2000 to 2001-2010 period found that attendance rates in the higher education increased by 71 percent for male students and 110 percent for female students in rural areas. In urban areas, the growth was 40 percent for males and 45 percent for females. Although the rise in percentage terms is a marked improvement over the decades, the data showed that the dropout rate also kept in pace. In 2009-10, the attendance rates were just 19 percent for males and 8 percent for females in rural areas; in urban areas, corresponding figures were 33 percent and 24 percent, respectively. This state of higher education compared badly with those in the age group of 5-14 years, where 87 percent of boys and 84 percent of girls were attending school in rural areas, and 91 percent of all boys and girls in urban areas. While current attendance rates indicate a positive trend for the future, existing educational levels of population in the age group of 15 years and above, continue to be dismal. This is much higher than the rural areas where only 3.7 percent of males and a mere 1.6 percent of females have gone up to graduation or beyond. What is even more alarming is that in 10 years between 1999-2000 and 2009-10, the graduate and above segment of the urban population declined by 5 percent among males, although it increased by 10 percent among females. Due to rural-urban differential, the new social demand for education in the rural areas is still driving educational levels higher. The proportion of graduates and above went up by 78 percent among females but only 12 percent in males in rural areas. In urban areas, about 15 percent of males and 11 percent of females are graduates or above. Interestingly, 'marriage prospects' for young females in the age group of (18-23 years) have tended them more to join higher education. At the same time, female students dropout from higher education when suitable marriage alliances are found elsewhere, especially in urban areas or abroad. Overall, the access to higher education is also low for females as compared with males. It needs to be recognized that although the enrolment ratio are generally lower for the female compared to the male, the female belonging to the lower caste and minority religious groups suffer more with regard to access to higher education than others (Srivastava and Sinha, 2008). According to them, there are inter-social group disparities in access to higher education like: poor–non-poor differential; and occupation, caste and poverty interface. There are significant differences in enrolment rates among the poor and non-poor. Among the self-employed cultivator, self-employed in non-farm sector, agriculture labor and other labor in rural areas; the enrolment is particularly low for the poor households against non- poor households. The main exclusionary divide as far as access to higher education is concerned is the rural-urban divide. Rural women and women from poverty level, almost without exception, have the lowest access to higher education. Amongst the rural women, it is essentially those from the lower rungs of socio-religious communities who have the lowest access in particular It is further pointed out more importantly, that the overall representation of women in higher education is therefore quite low and the concern here is to capture the gross quantum. In addition to enrolment, retention and completion is also major issue for women. She suggested that there should be avenues for continuing education for women who had interrupted educational trajectory due to marriage, family responsibility and/or child care. Hence, the traditional picture of Indian educational levels - like a pyramid - with a very wide base (of illiterates) tapering to a sharp point (of graduates) - is changing at the bottom but not much at the top (Subodh Varma, 2013) with little improvement of inequality at college/university level (Desai & Kulkarni, 2008).

Professor Yash Pal, former Chairperson of the University Grants Commission (UGC) suggested increase of funding for higher education could check the persistent high dropout rates in higher levels. However, there are several other systemic problems, but two of them are cited to highlight some of them – i) is the inadequate funds per se; and ii) more importantly is the gross under-utilization of even available funds - that too in backward states and particularly in tribal and some southern states where relatively better environment exists in terms of gender sensitivity. It is seen that out of the 8 percent of total UGC budget that is spent on women's scheme, as high as 95 percent is spent on hostels. However, the budgetary allocation is grossly inadequate and yet the

Plan-wise data for the years 1995-96 to 2005-06 show that although about 70 percent of allocated money for hostel construction is sought by educational institutes, about 40 percent is actually utilized as can be inferred from the utilization certificate (Zarabi, 2012).

Moreover, Central and State Governments are offering scholarships to promote higher education among students, belonging to the weaker sections of the society, who are unable to further their education for some reason or the other. There are a variety of scholarships – merit-based, need-based, student-specific, career-specific and college-specific. Central Scheme of Scholarship for College and University Students is a National Merit Scholarship Scheme. The objectiveof this scholarships scheme is to provide financial assistance to meritorious students from poor families from senior secondary to post-graduation level in Government Schools, Colleges and Universities, to meet a part of their day- to-day expenses while pursuing higher studies. It is renewed as a new Central Sector Scheme of Scholarship for College and University Students under XIth Five Year Plan in 2007-2012. These scholarships are awarded on merit basis to high achieving students (80th percentile in senior secondary examination of 10+2 pattern or equivalent). The number of scholarships allotted are in the ratio of 3:2:1 distributed for all subjects under Science, Commerce and Humanities disciplines for graduation and post-graduation studies (regular courses, not correspondence or distance mode) in colleges and universities and for professional courses, such as Medical, Engineering, Technology, Management, etc. The total number of scholarships (82000 fresh scholarships per annum, 41000 for boys and 41000 for girls) is divided amongst students passed from the State Boards based on the State's population in the age group of 18-25 years, Central Board of Secondary Education (CBSE) and Council for the Indian School Certificate Examination (CISCE). These scholarships are given to students under all categories ('general' and 'reserved' – SC, ST, MBC, OBC) having family income of less than Rupees 6 lakhs per annum. However, the rates of scholarship are merely nominal - i) Rupees 10,000 per annum at Graduation level for the first three years of College and University courses; ii) Rupees 20,000 per annum at Post-Graduation level; iii) Rupees 10,000 per annum in the 1st, 2nd and 3rd year and Rupees 20,000 per annum in the 4th and 5th year for Professional Courses.

Tamil Nadu Directorate of Collegiate Education also offers similar male and female inclusive scholarships for undergraduate, postgraduate and doctoral studies from Government and Government Aided Colleges and universities.

The well-known scholarship scheme is Waiver of Tuition fees - UG and PG. The State Government has been offering wavier of tuition fees upto undergraduate level for students since the academic year 2007-08. The Government has also waived the tuition fees for the students studying postgraduate courses from the academic year 2010-2011. Ph.D. Scholarships are available on merit basis to only 60 full time research scholars with a nominal stipend of Rupees 30,000 per annum (Rupees 3000 per month for 10 months a year) for the minimum period of 2 years. Government of India & Tamil Nadu Government Higher Educational Special Loan Scholarships are given to SC, ST, Converted Christian and Adi-Dravidar students; whose annual income of parents is below Rupees 50,000-1,00,000. Loan Scholarship Scheme was converted into Higher Educational Special Scholarship Scheme from 2002-2003 at the rate of Rupees 6500 per annum and free tuition fees.

Central and State Governments having recently realized that education is one of the most important means of empowering women with the knowledge, skill and self-confidence necessary to participate fully in the development process are offering 'women exclusive' scholarships. Pragati Scholarship has been launched by the Ministry of Human Resource Development, Government of India from the year 2014-15 to provide encouragement and support to the girl child to pursue technical education. 4000 scholarships are given under the Pragati Scheme for Girls and 1000 scholarships under the Saksham Scheme for the Differently-abled Students under both general and reserved categories (15 percent for SC, 7.5 percent ST and 27 percent for OBC). Pragati (Scholarship for Girl Students) is a scheme of All India Council for Technical Education (AICTE), aimed at providing assistance for advancement of girls' participation in Technical Education. Its objective is to give every young woman the opportunity to further her education and prepare for a successful future by "Empowering Women through Technical Education". 'One Girl' per family, where the family income is less than Rupees 6 lakhs per annum are selected on merit at the qualifying examination to pursue technical education (Degree or Diploma programme) in any of the AICTE approved institute through centralized admission process of the State/Centre Government. Pragati scholarship includes tuition fees of Rupees 30,000 and Rupees 20,000 incidental fees each year. Post-Graduate Indira Gandhi Scholarships are similarly available for single girl child pursuing postgraduate programmes in Sciences. UGC has announced Swami Vivekananda Scholarship from 2014-15 for single girl child (40 years for general and 45 years for the reserved category-SC/ST/OBC and Physical handicapped) pursuing regular full-time Doctor of Philosophy programme in Social Sciences in any recognized university/ institute. If in a family if there is one son and one daughter then girl child will not be considered for scholarship under the scheme. The amount of scholarship is: Rupees 8000 per month (for 10 months a year) in first two years and Rupees 10,000 per month for third and fourth year (extendable for fifth year in exceptional circumstances).

Tamil Nadu State Government Scholarships on 'women empowerment' are Periyar EVR Nagammai Free Education Scheme, which offers scholarships to women students since 1989. Government of Tamil Nadu Post-Matric Scholarship is offered to BC-MBC students and scholars whose parental annual income is below Rupees 1 lakh. Under this scheme, women students irrespective of their caste, creed and community and whose parental annual income does not exceed Rupees 50,000 per annum are exempted from payment of tuition fees in undergraduate courses. EVR Nagammai Scholarship is also given to the girl students pursuing postgraduate courses in Government and Aided colleges and State Universities in Tamil Nadu.

Therefore we can derive that students, whether male or female, who are high achievers (above 80th percentile in their respective streams), belonging to economically weaker sections (EWS) with parental income of Rupees 50,000-2,00,000 per annum (according to TN Govt.) and up to Rupees 6,00,000 per annum (according to Central Govt.) are encouraged for entry in higher education with tuition waiver and small amount of scholarships (a meager amount of Rupees 1000-3000 per month in UG, PG and PhD level), in order to take care only part of their daily expenses towards higher education. Interesting to note here is that all single girl child scholarships represented 'patriarchal mindset' as it takes for granted that 'only daughter' to parents needs financial help to complete education and join employment in order to look after her family. However, a girl child who has one or more brothers is to be dependent not on the Centre/State, but on the male members of her family, and her empowerment is not priority under Indian policy. Although from the above discussion we understand that Government has introduced several programmes and policies, including scholarships, since Tenth Five Year Plan (2002-2007) for the educational development of women in higher education which include: i) Increase in Women Enrolment Faculty-wise; ii) Construction of Women Hostels for Colleges; iii) Development of Women's Studies in Universities and Colleges; iv) Capacity Building for Women Managers in Higher Education; v) Establishment of Equal Opportunity Cells (EOC) for

SC/ST/OBC/Minorities; vi) Establishment of Residential Coaching Academy for SC/ST/ Minorities and Women in Universities and Colleges; vii) Post-Doctoral Fellowship for SC/ST; viii) Post-Graduate Scholarships for SC/ST students in professional courses; ix) Day Care Centres in universities and colleges; x) Indira Gandhi Scholarship for Single Girl Child for pursuing higher and technical education; xi) Doctoral and Post-doctoral Fellowships for Women (Zarabi, 2012). But in the absence of systematic database on how these programmes, policies and schemes actually work, been utilized/not utilized, benefitted, barriers by the end-users etc.; it becomes somewhat difficult to suggest effective interventions. Karuna Chanana (1993) demonstrated that the educational policy failed to integrate these functions which remain sectoral aims even at the conceptual level. Further, in the multi-cultural and multi-ethnic Indian society, the parameters of gender, caste, class, religion and region are crucial in determining access to higher education. Again, gender becomes the all-inclusive negative parameter conferring cumulative and competitive disadvantages on women. The educational policies and programmes are unable to encompass the complex social reality within a single framework and are, therefore, unable to bridge the gap between policy and practice. Hence the question arises, whether these 'tokenistic' policies, programmes and schemes such as scholarship, toward women empowerment can be 'drive enough' for young women to higher education or perhaps we need to explore other alternatives to motivate them to access and gain higher education and contribute to national development and progress.

'Women's Studies' as Discipline to Promote Higher Education for Women

With this understanding of 'symbolic' encouragement of women in higher education, this paper tries to explore whether Women's Studies can do 'real' justice to women in higher education in terms of enrolment, retention and return after career-break due to family obligations. Women's Studies as a discipline has created theories about 'women's issues' and its intersections with gender, race, ethnicity and sexuality - that offer important analytical frameworks for developing itself as a multicultural curricula. Women's Studies acts as a catalyst for the transformation of curricula into more inclusive frameworks of higher education. The Women's Studies programme was started as academic discipline due to the student unrest of 1960s and the subsequent changes to higher education. The 1970s produced serious interest in developing theory about the dynamics of feminist classrooms and the beginnings of a feminist pedagogy. These social and women's movements are beginning to transform higher education curricula through changes in course requirements and in course contents (Schmitz, Betty & Others, 1995).

Lack of Females' participation in education has been attributed to curriculum contents and pedagogical approaches that are biased toward males' interests (Sanders, Koch, & Urso, 1997; Shroyer, Backe & Powell, 1995). One significant challenge is culturally-grounded gender stereotyping, which has a substantial influence on children's self-concepts (Witts, 1997) and mindsets, which have life-long impact on their personalities. In a variety of ways, the media, peers and adults communicate and reinforce gender-based stereotypes (Martin, Eisenbud & Rose, 1995). Women's Studies creates awareness on how gender politics arises in everybody's personal life and why each of us needs to be sensitized and address gender injustice as when it takes place directly or indirectly to us (Connell, 2002).

Women's Studies in India historically traces the gender bias in Indian society that has been challenging and risking its social structures, education system and nation building. It is in fact the inter-disciplinarity of Women's Studies that made the discipline valuable. There is an urgent need of sensitizing younger generation with regard to the question of patriarchy. Over the last four and half decades there has been a spurt of studies on women being carried out both from within academic institutions and in the governmental and non- governmental sectors. Women's Studies uses feminist perspectives and concepts of patriarchy, gender division of labour, gender equality and justice in insightful ways. Particular attention is placed on inclusion of "missing women's issues" and "gender perspectives" in education for the development of gender-balance curriculum materials in Women's Studies and its shared borders with other areas of study - especially in Science, Mathematics, Medicine, Engineering and Technology (SMET). In the words of Sumi Krishna (2007), we need to recognize that the language and theories of Women's Studies and all other disciplines are socially-situated, that women are part of every discipline, but women are not a homogenous category, they are diverse among themselves.

Karuna Chanana (2007) stated that the disciplinary boundaries are socially created as women are not expected to work and earn in society. Therefore, disciplinary boundaries not only limit choices for women, but these also limit future options for "life chances" of women. As a result, for a majority of young women in academia and profession, higher education is not linked to their careers, but a matter of convenience decided by male members of the family and society. Professor Karuna Chanana in 2014 National Symposium pointed out high-rates of dropout among female students. Though there is unavailability of reliable, transparent and exhaustive statistics on access, participation and outcomes of girls' and women's education in India, some data at school level are available but not on higher education. A large majority of girls do not even finish school to enter college. Such differential enrolment among boys and girls, men and women indicate socially constructed gender bias and inequality in education. Both 'push-out' (by education institutions) and 'pull-out' (by personal-familial reasons) factors are at work against gender equality in Indian education system. These factors are responsible for dropout of girls and womenfrom education before or far-away from completion. 'Push-out' factors may be: infrastructure facilities (classroom, drinking water, toilet, transport, etc.); non- attendance due to distance and domestic work; language problem (mother tongue versus English/Hindi/State vernacular medium of instruction); academic and time demands; lack of mentoring, teaching and learning support. 'Pull-out' factors may be: social roles and obligations in family and community; safety and security of young women in public places; fee payment difficulty due to poverty or saving for marriage and dowry; early marriage and pregnancy; child/adult/elder care at home; distance, transport and mobility restriction; social traditions and norms for gender bias. Alternatives to overcome gender bias and prevention of dropout can be done by – education institution and community partnership; role-model, mentoring, tutoring and training for girls and women; bridging language and communication gaps, minimizing time spent in education institution for flexible learning and safety; offering need-based, career- and skills-oriented, technological and vocational education; free counseling to balance student and personal life; providing safe, fearless, healthy and sexual-harassment free campus; provision of drinking water and toilets, hostels and transport facilities; providing reservation or incentives to enter education institution and giving out scholarships to complete education; gender sensitization of families and communities to support education for girls and women in India for family, community, society and national progress; collaboration between the science and social science disciplines will encourage gender-sensitive and women-friendly policies in education and greater convergence and impact of educational policies and programmes on girls and women in India. In a single-sex school, college or in an all-women university, greater leadership roles are played by female students. Therefore, all-girls/women education institutions should prepare female students to take-up leadership roles towards making education women-friendly and qualitative experience - that can make society gender equal. There are many such resonances in the diverse experiences of study, interventions and activism that are shared, reflected upon and analyzed as the subject matter of Women's Studies.

METHODOLOGY

The research question pertinent to this study is 'can Women's Studies reduce dropout? Women's Studies Centres in Indian universities and colleges started in 1987 as a response to the call of the University Grants Commission (UGC) to address women's issues in higher education. Women's Studies Centres are initiated as a result of major concern to extend the understanding of *Women's Studies* beyond teaching and extend to study, advocacy and outreach for women's development and empowerment in society. As of now, there are almost 150 Women's Studies Centres being functional in Indian institutions of higher education. These centres are working individually and/or in partnership to place women and gender at the centre of its inquiry focusing mostly on multidisciplinary perspectives of class, caste, race, ethnicity, sexuality, religion, age, culture, and society. These inter-disciplinary centres are already contributing to the domain knowledge of Women's Studies through certificate, master, and study degree programmes. Similar functions are carried out by Women's Studies Centre of Avinashilingam Institute for Home Science and Higher Education for Women (Deemed University), Coimbatore, Tamil Nadu.

However, Women's Studies Centres across India still lack students to join the centre and gain knowledge in Women's Studies through M.A., M.Phil. and Ph.D. programmes. It is especially because of the inter-disciplinary nature of the centre and subject, and also because of the lack of career prospects (teaching, government offices, and NGOs) of students after completion of the courses. Moreover, Women's Studies attract only a handful of women students, either due to their passion for themselves and/or other women in the society; or due to their compulsion resulting from their poor performance and not meeting admission eligibility in other mainstream courses.

Nonetheless, there is also societal un-acceptance and stigma related to studying about women and working for women. The students and teachers of Women's Studies are regarded as 'feminist'; revolutionary against the patriarchal system; and threat to male dominance in family and society. Women's Studies Centres are not still fully integrated within the higher education institutions; whether colleges or universities are for women only, or are for both men and women.

Therefore, there is not only inhibition from male members of the society and in the higher education system for inclusion of Women's Studies as a discipline and allowing their wives, sisters, daughters and colleagues to study or work on women's issues. But there is also unexpected ignorance from female members of the society of accepting their own problems, challenges, and rights in society as well as their overt declination of facing any problems due to being women and/or allowing their sisters, daughters, friends and colleagues to study or work on women's interests. The women's issues are so sensitive within our culture and society and in higher education system that even in all-women's college and university, the Women's Studies staffs and students do not receive equal support and/or enjoy benefits. Irrespective of such women-unfriendly social conditions, Women's Studies Centres across Indian education institutions have been reasonably successful in initiating change in society through its teaching and non-teaching staffs and students. To prove or disprove this point, the Co-curricular Certificate Course on Women's Studies offered by the Women's Studies Centre (WSC) of Avinashilingam Deemed University for Women (ADUW) is analyzed through the survey and conversation responses from selective students enrolled between 2013-2015. WSC at ADUW conducts 6 month choice-based co-curricular certificate course on Women's Studies, open to all IInd and IIIrd year undergraduate students of the university across Arts, Humanities, Sciences, Social Sciences, Education, Engineering & Technology. Around 168 students were selected as the sample of study, all of whom are taught by the researcher - an Assistant Professor of Women's Studies. The data are collected from the classroom (focus group) conversation, individual survey questionnaire and student feedback form. At first, these college-going female students mindset towards reasons for dropout from education for young women was enquired. Next, their mindset towards completing undergraduate studies after studying the short certificate course on Women's Studies was also enquired. Data was analyzed quantitatively and qualitatively to understand whether Women's Studies as a course of study can influence the mindset of young female students (17-20 years) to complete undergraduate studies before early marriage and pregnancy.

FINDINGS AND DISCUSSION

I. Demographic-Socio-Economic Characteristics of Study

Table II
SOCIO-DEMOGRAPHIC-ECONOMIC BACKGROUND OF FEMALE STUDENTS WHO CHOSE TO STUDY WOMEN'S STUDIES

[N=168, n in %]

WS BATCH	Age (Yrs)			Birth Order				Siblings		Residence		Caste				Class					Family				Generation Educated		
	17-18	18-19	19-20	1st	2nd	3rd	4th	MALE	FEMALE	RURAL	URBAN	SC	ST	MBC	OBC	GC	UC	MC	LC	EWS	FARMING	NON-EMPLOYED	SELF-EMPLOYED	BUSINESS	1st	2nd	3rd
2015-2016	8	71	21	40	41	15	4	51	49	75	25	20	3	25	47	5	9	35	41	15	59	31	8	2	76	22	2
2014-2015	9	69	22	37	42	13	8	56	44	76	24	18	5	28	42	7	8	28	43	21	52	41	6	1	80	19	1
2013-2014	11	66	23	44	41	10	5	58	42	78	22	15	8	30	45	2	6	31	44	19	50	43	7	0	85	15	0
Total Average	9.3	68.7	22	40.3	41.3	12.7	5.7	55	45	76.3	23.7	17.7	5.3	27.7	44.7	4.7	7.7	31.3	42.7	18.3	53.7	38.3	7	1	80.3	18.7	1

Above Table II shows the socio-demographic-economic background of the female students who chose to study Women's Studies as a co-curricular credit course. Age-wise 9.3 percent female students are from 17-18 years, 68.7 percent are in the 18-19 years and 22 percent are in the 19-20 years of age group. 40.3 percent, 41.3 percent, 12.7 percent and 5.7 percent female students are respectively the first, second, third and fourth child in the family. 55 percent female students have brothers and 45 percent have sisters, thus more families have stronger patriarchal presence. Among these female students, 76.3 percent come from rural areas in and around Coimbatore District of Tamil Nadu. While only 23.7 percent are from urban and semi-urban areas – including Coimbatore, Tirupur, Erode, Salem, Madurai, Chennai, Ooty, Kotagiri of Tamil Nadu; Palakkad, Thrissur, Ernakulam, Wayanad from Kerala; Coonoor and Mysore from Karnataka; Chittoor from Andhra Pradesh. Caste-wise only 5.3 percent of female students are from Scheduled Tribes (STs), 17.7 percent from Scheduled Castes (SCs), 27.7 percent from Most Backward Classes (MBCs), 4.7 percent from General Category (GC) / Forward Castes (FCs), and in majority of 44.7 percent are from Other Backward Classes (OBCs). Class-wise, majority of female students of 42.7 percent belong to Lower Class (LC) [annual income between 2.5 to 5 lakhs], 31.3 percent belong to Middle Class (MC) [annual income between 5 to 10 lakhs], 18.3 percent belong to Economically Weaker Section (EWS) [annual income is between Nil to 2.5 lakhs], and only 7.7 percent belong to Upper Class (UC) [annual income above 10 lakhs]. The female students are in majority of 53.7 percent belong to traditional patriarchal rural farming community, 38.3 percent from family of industrial labour and employee, 7 percent belong to self-employed and professional family, and only 1 percent is from entrepreneurial or business family. Therefore, the socio-demographic-economic characteristics of the female students enrolled in Women's Studies as respondents signify that most of them are brought-up in traditional patriarchal culture under random practices of social bias and gender stereotypes against girls' and women's needs and for their lower status *vis-à-vis* boys and men in society. In this case, we have to keep in mind that Avinashilingam Deemed University for Women provides free and subsidized education for rural girls and women for their upliftment with power of education and values of tradition and spiritualism. Due to its decades-old contribution towards community development and women empowerment since 1987, it draws female students in majority from rural background and minority from urban-cosmopolitan setting of Tamil Nadu and nearby States of Kerala, Karnataka and Andhra Pradesh. Therefore, these female students are mostly raised in and exposed to tradition of Indian culture of patriarchal dominance and gender discrimination.

Thus, their choice to study Women's Studies as Co-curricular Course in itself is progressive and reflected in their desire to change gender-relations in family and break gender- stereotypes in society.

II. Factors and Reasons for Dropout

Table III
DETERMINING FACTORS AND REASONS FOR DROPOUT BY WOMEN FROM EDUCATION AS STATED BY YOUNG FEMALE STUDENTS (17-20 YEARS)

[N=168, *n* in %]

No.	Factors	Reasons	Priority
**Factors and Reasons for Dropout in Order of Importance**			
1	**Reproductive Demand**	Early Marriage & Pregnancy	87
2	**Safety & Security**	Sexual Harassment and Gender-based Violence inside and outside Campus	82
3	**Cultural Bias**	Gender Stereotypes against Women in Society	81
4	**Family Demand**	Home Care, Child, Adult & Elder Care	79
5	**Economic Demand**	Child & Forced Labor for Family Maintenance, Earning/Saving for Marriage Costs & Payments	76
6	**Academic Demand**	Medium of Instruction (English vs. Native Language Problem), Lack of Study Interest due to Subject Chosen by Parents, Lack of Understanding and Training to cope with Higher Education Method	73
7	**Social Restriction**	Problem of Mobility due to Distance and Transportation to-fro Education Institution	65
8	**Time Demand**	Conflict between Domestic Work and College/ University Timing	56
9	**Communal Support**	Lack of Role-model & Mentor, Teaching & Learning Facilities, Governmental Incentives, Family & Community Encouragement	38
10	**Health & Environment**	Lack of Infrastructural &Sanitation Facilities (Classroom, Laboratory, Common-room/ Rest- room, Drinking Water, Canteen, Toilet, Hostel, etc.)	29

Table III explains the societal and familial priorities against education for women and thus the stated reasons for dropout by young women from completing their higher education. Reproductive role of women is so demanding in society that the dropout from education primarily occurs due to early marriage and immediate pregnancy in a physically and mentally premature age of 18-20 years. Therefore in most cases young women fail to cope with the simultaneous demands of married life, home care and child care at this tender age. Sexual and gender-based violence in public and private places is another major deterring factor for dropout, since young girls are traditionally guarded by family to protect their purity and virginity for marriage. Gender stereotypes are rampant and constraints girls' and women's freedom of choice and voice, independence and mobility, development and empowerment. Gender stereotypes are over-generalizations of male versus female characteristics of an entire group based on their gender-roles in society. Gender Stereotypes are fixed social ideas about men's and women's traits and capabilities and how they should behave gender-appropriately in family, community and society. In every society there is positive stereotype for men, but negative stereotype for women. Gender stereotypes are thus based on the cultural myths to safeguard the higher position of patriarch and validate socially accepted norms to subjugate women by men in society. Girls and women's domestic work in family and care for members (child/ adult/aged) are superimposed as 'common-good' against their own needs and development or 'personal-good'. Hence, they are expected to sacrifice education for economic demands of family maintenance and/or earning/ saving for their own or siblings' costs of and payments for marriage. Social restrictions and family-time demands constantly conflict with women's education and development. Lack of support from government (Centre and State), education institution, family and community make it even more difficult for women to continue their higher studies. Health and environment needs for women in education institutions are also neglected leading to their dropout. Their gender-specific needs like separate common-room or rest- room and toilets are necessity for young women to feel safe and secure when away from home environment. Nonetheless, academic demands are also high in higher education – like: foreign (English) language of instruction, lack of interest in subject due to parents' choice than their own, and lack of understanding and training to cope with the studying and learning methods for higher education. All these socio-cultural-economically interdependent factors add up to substantial reasons for dropout by young college/university going women from higher education.

III. Impact of Women's Studies Course on Female Students

Table IV
SCOPE OF WOMEN'S STUDIES AS RECOGNIZED
BY THE FEMALE STUDENTS (17-20 YEARS)

[N=168, *n* in %]

No.	Scope of Women's Studies	Positive Responses	Neutral Responses	Negative Responses
1	Questions and Breaks Gender Stereotypes present in Society	89	6	5
2	Offers Women-friendly Education and Knowledge, Skills and Leadership	83	11	6
3	Empowers Women and Builds Capacity for Self and Family Empowerment	74	22	4
4	Gives Various Career Choices and Economic Opportunities for Women	55	31	14
5	Helps Women to become Socially Independent and Agents of Social Change	51	40	9

It was enquired from the female students what they understood as the importance of Women's Studies as an academic discipline. It was confirmed by 89 percent of female students that Women's Studies Course raised their awareness against social bias and broken prevalent gender stereotypes against girls and women in society. According to the overwhelming majority (78.5 percent) of female students believed that Women's Studies Course offered women-friendly education and knowledge, skills and leadership, women's self and family empowerment. However, just little above the majority (53 percent) of female students felt that the subject provides awareness on various economic opportunities and career choices for women and helps women to become socially independent and motivates them to become agents of social change. Above understanding by comparatively smaller percentage of female students signifies that most young women due to patriarchal dominance are hesitant to choose economic opportunities for themselves and take-up leadership roles in society.

Table V

**IMPACT OF WOMEN'S STUDIES COURSE ON THE
MINDSET OF YOUNG WOMEN AS RECOGNIZED
BY THE FEMALE STUDENTS (17-20 YEARS)**

[N=168, *n* in %]

No.	Women's Studies Impact on Female Students' Mindset towards Dropout	Positive Mindset	Neutral Mindset	Negative Mindset
1	Education should be completed before Early Marriage and Pregnancy	92	5	3
2	Completion of Education is important for Socio-Economic Independence for Women	88	8	4
3	Domestic Work can be Balanced with Study or Job	50	26	24
4	Women should choose their Subjects and Careers of Personal Interest	83	12	5
5	Empowered Women should make Education and Profession Women-friendly for other Women	77	23	0

It was also found that Women's Studies had influence on the mindsets of female students as 92 percent female students agreed to complete higher education before marriage and pregnancy. The female students realized the fact that completion of higher education with marital family and childcare demands would be antagonistic and stressful family life and eventually dropping-out decision would be enforced upon them by the family members due to less scope and support for study-work-life balance. Female students also understood the negative effect of unfinished education upon their life-chances in unforeseen circumstances. Thus 85.5 percent women perceived that women should complete education to gain life-skills, career-choice and socio-economic independence. However, half of the female students also expressed doubts in whether socially expected domestic work by women could be balanced along with study or job. This apprehension could be because of women's domestic and reproductive roles are more demanding than their productive (economic) roles. Therefore, 77 percent of students collectively felt that women need to voice and support for women's development and empowerment by making education and profession women-friendly. By 'women-friendly' they meant means and ends, processes and outcomes, policies and programmes to benefit the needs and interests of girls and women not as a homogenous but as a diverse group.

Table VI
CORRELATION MATRIX FOR REASONS OF DROPOUT FROM EDUCATION AMONG FEMALE STUDENTS (17-20 YEARS)

[N=168, Pearson's r]

Correlation	Reproductive Demand	Safety & Security	Cultural Bias	Family Demand	Economic Demand	Academic Demand	Social Restriction	Time Demand	Communal Support	Health & Environment
Reproductive Demand	1.000	.633**	.612**	.587**	.551**	.520*	.451*	.454*	.378	.285
Safety & Security	.633**	1.000	.637**	.575**	.510*	.500*	.481*	.456*	.328	.217
Cultural Bias	.612**	.637**	1.000	.579**	.536*	.555**	.439	.417	.301	.214
Family Demand	.587**	.575**	.579**	1.000	.575**	.489*	.423	.475*	.388	.200
Economic Demand	.551**	.510*	.536*	.575**	1.000	.627**	.546**	.497*	.444	.364
Academic Demand	.520*	.500*	.555**	.489*	.627**	1.000	.521*	.425	.307	.199
Social Restriction	.451*	.481*	.439	.423	.546**	.521*	1.000	.496*	.319	.211
Time Demand	.454*	.456*	.417	.475*	.497*	.425	.496*	1.000	.393	.176
Communal Support	.378	.328	.301	.388	.444	.307	.319	.393	1.000	.243
Health & Environment	.285	.217	.214	.200	.364	.199	.211	.176	.243	1.000

** / * Correlation is significant at the 0.01 level (2-tailed)

Table VI shows that among female under-graduate students in the age-group of 17-20 years, there are more or less strong correlations between the reasons for dropout like – reproductive demand, safety and security, cultural bias, family demand, economic demand, academic demand, social restriction, and time demand. However, no significant correlations are found among the sample of female students in this age-group supporting the dropout factors like – communal support (governmental incentives, family and community encouragement for higher education) and health and environment (lack of infrastructural and sanitation facilities in education institutions). It is interesting to note that in reality, very little has been done at policy level by Central and State Government to encourage higher education and reduce dropout among women; so as at grassroots level by community and family due to traditional power and control of patriarchy on girls and women and for more priority on women's reproduction (marriage and pregnancy) than production (education and work) needs in Indian society. The above results also strongly suggest that mindset changes are indeed needed in Indian society at all levels.

Table VII
RELATIONSHIPS BETWEEN WOMEN'S STUDIES COURSE AND MINDSET ON DROPOUT FROM EDUCATION AMONG FEMALE STUDENTS

Women's Studies Course Sensitizes Students against Dropout before completing Education			
Variable	Yes %	No %	*p*-value
Age			**0.013***
17-18	50.1	49.9	
18-19	56.1	43.9	
19-20	57.6	42.4	
Birth Order			**0.223**
1st	79.3	20.7	
2nd	73.4	26.6	
3rd	72.1	27.9	
4th	68.8	31.2	

Siblings			**0.795**
Male	74.8	25.2	
Female	73.7	26.3	
Residence			**0.017***
Rural	51.5	48.5	
Urban	57.5	42.5	
Caste			**0.002***
Scheduled Caste (SC)	53.8	46.2	
Scheduled Tribe (ST)	51.7	48.3	
Most Backward Class (MBC)	53.2	46.8	
Other Backward Class (OBC)	61.3	38.8	
General Category (GC)/Forward Caste (FC)	65.5	34.5	
Class			**0.001****
Upper Class (UC)	61.3	38.7	
Middle Class (MC)	79.4	20.6	
Lower Class (LC)	68.4	31.6	
Economically Weaker Section (EWS)	48.6	51.4	
Family			**0.861**
Farming	74.8	25.2	
Non-Farming	72.7	27.3	
Self-Employed	73.6	26.4	
Entrepreneur/Business	24.5	75.5	
Generation Educated			**0.279**
First	56.9	43.1	
Second	51.0	49.0	
Third	48.8	51.2	

Note: *p*-values are for one-tailed Pearson's Chi-Squared Test (χ^2).
Level of Significance: *$p<0.05$ and **$p<0.001$

Table VII gives the measures of association between female students' socio-demographic-economic backgrounds and mindset for reduction of dropout due to

Women's Studies Course. It was found from the survey responses that the variables like – age, residence, caste and class are significantly related to the mindset towards reduction of dropout from education due to enrolment in Women's Studies co-curricular course. Age (17-18, 18-19, 19-20 years), Residence (rural and urban) and Caste (Scheduled Caste, Scheduled Tribe, Most Backward Class, Other Backward Class, General Category / Forward Caste) variables are statistically significant at 5 percent or significant at the 0.05 level and Social Class (Economically Weaker Section, Lower Class, Middle Class, Upper Class) variable is statistically highly significant at 1 percent or highly significant at the 0.001 level with the female students' mindset for dropout reduction against early marriage and pregnancy. It can be derived from table VII that, this particular age group (17-20 years) of female students is at high risk for early marriage and pregnancy as they are in majority from rural and semi-urban background, born and brought-up in traditional patriarchal family. Patriarchal family is dominated by male head of the household and fathers or father-figures hold authority over family members, especially on women and children. Therefore female students undergo family pressure for marriage as soon they turn legal marital age of 18 years. Marriage and pregnancy are cited to be the highest priority for female students for dropout from education. Social Caste and Class are also determining factors for or against dropout from education for women. The study shows that Safety and Security for women in Indian society is a 'family priority' (82 percent, as per *Table 3*) and it may be inferred from the data that it is a major 'push factor' for young girls to accept early marriage to save themselves from wide-spread sexual harassment and other gender-based violence in public places. Since, married women are culturally respected as 'others' property' (husband and marital family) and therefore relatively safe as believed by parental family.

It was found from the survey that in all caste-communities and social class-families dropout from education and job is widely practiced by girls and women due to parental and/or marital family pressure. However, Women's Studies course was found to raise awareness on the need of completion of women's education before marriage and pregnancy for future life-chances and socio-economic independence. Women's Studies was found to sensitize the female students to balance study-life for overcoming dropout from education.

CONCLUSION

In conclusion, we can infer from the survey responses, classroom conversations and feedback forms collected from 168 female students across disciplines enrolled in choice-based Women's Studies co-curricular course, that it does make female students aware about girls and women specific socio-economic needs and problems, and sensitizes them to overcome dropout from education due to early marriage and pregnancy. The study also shows that 'dropout' is significantly related to age (17-20 years), residence (rural and urban), social castes and classes, and safety and security of female students and can be significantly reduced by Women's Studies, which aims to create gender sensitization. Women's Studies as a curriculum breaks gender-stereotypes and creates awareness about gender equality and need for completion of higher education among women for future life-chances.

In fact, the research study finds that women empowerment policies, programmes and schemes (scholarships) can bring only top-down (superficial) changes in society. However, Women's Studies as a discipline is more impactful on students, and more so on female students, as they can relate to their own and shared experiences in family, community and society. Therefore, Women's Studies helps female students from within, encourage them to rethink their life and career, choices and voices, mindsets and attitudes towards gender equality and women empowerment. Such individual changes from within oneself in each and every student of Women's Studies can make greater bottom-up changes in wider society. Women's Studies can foster change in higher education through pragmatic curriculum and experiential learning; knowing about society and its positive and negative influences; understanding gender differences, stereotypes and discriminations; challenging social mindsets and public attitudes; and finally changing self, family, community and society. Therefore, impact of Women's Studies may be sustainable on young women (17-25 years), who will be motivated to enter higher education, continue enrolment, resist dropout and return to education after a career-break due to family obligations.

According to this study, Women's Studies as a discipline has more potential to create women-resources benefitting the higher education, workforce and growth and development sectors of India. However, it is to be kept in mind that the present study is done within an all-women university set-up, wherein female students are in continuous encouragement to excel in their life and career. Thus, it will be interesting to extend the research study in co-education environment to compare the impact of Women's Studies on female students in higher education in terms of enrolment and dropout.

The cooption and vocationalising of Women's Studies and its move away from academic activism has to be understood in the context of students' legitimate aspirations. Perhaps more progress has been made by mobilizing outside the academy than within it. Eventually, Women's Studies has expanded in itself to *gender studies* in order to provide alternative 'knowing' and interdisciplinary ways of approaching same problem areas and to be more inclusive in postmodern society - where gender divisions and gender diversity co-exist. Women's Studies has further extended itself to Gender Studies to focus on the issues of culture, identity, celebrating difference and complementarity character of both genders. The teaching of feminist ideology and gender diversity facilitate society's reflection on women's everyday life experience. Gender sensitization training programme in educational institutions can promote gender equality by identifying where the gender disparities are widest, what factors contribute to gender disparities, and which interventions are most likely to be effective for gender equality and equity. Thereby the academic-activist gap could be bridged in order to initiate change in individual (especially students) and social mindset and public attitude towards women's equity and equality, development and empowerment in India.

REFERENCES

Chanana, K. (1993). Accessing higher education: the dilemma of schooling women, minorities, Scheduled Castes and Scheduled Tribes in contemporary India. *Higher Education, 26*(1), 69-92.

Chanana, K. (2004). Gender and disciplinary choices: Women in higher education in India. In *UNESCO Colloquium on Research and Higher Education Policy. 'Knowledge Access and Governance: Strategies for Change'. Paris* (Vol. 34, December).

Chanana, K. (2007). Globalisation, higher education and gender: Changing subject choices of Indian women students. *Economic and Political Weekly,* 590-598.

Connell, R. W. (2002). *Gender: Short introductions.* Polity Press & Blackwell Publishers.

Desai, S., & Kulkarni, V. (2008). Changing educational inequalities in India in the context of affirmative action. *Demography, 45*(2), 245-270. MHRD (2014).

Educational Statistics at a Glance: Handbook. Ministry of Human Resource Development, Bureau of Planning, Monitoring & Statistics, Government of India. New Delhi: India.

John, M. E. (2003). The encounter of sociology and women's studies: Questions from the borders. *The Practice of Sociology*, 258-284.

Gandhi Kingdon, G. (2002). The gender gap in educational attainment in India: How much can be explained?. *Journal of Development Studies, 39*(2), 25-53.

Krishna, S. (Ed.). (2007). *Women's livelihood rights: recasting citizenship for development.* India: SAGE Publications.

Leach, M., & Davies, B. (1990). Crossing the boundaries: Educational thought and gender equity. *Educational Theory, 40*(3), 321-332.

Raju, S. (2008). Gender differentials in access to higher education. *Higher Education in India*, 79-102.

Rege, S. (2003). *Sociology of gender: the challenge of feminist sociological knowledge.* India: Sage Publications.

Schmitz, B., Butler, J. E., Rosenfelt, D. & Guy-Sheftall, B. (1995). Women's Studies and Curriculum Transformation. In *Handbook of Research on Multicultural Education*. James A. Banks and Cherry A. McGcc Banks (Eds.). New York: Macmillan.

Srivastava, R. S., & Sinha, S. (2008). Inter-social groups disparities in access to higher education. *Higher Education in India*, 103-110.

Uberoi, P. (1995). Problems with patriarchy: Conceptual issues in anthropology and feminism. *Sociological Bulletin*, 195-221.

Varma, S. (2013). More students opt for higher education, but even more drop out: Survey. The Economic Times: Education. TNN, 31 Aug, 2013, 09.07AM IST.

Zarabi, D. (2012). Women in Higher Education – the Challenges Ahead. *Indian Journal of Adult Education, 73*(1) (January-March).

SKILL TRAINING FOR SELF EMPLOYMENT

M. Kanimozhi[1] and K. Amutha[2]

[1]Dr. M. Kanimozhi, Assistant Professor, Department of Costume Design and Fashion, PSG College of Arts and Science, Coimbatore, Tamil Nadu. Email: mjkani@gmail.com

[2]K. Amutha, Assistant Professor, Department of Textiles and Apparel Design, Bharathiar University, Coimbatore, Tamil Nadu. Email: ammusuman@rediffmail.com

ABSTRACT

The uneducated house wives from the rural background of Salem city were selected as samples to endeavor a tie and dye class for a period of three months. They were given absolute orientation regarding, selection of fabric, dyes and materials required. The various types of tie and dye techniques were explained to them in an elaborate manner. Designing, preparations of dye bath and application of dye on the material were also taught to them in a detailed way. Lecture cum demonstration method was adopted for conducting the classes. The raw materials required were provided to the women and they were helped to do tie and dye design on plain material. Through personal and canvassing they procured orders for tie and dye articles from Women's Club, Self-Help Groups and colleges. The profit thus obtained was distributed among the house wives and the feedback regarding the programme was collected.

Keywords: tie and dye, house wives, design, demonstration, feedback

INTRODUCTION

The condition of women is more miserable in rural India with respect to various socio-economic aspects. Most of the rural women are uneducated state Kandasamy and Smarandache (2005). Rural women are still poverty stricken. They are engaged in unskilled and low paid jobs in the fields, construction areas and industry refers Tanaka (2003). The polluting atmosphere in these work spots affects the health of rural women very badly. They are neither able to carry out the job outside properly nor take care of the children well.

The only way to solve the problem of rural women is to train them for self-employment. It is with this objective in mind, an attempt has been made in this study to train rural women in tie and dye technique.

METHODOLOGY

1. Selection of Sample

Women's status is a replication of her socio-economic status. Since the purpose of this research is to help the selected subjects to improve their socio-economic status by increasing their income through tie and dye method, ten women residing in the rural background of Pottenari and Mechari Districts were selected as the samples for the study.

2. Selection of Area for the Class

The community hall intended for the welfare of the workers of Jindal South West (JSW) steel limited was chosen as the class room for conducting the tie and dye course, as it was available free of charge and also the samples had a free access to this hall.

3. Organizing the Class

The classes were conducted from 1.00 P.M. to 4.00 P.M. based on the convenience of the samples for 30 days. During the training period, the investigator trained the subjects regarding the selection of materials for the tie and dye, different types of dyes available in the market, appropriate dye for the particular materials, dye calculation, dyeing procedure and after treatment of the dyed materials.

4. Teaching Methods

Lecture cum demonstration method was chosen as the teaching technique, as it suited the educational level of the samples.

5. Selection of Raw Materials

Fabrics suitable for tie and dye are cotton and silk. Cotton fabrics are suitable for any method of dyeing and can be worn round the clock. Hence, cotton material was preferred for the study.

6. Selection of Design

There are plenty of designs in tie and dye method. For this study six common designs which are suitable for blouse, duppattas, hand kerchiefs, midi top, salwar, kameez and cushion covers were selected, since they were attractive. The designs selected include knotting, pleating, object tyeing, twisting, marbling and point tyeing.

7. Selection of Dyes

The dyes selected for this study include reactive and vat dyes.

8. Pre-treatment of Fabric for Tie and Dyeing

The pre-treatment given for cotton is desizing which helps to remove the sizing material present in the fabric thus helps in equal dye absorption remarks Battan *et.al.* (2012).

9. Application of Design on the Fabrics

The designs namely knotting, pleating, object tyeing, twisting, marbling and point tyeing were selected for this study. The designs were introduced in to the fabrics and tied securely to prevent the penetration of dyes.

10. Procedure for Dyeing

The dye powder was made into a thorough paste using wetting agent. Boiling water was added to it and the solution was stirred well. Caustic soda was added followed by sodium hydro sulphite with constant stirring. The fabric to be dyed was dipped in the dye bath at 40°C. Finally the fabric was rinsed thoroughly in soft water.

11. After Treatment

The dyed fabrics were dried in shade without removing the thread in order to prevent the merging of colour.

12. Procuring Orders

The investigator and the students procured orders for tie and dye samples from the Women's club, self-help groups and also from the various colleges through personal and canvassing.

13. Price Fixation

Price for the tie and dye samples made by the students were fixed based on the total expenditure of raw materials plus profit. The profit thus obtained was distributed among the students.

14. Feedback Regarding the Programme

Through personal interview, the investigator collected the views of the samples regarding the content of the course, duration, teaching method, income generation and problems faced.

RESULTS AND DISCUSSION

The results of the study are discussed under the following heads.

1. Time Consumption for Individual Designs

The time consumed by the individual samples for aspects like desizing, cutting, ironing, designing, dyeing, starching and ironing were listed in Table I. Variation in time consumption was noticed mainly in the case of designing and tyeing. The dyeing time ranges from 30 to 45 min. For tie and dye blouse samples the time consumed ranges from 80 to 90 min. The time consumed for designing single piece of hand kerchief ranges between 45 to 50 min. The time taken for tie and dyeing of duppata varies from 112 to 162 min. The duration taken for completion of cushion cover and miditop varies between 86 to 101 minutes respectively.

Table I
TOTAL TIME CONSUMED FOR ONE PIECE
OF EACH DESIGN (IN MINUTES)

Items & Designs	Desizing & Washing	Cutting	Ironing	Designing	Tyeing	Dyeing	Un-Tyeing	Starching & Ironing	Total
Blouse									
A	4	4	2	10	10	40	5	15	90
B	4	4	2	10	10	40	5	15	90
C	4	4	2	5	5	40	5	15	80
D	4	4	2	5	5	40	5	15	80
E	4	4	2	5	5	40	5	15	80
F	4	4	2	10	10	40	5	15	90
Hand kerchief									
A	1	-	1	3	3	30	3	5	46
B	1	-	1	5	5	30	3	5	50
C	1	-	1	3	3	30	3	5	46
D	1	-	1	2	3	30	3	5	45
E	1	-	1	2	3	30	3	5	45
F	1	-	1	5	5	30	3	5	50

Duppata									
A	8	10	6	15	20	45	10	18	132
B	8	10	6	30	30	45	15	18	162
C	8	10	6	15	20	45	10	18	122
D	8	10	6	10	10	45	5	18	132
E	8	10	6	10	10	45	5	18	112
F	8	10	6	30	30	45	15	18	162
Cushion Cover									
A	6	5	5	5	5	40	5	15	86
B	6	5	5	15	10	40	5	15	101
D	6	5	5	10	5	40	5	15	91
E	6	5	5	5	5	40	5	15	86
Miditop									
D	5	5	5	5	5	40	5	18	88
E	5	5	5	5	5	40	5	18	88
Salwar									
B	7	7	7	15	10	40	5	18	109
D	7	7	7	10	5	40	5	18	99
E	7	7	7	10	5	40	5	18	99
F	7	7	7	15	10	40	5	18	109
Kameez									
B	7	7	7	15	10	40	5	15	106
D	7	7	7	10	5	40	5	15	96
E	7	7	7	10	5	40	5	15	96
F	7	7	7	15	10	40	5	15	106

A – Knotting, B – Object Tyeing, C – Pleating, D – Twisting, E – Marbling, F – Point Tyeing

2. Cost Incurred for the Designs

The total cost incurred on tie and dye work is given in Table II. It was evident that the cost incurred on tie and dye work varies depending upon the item on which it was done. The total cost included the expenditure on the purchase of fabric, dye, thread and fuel cost. As far as blouse is concerned the cost varied from Rupees 98 to 103 per item. The total cost for each hand kerchief was Rupees 12 to 15 depending upon the nature of the design. The expenditure on dupattas varied from Rupees 150 to 155 and on midi top Rupees 108. The expenditure on cushion covers was Rupees 65 to 70. Salwar Kameez cost Rupees 171 to 181 respectively.

Table II
COST INCURRED IN RUPEES FOR TIE AND DYE DESIGNS

Items	Size	Cloth Value (₹)	Dye Variety	Dye Cost (₹)	Cost of Fuel (₹)	Allied Material Cost (₹)	Wages (₹)	Total Cost (₹)
Blouse								
A	100x80	50.00	Reactive	20	6	7	18	101
B	100x80	50.00	Reactive	20	6	7	20	103
C	100x80	50.00	Reactive	20	6	7	15	98
D	100x80	50.00	Reactive	20	6	7	18	101
E	100x80	50.00	Reactive	20	6	7	15	98
F	100x80	50.00	Reactive	20	6	7	20	103
Hand Kerchief								
A	32x32	3	Reactive	1	1	2	5	12
B	32x32	3	Reactive	1	1	2	8	15
C	32x32	3	Reactive	1	1	2	7	14
D	32x32	3	Reactive	1	1	2	5	12
E	32x32	3	Reactive	1	1	2	5	12
F	32x32	3	Reactive	1	1	2	8	15
Dupattas								
A	90x250	96	Procion	21	4	9	20	150
B	90x250	96	Procion	21	4	9	22	153
C	90x250	96	Procion	21	4	9	25	155
D	90x250	96	Procion	21	4	9	22	152
E	90x250	96	Procion	21	4	9	20	150
F	90x250	96	Procion	21	4	9	23	153
Midi Top								
D	120x150	65	Procion	20	4	4	15	108
E	120x150	65	Procion	20	4	4	15	108
Cushion Cover								
A	60x120	25	Procion	20	4	6	10	65
B	60x120	25	Procion	20	4	6	15	70
D	60x120	25	Procion	20	4	6	13	68
E	60x120	25	Procion	20	4	6	10	65
Salwar Kameez								
B	120x300	100	Procion	30	4	12	35	181
D	120x300	100	Procion	30	4	12	30	176
E	120x300	100	Procion	30	4	12	25	171
F	120x300	100	Procion	30	4	12	35	181

3. Total Income Earned by the Selected Subjects

The total income for three months from December to February were calculated and depicted in fig.5. In the first month the total income was Indian Rupees (INR) 11,324. In the second and third month the total amount earned was Rupees 11,885 and Rupees 12,085 respectively. The total of the same worked out to Rupees 35,295.

Figure 1
INCOME EARNED BY INDIVIDUAL SUBJECTS

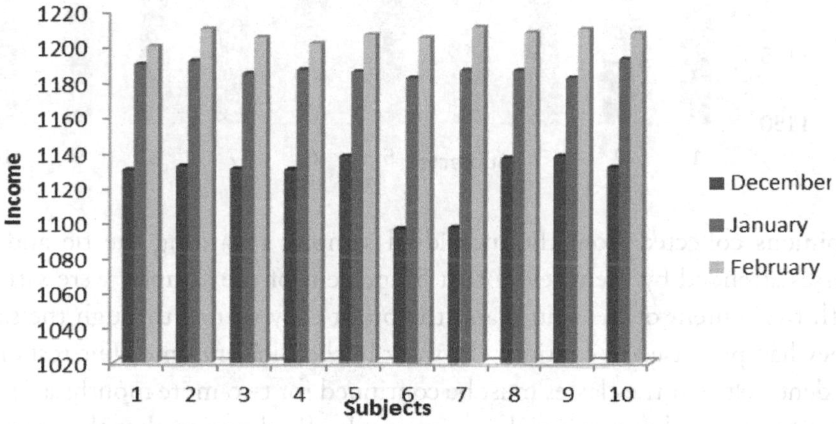

4. Income Earned by the Individual Subjects

Average income earned by each of the individual samples is presented in Fig.2. On an average the samples have earned from Rupees 1161 to Rupees 1177 per month, irrespective of the items and the nature of design done by them.

Figure 2
INCOME PROFILE OF THE SELECTED SUBJECTS

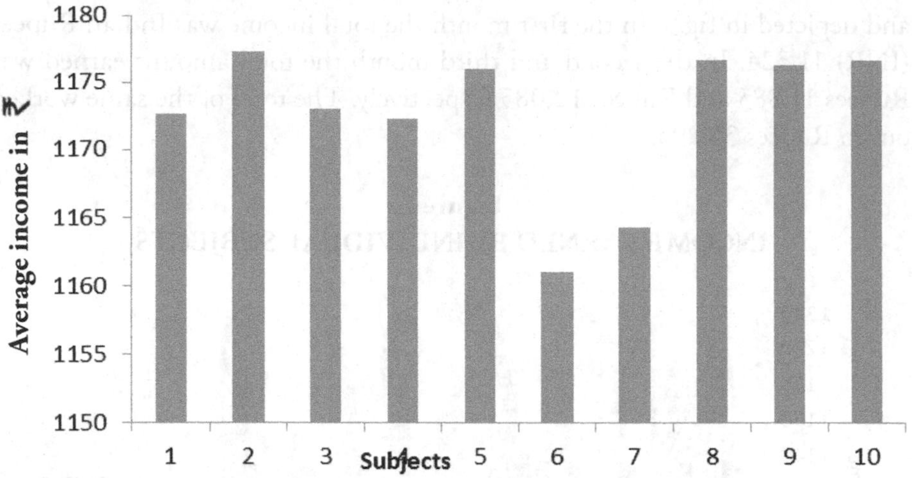

Opinions collected from the individual samples regarding the tie and dye classes attended by them reveal that 55 percent of the samples were satisfied with the content of the course and the profit they gained through the same. They had promised to continue the work in their leisure time. The rest of the students felt that the classes must be continued for two more months and they must be supplied raw materials at a very subsidised rate so that their earning will also be increased.

CONCLUSION

Thus tie and dye work improved the economic status of the girls. Among the students 55 percent of the members were satisfied with the classes on tie and dye work. The others expressed problem regarding duration and procurement of raw material. Regarding duration, they suggested that the classes must be extended for two more months. They wanted help regarding the procurement of raw materials at a subsidized rate, so that their income could be increased.

REFERENCES

Battan, B., Dhiman, S.S., Ahlawat, S., Mahajan, R. and Sharma, J. (2012), 'Application of Thermostable Xylanase of *Bacillus pumilus* in Textile Processing', Indian Journal of Microbiology, Vol.52, No.2, June, Pp. 222–229.

Kandasamy, W.B.V. and Smarandache, F. (2005) Fuzzy and Neutrosophic Analysis of Women with HIV/AIDS: With Specific Reference to Rural Tamil Nadu in India, 7th edition, USA: Infinite Study Publisher.

Tanaka, Y. (2003) Japan's Comfort Women, London: Routledge Publisher.

http://ww w.f ibre2fashion.com/industr y-article/33/3248/committed-to-colours3.asp

http://craftbits.com/project/tie-dye-effects/

EMPOWERMENT OF WOMEN THROUGH HANDICRAFTS FROM AGAVE *AMERICANA* FIBRES

R. Sunitha[1] and G. Krishnabai[2]

[1]Dr. R. Sunitha, Assistant Professor, Department of Textiles and Clothing, Avinashilingam Institute for Home Science and Higher Education for Women, Coimbatore, Tamil Nadu. Email: sunitha1976adutex@gmail.com

[2]Dr. G. Krishnabai, Retired Dean, Faculty of Home Science, and Retired Head of the Department and Professor of Textiles and Clothing, Avinashilingam Institute for Home Science and Higher Education for Women, Coimbatore, Tamil Nadu. Email: krishna_1946@yahoo.co.in

ABSTRACT

The purpose of the study is to innovate eco-friendly fashionable products and at the same time bring out the job potentialities in procuring raw materials and manufacturing the products. This may motivate women to become entrepreneurs at minimum investment. This study exhibits vividly that it is cent percent possible to extract fibres from the leavers of non-food crop Agave *americana*. These fibres also have good affinity towards dye. These also lend themselves to prepare handicraft items and accessories.

Keywords: Agave *americana*, entrepreneurs, handicrafts and accessories

INTRODUCTION

India is a tropical country blessed with plenty of renewable resources obtainable from plant kingdom. The natural fibres are eco-friendly as they are biodegradable in nature. The plant fibres obtained from stem are soft when compared to the fibres obtained from leaves. So the leaf fibres are restricted to only limited uses due to their hard nature. Keeping this in view, the study has been focused on extraction and processing of the fibres so as to lend themselves to various end uses for handicrafts and fashion accessories. The handicrafts provide several job opportunities for women. Accessories are given much importance in fashion world helping women in generating their income. Entrepreneurship for women would surely empower them. This study focuses on how the abundantly available natural minor fibres are extracted, to be utilized to empower women through self-employment.

Hence the specific objectives of the study are to:

1. extract the fibres from the leaves of Agave *americana* using various methods and determine the best out of them
2. study the effect of processing on the fibres
3. find the properties of the fibres at different stages of maturity of the plant
4. produce various handicrafts and accessories to create job opportunities for women

METHODOLOGY

The matured leaves were cut from the Agave *americana* plants and fibres were extracted from these leaves by various methods. The method used for extraction of fibres was of great importance since the quality as well as the quantity of extracted fibres strongly influenced by the method of extraction.

1. Extraction of the Fibres from the Leaves

The fibres were extracted by the following methods.

1.1 Stagnant Water Retting

Franck (2005) feels that retting is quicker in soft water than in hard water and also adds that the colour and lustre of the fibres are remarkably improved by using soft water. Considering this fact, soft water was used not only for retting but also for the whole process.

The fresh Agave *americana* leaves were pounded, and made into bundles and immersed in stagnant water for fungal action for required period. The gas formation indicates the commencement of fungal action says Stout (1970). Retting in water is caused by micro-organisms which soften and disintegrate lignin and hemicellulose. After softening, the fibres can be stripped easily from the rest of the leaf, express Pardeshi and Paul (2003). The completion of the retting process took 23 days. Then the retted leaves were taken out and scraped to remove the decomposed matter surrounding the fibres. The extracted fibres were then washed thoroughly, dried and combed.

1.2 Chemical Retting

In chemical retting, the leaves were subjected to alkali. As suggested by Corbman (1983), sodium hydroxide was used for chemical retting. The concentration of 0.5 percent was used for the process as it was proved to be the best concentration for chemical retting. After 20 days when the retting was completed, the retted leaves were taken out and scraped to separate the fibres. The extracted fibres were then washed thoroughly in fresh water, dried and combed.

1.3 Decortication

Hall (2004) suggests that the leaves are fleshy and require mechanical decortication for separation of the fibres. The investigator decorticated the leaves for the extraction of fibres as instructed by Doraisamy and Chellamani (1993). The leaves of equal length were arranged together and fed into the decortication machine. As the drive rotates three to five leaves were fed between the drum and the backing plate. Owing to the crushing, beating and pulling action, the pulpy material was removed. When it was half way through, the leaves were slowly pulled and the other half was fed in the same manner as before. Then the fibres were washed, dried and combed when they were slightly wet, using a suitable brush.

2. Fibres from Plants of Various Stages of Maturity

The leaves from plants of different stages of maturity were cut and collected. Fibres were then extracted from the leaves by decortication and analyzed.

3. Processing of the Fibres

3.1 Scouring: The scouring process is done to remove the nitrogenous matters and to make the operations of bleaching and dyeing efficient say Modi and Garde (1995). The parameter and the operational range are given in the Table I.

Table I
RECIPE USED FOR SCOURING OF FIBRES

No.	PARAMETER	OPERATIONALR ANGE
1	Sodium Carbonate	2-3%
2	Sodium Silicate Wetting	1.0-1.5%
3	Agent	0.1%
4	Material to Liquor Ratio	1 : 4
5	Temperature	60°C
6	Time	10 Hours

After scouring process, the liquor was drained off and the fibres were washed thoroughly in cold water.

3.2 Bleaching: Bleaching is done using Hydrogen peroxide. This is done to brighten the fibres and to improve the dye affinity.

3.3 Dyeing: Needles (2001) is of the opinion that direct dyes penetrate cellulosic fibres readily, have good affinity for these fibres and are reasonably colour fast. Taking this into consideration, the investigator selected direct dye of two colours namely blue and orange for dyeing the Agave *americana* fibres. The dyeing procedure was carried out as instructed by Shenai (1983). Amount of dye solution was calculated using the following formula.

$$\text{Amount of solution to be taken in cc} = \frac{w \times p}{c}$$

where   w = weight of the material, p = percentage of solution and
c = concentration of the prepared solution

The required amount of dye was dissolved in cold water. The fibre skeins were entered into the dye bath and stirred well for 20 minutes, then the temperature was slowly raised to 60°C and common salt was added (10 percent of the weight of the material). The temperature was then raised to 100°C and dyeing was continued at the same temperature for 30 minutes. The fibres were then taken out from the dye bath, given soap boiling for 15 minutes and then washed thoroughly with cold water and then dried under shade. Fibre swatches are given in Appendices 1f and 1g. These coloured fibres were used for making accessories and handicraft items.

4. Preparation of Handicraft Items and Accessories

The dyed fibres are made into handicraft items like bags, wall hangers and decorative pieces. These fibres are also utilized to make fashionable accessories (Plate 1).

5. Evaluation and Estimation of Cost

5.1 Evaluation of Extracted Fibres

The fibres extracted by various methods were evaluated for various parameters such as general appearance, colour, luster and texture. These were judged visually by a set of 25 Post Graduation students belonging to Textiles and Clothing Department. Their ratings were consolidated and recorded.

The fibres were also evaluated for essential parameters like length, diameter, force and elongation. The tests were carried out to compare the method of extraction as well as the maturity of fibres.

PLATE 1 – PRODUCED PRODUCTS

The cost of the fibres was then calculated.

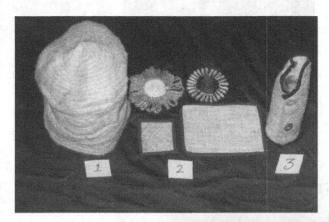

1. TEA COZY
2. TABLE MATS
3. FEEDING BOTTLE CASE

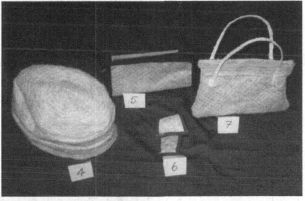

4. CAP
5. PURSE
6. CELL PHONE CASE
7. HAND BAG

8. APPLIQUE
9. BRACELET
10. WAIST BAND
11. GARLAND
12. LETTER HOLDER

13. DUSTER
14. WALL HANGER
15. BIRDS NEST
16. PHOTO FRAME
17. DOLLS
18. FIBRE FOUNTAIN

FINDINGS OF THE STUDY

The findings of the study are expressed under:

i. Visual Evaluation of Extracted Fibres

Table II
VISUAL EVALUATION OF EXTRACTED FIBRES (%)

No.	Samples	General Appearance			Colour			Lustre			Texture		
		Good	Fair	Poor	Bright	Medium	Dull	Good	Fair	Poor	Soft	Coarse	Very Coarse
1	Decorticated	80	20	-	56	40	4	60	40	-	68	32	-
2	Stagnant Water Retted	12	80	8	24	52	24	20	68	12	12	72	16
3	Chemical Retted	4	24	72	8	36	56	8	40	52	8	28	64

The above Table II reveals the following findings:

- **General appearance:** The decorticated fibres were rated as good in appearance by 80 percent of the judges whereas stagnant water retted fibres were rated as fair by 80 percent of the judges. About 72 percent of the judges rated the chemical retted fibres as poor in appearance.

- **Colour:** The colour of the decorticated fibres were rated as bright by 56 percent of judges, whereas stagnant water retted fibres were rated as medium by 52 percent of the judges. The chemical retted fibres were rated as dull by 56 percent of the judges.

- **Lustre:** The decorticated fibres were rated as good in lustre by 60 percent of the judges, whereas stagnant water retted fibres were rated as fair in lustre by 68 percent of the judges. The chemical retted fibres were rated as poor in lustre by majority of the judges.

- **Texture:** The decorticated fibres were rated as soft in texture by 68 percent of the judges, stagnant water retted fibres were rated as coarse by 72 percent and chemical retted fibres were rated as very coarse by 64 percent of the judges.

It could be concluded that the decorticated fibres are good in general appearance and lustre, bright in colour and soft in texture. So, the fibres extracted by the process of decortication could be called as the best of all the three methods. Hence the decorticated fibres could be utilized for making handicrafts and other accessory items.

ii. Physical Tests

- **Length:** The length of the Agave *americana* fibres was found to be 100-125 cms.

- **Diameter:** Higher the diameter, lesser is the spinnability of the fibre express Ashwini *et.al.* (2004). The diameter of Agave *americana* fibres viewed under the projection microscope ranged from 150µm to 300 µm. The average was found to be 235µm.

iii. Characteristics of the Fibres Extracted by Various Methods

The characteristics of the fibres based on various methods of extraction are given in Table III.

The force in grams required to rupture the fibre obtained by chemical retting, ranged between 434.03 and 2007.78 with an average of 1153.89. This was followed by decorticated fibres with an average of 724.14 and stagnant water retted fibres with an average of 300.34. The elongation of decorticated fibre ranged from 3.19 to 9.39 percent with an average of 5.98 percent. The fibre extracted by stagnant water retting ranged between 1.18 percent and 9.19 percent with an average of 6.01 percent, followed by chemical retting with an average of 3.92 percent. Basra (2002) feels increased elongation is associated with improved quality of the yarn, which in turn improves the quality of the fabric.

Table III
FIBRE CHARACTERISTICS BASED ON VARIOUS EXTRACTION METHODS

No.	Extraction Method	Force (gram)			Elongation (percent)			Time of Rupture (seconds)
		Minimum	Maximum	Average	Minimum	Maximum	Average	
1	Decortication	309.19	1152.93	724.14	3.19	9.39	5.98	16.85
2	Stagnant Water Retting	37.21	499.79	300.34	1.18	9.19	6.01	12.30
3	Chemical Retting	434.03	2007.78	1153.89	1.60	5.88	3.92	2.42

The time required to rupture, in seconds, for decorticated fibres was found to be the highest of 16.85 followed by water retted fibres of 12.30 and chemical retted fibres of 2.42. Among all the three methods, force and elongation of the decorticated fibres were found to be moderate. The time taken for rupture was found to be maximum in the case of decorticated fibres. The fibre extracted through decortication method is strong enough to do embroidery, and other surface embellishments. These fibres could be utilized for making all accessories as these are stronger.

iv. Fibres from Plants of Various Stages of Maturity

Table IV
FIBRE CHARACTERISTICS BASED ON
VARIOUS STAGES OF MATURITY

No.	Stages of Plant	Force (gram)			Elongation (percent)			Time of Rupture (seconds)
		Minimum	Maximum	Average	Minimum	Maximum	Average	
1	Matured	857.36	1946.28	1341.38	4.04	7.25	5.89	3.53
2	Moderate	380.47	1003.77	708.72	1.60	5.88	3.92	2.42
3	Tender	207.77	1141.35	658.20	1.20	5.63	3.81	2.34

Table IV reveals that the force, in grams, required to rupture the fibres was found to be the highest for matured fibres namely 1341.38 followed by moderate and tender fibres as 708.72 and 658.20 respectively. The elongation percentage of matured fibre ranged between 4.04 and 7.25 with an average of 5.89 which is the highest among the three samples. This was followed by moderate fibre with an average of 3.92 and the tender fibre of 3.81. The time taken for rupture by the matured fibre was the highest of about 3.53 seconds followed by moderate fibre of 2.42 seconds and tender fibre of 2.34 seconds. Among the three stages of growth of the fibres, it was found that the matured fibres required the maximum time for rupture with a maximum elongation and force. So, matured fibres proved to be the strongest of all the three. Hence the matured fibres could be utilized for making handicraft items and other accessories.

v. Evaluation of the Prepared Handicraft Items

The handicraft items were prepared by the scholar for evaluation. The items namely wall hangers, photo frame, decorative piece, ear rings and slippers were prepared. These were evaluated for their beauty and other decorative aspects which gave best results as per the evaluation of the judges. The cost estimation of the products is expressed in the Table V.

Table V
COST ESTIMATION OF PRODUCTS

No.	Particulars	Cost in Indian Rupees (₹)
	Preparation Cost	
1.	Fiber Extraction	15/ Kg
2.	Fiber Bleaching	10/Kg
3.	Fiber Dyeing	5/Kg
4.	Spinning and Miscellaneous Expenses	2/Kg
	Selling Price in Total	32/Kg

From 1 Kg of extracted, bleached and dyed fibres, decorative pieces - 3 wall hangers, 5 table mats, 2 bags, and accessories - 10 earrings and 2 garlands were prepared.

vi. Estimation of Costs

The products made out of the fibres were also cost effective. Any entrepreneur can be successful with limited investments. Women can do this at home as these do not need much of space or investment. This also gives more benefit when it is produced in large scale.

CONCLUSION

Thus from the findings of the study it is clear that strongest fibres are obtained from matured leaves of Agave *americana* plant through decortication. These fibres are strong enough and have good affinity towards dye to be converted into handicraft and accessory items.

These when dyed give wonderful bright colours. Women can do this at home as these do not need much of space or investment. This also gives more benefit when it is produced in large scale. Women can become successful entrepreneurs by starting the business of making handicraft items with this fibre and other minor fibres. Fashionable eco-friendly accessories also could be made from such minor fibres which have high potentiality for export value.

REFERENCES

Basra, A.S. (2002), Cotton Fibres, Developmental Biology, Quality Improvement and Textile Processing, CBS Publishers and Distributors, New Delhi. Pp. 207.

Corbman, B.P. (1983), Textiles Fibre to Fabric, Mc Graw Hill, New Yok. Pp. 259.

Doraisamy, I. and Chellamani, P. (1993), Pineapple Leaf Fibre, Textile Progress, Vol. 24, No.1, Textile Institute, Manchester, Pp.1-5.

Franck, R.R. (2005), Bast and Other Plant Fibres, The Textile Institute, Woodhead Publishing Limited, Abington Hall, Cambridge: England. Pp. 31, 233.

Hall, A.J., (2004), The Standard Handbook of Textiles, Woodhead Publishing Limited, England. Pp. 27.

Modi, J.R. and Garde, A.R. (1995), Chemical Processing of Cotton and Polyester- Cotton Blends, Textile Association of India, Ahmedabad. Pp. 5, 12.

Needles, H.L., (2001), Textile Fibres, Dyes, Finishes and Processes, Standard Publishers, New Delhi. Pp. 148, 167.

Pardeshi, P.D. and Paul, R. (2003), New Cloth Market, Vol. 17 (Nov). Pp. 29, 231.

Sen, K.K. and Sen, S.K. (1994), Glucon Type of Gum From Ramie, Research and Industry, Vol. 39, No.4, Pp. 224.

Stout, E. (1970), Introduction to Textiles, John Wiley and Sons, New York, Pp. 81, 82.

VOCATIONAL EDUCATION AND SKILL BASED TRAINING FOR WOMEN IN INDIAN PRINT SECTOR

S. Ambika[1] and T.K.S. Lakshmi Priya[2]

[1]S. Ambika, Assistant Professor, Department of Printing Technology, Avinashilingam Institute of Home Science and Higher Education for Women, Coimbatore. Email: ambikathir06@gmail.com

[2]Dr. T.K.S. Lakshmi Priya, Professor, Department of Printing Technology, Faculty of Engineering, Avinashilingam Institute for Home Science and Higher Education for Women. Email: tkslp.dr@gmail.com

ABSTRACT

India, with more than billion residents, has the second largest education system in the world. Yet there is a gap between the qualities of those who pass out and the expectations of the industries, which limits their scope to compete globally. One approach to bridging the gap is by integrating academic skills and vocational skills and preparing the students for demand based employment. The Print Sector also faces this problem of lack of suitable candidates for the job requirements. Even in countries where gender equality is formally achieved; there frequently remain disparities between women and men with regard to employment and career opportunities. Women often do not have access to certain sectors or field of occupation (Gender in Technical and Vocational Education and Training, TVET). Especially in the print sector women are engaged in limited segments like bindery section. In this paper we provide - (i) our study of the Print Sector, (ii) the associated vocational skills and education especially for women, where there is a large scope for women as employers and employees. We provide our (iii) suggestions for improving the scenario by exploring the different fields in print sector where women can be suitably engaged, in order to bridge the gap between the industry and academia.

Keywords: vocational education, print skills, women's education

INTRODUCTION

While higher education aims at developing the technical and theoretical skills thereby making the students employable at higher levels, vocational education imparts hands-on training so that the candidates are ready for self-employment or become entrepreneurs.

Job opportunities in India, at all levels of any organization's hierarchy, are huge (All India Management Association, 2003). In India vacancies and unemployment exist as two large mutually exclusive entities. This gap needs to be bridged by equipping the unemployed with 'required' skill sets. This fact has already been identified by the authorities in the Government and Education sectors and initiatives have been taken to promote vocational schools (Planning Commission, 2007).

Although it is clear that the vocational training system is the bridge to be taken by job-seekers, especially with 28 percent of Indians in the below poverty line (TVET), only about 3 percent of the students at the higher secondary level enrol for vocational training (World Bank, 2006). Among these, the statistical report says that the percentage of women candidates enrolling in ITI'S (Industrial Training Institute) is much lower than men.

Figure 1

MALE AND FEMALE ENROLMENT RATIO IN
TRADITIONAL COURSES ACROSS INDIA

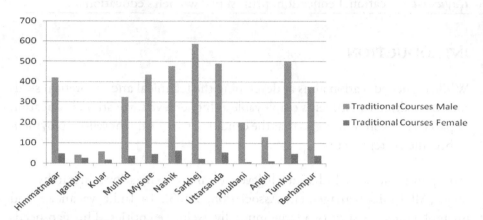

Source: www.peoplefactorindia.com/frameworks/women-in-itis-2

Figure I indicates that the percentage of women candidates' enrolment in ITIs is comparatively less than the number of male candidates. There are many ways to improve this scenario. One way is to identify vocational courses which have a large scope for employment opportunities which are more suitable for women. Enrolment in any vocational stream has a direct relationship with the employment opportunities available. This state-of-affairs motivated us to explore the potential within our domain of specialization – the Print Sector and to identify the scope for vocational training in the Print Sector for women, where the requirement of trained employees is more. Considering the constraints and barriers for women in undergoing vocational training, we have identified few areas in Print the sector where women can be given vocational training through which they can turn out to be entrepreneurs or employees. We present in this paper the results of our study.

In Section 2, we present the global and Indian Print Sector with its rich repository of vocational skills. In Section 3, we give an overview of vocational education in India for women and bring out the need for focusing on courses related to skills required by the Print Sector. In Section 4, we provide our suggestions for such training courses before concluding the paper in Section 5.

An Overview of the Print Sector

Print has facilitated the dissipation of knowledge to people on a mega scale, ever since the Stone Age when cavemen created images on the cave walls. A major break-through in the Print evolution was the invention of a mechanized printing unit in the 10th Century. Over the centuries the Print industry has percolated into all major and minor commercial and non-commercial industries. This sector comprises of the Printing Presses, the Packaging, Graphic Arts, Digital printing, e-publishing and advertising industries. The chemical and ink industries, machine manufacturers, paper, ceramic and glass industries, are a few of the feeders to the Print Sector. Market analysis indicates a compound annual growth of 5-10 percent for the various segments of the Print Industries (https://www.smitherspira.com).

In India, the Printing Industry is valued at about 10.6 billion Euros as per 2006 statistics and estimated growth rate of about 12 percent (http://italiaindia.com/index.php?/publications/P12). More than 75 percent of the Indian Print Industries are family owned. Newspapers dominate the market share among the Printed products while the Offset Printing dominated the market share among the various others as illustrated in Figure 2.

Figure 2
MARKET SHARE OF PRINT SECTOR

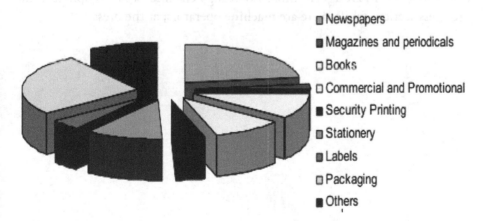

□ Newspapers
■ Magazines and periodicals
□ Books
□ Commercial and Promotional
■ Security Printing
□ Stationery
■ Labels
□ Packaging
■ Others

a. Market share of End Use Sectors

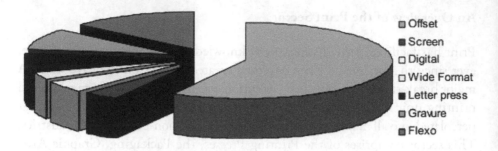

b. Market share based on Technology used

Source: www.italiaindia.com

Having highlighted the significance and enormous size of the Print sector, we move on to explore the spectrum of jobs available in these industries. We have categorized the jobs based on the three primary sections of the Print Industry viz., Pre-press, Press and Post-press.

Table I indicates the typical skill-based jobs under these three sections of each Industry which produces a specific range of products. For instance, the Newspaper Industry which primarily prints newspapers daily both as printed copies and in the digital form, has employees working as Proof-readers, Desktop Publishing (DTP) Designers, Story Boarding Personnel, and Compilers in the Pre-press section, while there are machine operators, at the press.

Table I

A SAMPLE SKILL-ORIENTED JOB MATRIX
FOR THE PRINT SECTOR

S. No.	Industry Segment	End Uses	Typical Jobs in Various Sections of a Print Sector Industry		
			Pre-press	Press	Post-press
1.	Newspaper Industry	Newspapers - Paper and Digital	Proof Reading, DTP, Story Boarding, Compiling	Screen Printing Operations	Binding, Folding, Wrapping
2.	Book Publishing Houses	Books, Journals, Magazines, Newsletters, Periodicals	Desk Top Publishing, Plate Making Operations	Production Planning	Book Binding, Cutting and Finishing Operation
3.	Animation Industry	Animated Films, Cartoons, Educational CDs	Avatar Designers, Media Animation, Rendering	2D & 3D Animation Courses, Web Animation Designing Courses	
4.	Photo Industry	Photos On Paper, and Non- Paper Substrates	Editing, Correction, Enhancement	Photography Certificate Course	Photo Lamination
5.	E-Publishers	Websites, Portals, E-Books	Proof Reading, Scanner Operation, E-Publishing	-	-
6.	Packaging Industries	Wrappers, Tetrapacks, Cartons,	Packaging Design	Flexographic Machine-Operation, Hand-Made Packaging, Label Making	Tool and Die-Making, Corrugation Board Making
7.	Commercial Printers	Invitation/ ID/Visiting/ Handouts/ Fliers	Desk Top Publishing, Image Carrier Making	Screen Printing, Offset and Flexo Machine Operation	Guillotine Cutting Operation, Lamination, Folding Machine Operation
8.	Advertising Agencies	Advertisements, Short Films, Hoardings	Modeling, Short Film Making	Printing Banners, Buntings, Posters	Public Relation

Vocational Aspects, Education and Training – Scope for Women

Due to its origin as a family-owned business, the Indian scenario of the Print Industry showcases entrepreneurial characteristics. It is therefore a direct candidate for vocational skill based business which includes everyone in the family, including women, children, senior citizens and the physically challenged (if any). All business houses, are 2, 3 or multi-tiered consisting of (i) proprietor (or equivalent), (ii) manager (optional) and (iii) worker. While proprietors and managers may possess academic skills, workers are vocationally trained personnel.

To cope with the advancements in technology, print industries must exhibit dynamic adaptation to market changes and customer requirements. Thus, several successful Printers in India who have been holding fort for 3–4 generations, evolved onto multifunction printing houses. Such environments mandate highly trained and dynamic persons with appropriate skills for employment. On similar lines, even small level start-ups and Print houses can sustain if the personal are sufficiently skilled.

Although providing skill-based training to unemployed women forms the first step to make unemployed women employable in the Print Sector, reports indicate that percentage of women candidates enrolling in ITI'S (Industrial Training Institute) is much lower than men. Further, among the vocational training courses offered to women, Wellness and Healthcare sector is being focused currently (www.kenresearch.com).

Since the Print Sector can accept women either as (i) skilled personal or (ii) with academic background, we have explored the suitability of women in these two roles which is presented in Tables II and III respectively.

Table II
SUITABILITY OF A VOCATIONALLY TRAINED WOMAN
IN SMALL & MEDIUM ENTERPRISE (SME)

Existing Benefits		Lacuna
• Can be easily trained according to the profile of the press		• Resistance to change from what they learn in the training centres
• Specific classes of vocationally trained women can quickly acquire new skills (example- DTP)		• Lack of awareness in using quality control equipments, because vocational training centres cannot afford to invest on high cost quality inspection equipments
• Small duration for training		• Lack of vertical mobility and transfer of credits for deserving candidates
• Easy labor availability	**Employing Vocationally Trained Women by small/medium entrepreneurs in India**	• The prevailing *Low prestige* attached to vocational training
• Trained women can quickly learn the required skills to work in the commercial printing unit compared to untrained workers		• Vocational training and vocational education are dealt with separately
		• Presently communication/ soft skills are poor
• Initial training period can be minimized		• Lack of adaptability to an entirely new technology eg. manual pre-press to digital pre-press
		• Women cannot be employed directly into production sector

Table III
SUITABILITY OF AN ACADEMICALLY SKILLED PERSON IN SME

Existing benefits		Lacuna
• Conceptually strong		• Insufficient practical knowledge
• Possesses managerial skills		• Requires to be trained after employment
• Sufficient communication skills		• Less knowledge about commercial printing press
• Understands the concepts of printing from the grassroot	**Employing an academically skilled Women in small/medium entrepreneurs in India**	• Initially need to pay more, without productivity
• Quickly learns the profile of the company and work better		• Risk of quitting the job any time after training
• Can sustain in any department, pre-press, post press, press, etc.		• Lacks knowledge spanning pre-press, press and post-press
• Theoretical knowledge about current developments		• Gap between current industrial and technical developments and skills required for it

We find that academic skills without vocational skills, and vice-versa would result in poor quality, performance and more production time. It is essential that these two skill sets are integrated to a certain level. Present scenario in India is that these two skills are independently offered and hence a gap exists between workers and managers. This state of affairs affects the Small and Medium Enterprise (SME) sector, the worst. Since the SMEs form a large group in India and cannot be ignored, we must focus on bridging this gap.

Suggestions for Educating Women for Print Sector Jobs

Printing industries are moving towards a digital world. It is no more a men oriented industry working with the machines day long. Printing sector goes digital where women can have a comfortable working environment. The growth in the digital technology grows day by day in a faster rate. But to keep pace with the fast developing technology, the women employee involved in the Print sector must be able to possess the following abilities:

1. ability to accept the change in technology and adopt it
2. awareness to old techniques and tips, in spite of being obsolete
3. ability to integrate concepts and application
4. have a futuristic view – foresee the progress of the Print Sector

In order that these abilities are acquired, higher education and vocational education must be integrated.

1. The curriculum must contain an industry visit and placement component in each course
   a. For example: A course on quality control may be provided with quality control practicals. In addition, visits and placements to appropriate industries concerned with quality, must be provided

2. Every practical course must include experiments at two levels
   a. Level 1: study of the concept
   b. Level 2: basic experiments on the concept
   c. Level 3: an application oriented experiment

3. Students must undergo multiple certificate courses in specific areas
   a. Language skills: proof reading, drafting, technical writing, etc.
   b. Computer skills: software installation, hardware troubleshooting, networking, etc.
   c. Aesthetic skills: colour combination and choice

4. Curriculum must be flexibly designed to accommodate industry requirements without major change to the syllabus
5. Mandatory periodic training for teachers and support staff
6. Mandatory industry-institute interaction

Although some educational institutes in India are plasticizing some of these tips, a national level improvement in curricula is required.

Vocational Skill Requirement in Print Sector

The printing process has three stages: pre-press, press, and binding or finishing. In small print shops, the same person may take care of all three stages. In such a case the required skill sets that are required to accomplish the tasks are:

Table IV
SKILL SETS REQUIRED TO WORK IN A SMALL PRINT SHOP – MULTI TASKING

• Review Job Orders – Includes Quantities to be Printed, Paper Quality, Ink Colour, And Special Printing Instructions • Pre-flighting • Arrange Pages so that Materials can be Printed • Basic Computer Knowledge • Minimal Press Operation • Collect and Inspect Random Samples during Print Runs to Identify any Needed Adjustments • Guillotine Machine Operation • Finishing and Binding Operations

However, in most print shops, workers specialize in an occupation that focuses on one step in the printing process. Skill sets required to work in each of such area:

Table V
SKILL SETS REQUIRED TO WORK IN SPECIFIC WORK AREA

Skill Sets Required to Work in as Prepress Technicians
• Pre-flighting – check the job for completeness • Computer Knowledge • Designing Software • Skills to Operate Direct-to-Film/Plate • Knowledge in Colours • Basic Knowledge in Press Operation
Skill Sets Required to Work as Press Operators
• Prepare, Run, and Maintain Printing Presses (special skill sets required for operating each of the printing process like- Offset Lithography, Gravure, Flexography, Screen) • Colour Matching Skills • Proof Images

Skill Sets Required to work as Print Binding and Finishing Workers
• Gathering • Collating • Folding • Skill to work in Laminating, Folding, Perfecting, Collating, Cutting Machine, etc. • Saddle Stitching • Binding Operations • Basic Knowledge about Paper

CONCLUSION

The importance of women empowerment for social progress and economic development is undisputed. The concept of vocational training is considered with top priority in developing countries like ours. Several initiatives are being taken by our government. However, significant improvements are yet to come up. The concept of vocational training for women can give a great opportunity for the underprivileged girl students to get to master a particular skill, by which they can confidently face the world. The massive scope of skill based training in the print sector which we have identified in this paper- more suitable for women, will definitely give them an opportunity to get themselves employed in a decent job. With the improved skills they can turn out to be an entrepreneur with a minimum investment. However, significant improvements are yet to come up. Print Sector which encompasses designing, printing and packaging, spans from small in-house job-workers to large multinational companies. In order to uplift the Print Sector, especially SME, it is necessary to integrate higher education and vocational education. On these lines we have given some of our suggestions, which would make our Print Industry ready for global competition.

REFERENCES

All India Management Association (February 2003), *India's New Opportunity – 2020*, New Delhi: PMDL Design Private Limited.

Gender in Technical and Vocational Education and Training (TVET), http://www.wiram.de/gendersourcebook/cooperation/cooperation_TVET. html, Last accessed 22.12. 2012.

People Factor Strategic HR Solutions Company, *Why Are The Women Absent From The 'Indian Skill Story'*. Online available at: www.peoplefactorindia. com/frameworks/women-in-itis-2, Last Accessed 27.8.2014.

Planning Commission, Government of India (May, 2007), *Report of the Task Force on Skill Development*, New Delhi.

Prakash, Ved, University Grants Commission (2011), *Inclusion and qualitative Expansion of Higher Education-Compilation Based on the deliberations of Working Group for Higher Education in the 12th Five-Year Plan (12012-17)* 1st ed. New Delhi: VIBA Press Pvt. Ltd.

TeamLease Service Pvt. Ltd. (2010), *India Labour Report 2009*. Available: www. teamlease.com, Last accessed 22.12. 2012.

UGC Committee (4th March 2011), *Report UGC committee prepare detailed project report,* Online available at: http://mhrd.gov.in/content/report-ugccommittee, Last accessed 27.08.2014.

World Bank (2006), *Skill Development In India The Vocational Education And Training System, 1st Edition*, South Asia Region.

http://italiaindia.com/index.php?/publications/P12, Last accessed 16.09.2014.

https://www.kenresearch.com, Last Accessed 27.08.2014.

https://www.smitherspira.com/market-reports/printing-industry-market-trends-statistics-report.aspx, Last accessed 16.09.2014.

GREEN TECHNOLOGY FOR RURAL WOMEN

D. Sumathi

[1]Dr. D. Sumathi, Assistant Professor in Resource Management, Avinashilingam Institute for Home Science and Higher Education for Women. Coimbatore, Tamil Nadu. Email: sumidhans@gmail.com

ABSTRACT

Major Indian population is widely spread among many small and isolated villages. So their enormous energy needs can hardly be expected to be met by commercial energy sources. Renewable energy sources have an important role to play in the development of such isolated villages, because they require minimum infrastructure development and they are environmentally friendly with the inmates. In view of the problematic arrivals in recent years, namely fuel crisis and environmental pollution, worldwide attention has been attracted by the biogas technology. Biogas technology is an apt solution for offering fuel, fertilizer and sanitation in the environment. The major problem in India is human night soil management. Improper management of human excreta has been a major threat to environment as well as for health of the population in the country. In India, the practice of open defecation had been a major problem. So, the multifaceted problems facing the rural households such as non-availability of clean energy, indoor pollution and insanitary surrounding due to open defecation can be evacuated in course of time by night soil/ garbage based Community Biogas Plant. Such innovative programme has been considered as a real boon to the households. However, the evaluatory studies in this direction are less. This study has been framed in order to assess the benefits accrued in qualitative and quantitative terms by installing

Community Biogas Plants. The research is indebted to the guidance of (Late) Dr. Sathyavathimuthu, Professor of Resource Management.

Keywords: community biogas plant, environmental sanitation, night soil

INTRODUCTION

India is on the brink of a massive waste disposal crisis and is likely to face a massive crisis situation in the coming years. Till recently, the problem of waste has been seen as one of cleaning and disposing rubbish, but a closer look at the current and future scenario reveals that waste needs to be treated holistically, recognizing it as a natural resource with impact on health (Govindaraja and Sacratees, 2012). It is ironical that when there is great need for conserving energy and exploring the possibilities of newer sources, a large quantum of energy is allowed to go unutilized in the form of waste as a result of human activities of production and consumption (Sinha, 2002). Organic wastes which are produced in large quantities all over the world create major environmental and disposal problems (Baby and Govindarajalu, 2012). These materials cause major unpleasant odour problems and need a large land area for disposal and are often a source of contamination of ground water (Kannaiyan and Lilli, 1999; Edwards and Bater, 2002). Yet in the rural areas majority of them go to the fields for defecation and thereby pollute the environment with human excreta. Poverty, ignorance, customs, tradition and superstitious beliefs, high cost and non-availability of space in the households are the reasons for many of them to refrain themselves in having a sanitary latrine. So, the multifaceted problems facing the rural households can be mitigated through the night soil/garbage based Community Biogas Plant.

METHODOLOGY

This phase of the study has been done in two villages of Sathyamangalam Taluk in Erode District. The presence and successful running of the Community Biogas Plant in this region is the major reason for this consideration. All the 312 households spread in the villages were surveyed. In depth open-ended interviews, direct observation of behaviours and interactions and participatory methods have been adhered to collect qualitative data. Quantitative approach was used for measurable aspects such as time use, expenditure on fuel, recovery of money. The quantum of the major resources fuel energy and money recovered by the homemakers using biogas instead of traditional fuel were studied. Few examples of Community Biogas Plant successfully running in Tamil Nadu are in the villages like Kovanur, Saravanampatty and some villages are now yet to install.

RESULTS AND DISCUSSION

Socio-Economic Profile: The socio-economic profile of the households includes social, educational and economic status of the households in selected villages. The distribution of households based on household structure and size are presented in Table I.

Table I
SOCIAL STATUS

Particulars	Households	
	N:312	Percentage
Household Structure		
Nuclear	266	85
Joint	46	15
Household Size		
Small (1 – 3)	65	21
Medium (4 – 6)	212	68
Large (>6)	35	11

Changes in the social structure, higher education, generation gap, availability of lucrative jobs in the urban areas, education and above all, changes in the value system are the major reasons for breaking up joint family system and setting up nuclear families. The data highlights the fact that 85 percent of them adopt nuclear family system.

Economic Status: The study of rural population is incomplete without the analysis of their economic status.

Table II
ECONOMIC STATUS

Particulars	Households	
	N:312	Percentage
Occupation - Heads of Family		
Coolie	112	36
Agriculture Laborers	93	30
Employed in Industries	68	22
Self-Employed	20	6
Government Employees	19	6
Occupation - Homemakers		
Coolie	134	43
Agriculture Laborers	98	32
Self-Employed	51	16

Daily wage earning for their livelihood is still prominent in the rural areas as 36 percent of head of families and 43 percent of homemakers are working as coolies. 22 percent of head of the families are permanently employed in the Bannari Amman Sugar Factory which is located nearer to their area. As agriculture is one of the predominant occupations in surrounding area of the villages, 30 percent of head of the families and 32 percent of homemakers are agricultural laborers. Self-employment like running petty shops, mending slippers, selling vegetables is pursued by 6 percent of head of families and 16 percent of homemakers. It is amazing to know that 6 percent of heads of family are employed in Government jobs.

According to HUDCO classification, 57 percent of the households irrespective of the occupational category are earning less than Indian Rupees (INR) 5000 per month belonging to low income category. Thirty three percent of households are middle income families earning Rupees 5000-7000 and only a few of them are high middle income families earning monthly income of Rupees 7000-9000.

Fuel Management Practices in Households

Table III illustrates the fuel usage pattern of the households.

Table III
FUEL USAGE PATTERN

Fuel usage	Households	
	N:312	Percentage
Firewood, Barks and Twigs	109	35
Firewood	93	30
Firewood and Kerosene	33	10
Firewood and Biogas	62	20
LPG	15	5

Out of the 312 families surveyed, only 15 households are using LPG for their cooking requirements. None of the agricultural labor families or the daily wage earning families is using LPG due to their low economic status. The introduction of Community Biogas Plant (CBP) to supply biogas is a boon to these households, so 62 households made use of this opportunity and perform their daily cooking using biogas.

Though the CBP is constructed for the benefit of the rural households, 250 families are not utilizing this facility. With adequate motivation and guidance the village women could make significant use of available resources.

Resource recovery of firewood after installation of CBP is presented in Table IV.

Table IV
RESOURCE RECOVERY OF FUEL ENERGY

(Total No. Families: 62)

Members	Families	Mean Fuel Consumption/ Day/Family				Mean Fuel Consumption/ Month/Family			
		Before (kg)	After (kg)	Fuel Saved (kg)	Amount Saved (₹)	Before (kg)	After (kg)	Fuel Saved (kg)	Amount Saved (₹)
2	9	2.20	0.40	1.80	12.6	66.0	12.0	54.0	378.00
3	13	2.33	0.80	1.53	10.71	69.9	24.0	45.9	111.30
4	28	2.57	0.90	1.67	11.69	77.1	27.0	50.1	294.00
5	7	2.87	1.80	1.07	13.09	86.1	54.0	32.1	224.70
6	5	3.07	1.93	1.14	13.51	92.1	57.9	34.2	239.40
				'F' value	15.50**	8.209**			

**Significant at one percent level

Figure 1
MEAN FUEL CONSUMPTION

The consumption of fuel varied with the number of members in the family. On average they saved firewood ranging from 32 kg to 54kg per month. Similarly a sum of Rupees 111-378 per month could be recovered through the use of biogas. The proportion saved from the fuel budget was reported to be spent on items such as education of children, buying additional clothing and acquisition of capital goods. This fact denotes that if all the homemakers effectively use the gas plant, a considerable amount of fuel and money could be recovered.

Benefits Accrued

The informal interview conducted with the 62 homemakers who accepted the technology in using biogas for cooking, narrated their experience indicated the impact. Table V indicates the benefits enjoyed by the homemakers with the technology.

Table V
REASONS FOR ADOPTION

Reasons	Households*	
	N:62	Percentage
Relieves Drudgery	62	100
Clean and Hygienic Indoor Environment	60	97
Saves Time	60	97
Prestigious Issue	58	94
Free from Eyestrain	57	92
Soot Free Utensils	56	90
Safe Drinking Water	52	84
Opportunity to Share Ideas with Friends	51	82

* Multiple responses

The homemakers who adopted this technology for a period of two years expressed the numerous benefits in using night soil based biogas for cooking. Earlier, the homemakers faced several drudgery using conventional fuels such as walking long distances to collect; spending lot of time in collection; difficulty in lighting the fire and smoky kitchen. The respondents are highly conscious of many problems in their fuel management practices and all of them welcomed the idea of introduction of CBP.

Eighty four percent of the homemakers boil water for drinking purposes using biogas, a fuel available free of cost. Rural women have limited opportunity to interact with friends and share their views and ideas, since they leave home for their employment and return only late in the evening. Hence cooking in the community kitchen along with their friends is preferred by 82 percent of the women.

These reasons clearly show that it is not only the technological competence that is important for women but equally important are the social benefits of the technology to women.

Table VI
REASONS FOR NON-ADOPTION

Reasons	No. of Women*	
	N:250	Percentage
Distance from the Households	244	98
Carrying the Vessel and Food Items	226	90
Not Able to Cook All the Items	215	86
Change in the Taste of Food	206	82
Psychological Barrier	123	49
Availability of Other Fuels	96	38
Non-Acceptance of Male Members	86	34
Afraid of Operation	59	24
Unable to Use Mud Pots	19	8

* Multiple responses

Ninety percent of the homemakers mentioned that the community kitchen is located far away from their households; so they feel discomfort in carrying the vessels to the area. In Eighty two percent of the families they were addicted to the taste of foods prepared using firewood as fuel. Thirty eight percent of the homemakers were using other fuels such as Kerosene and Liquid Petroleum Gas (LPG) for their cooking. Technological solution to the problem is often gender biased as can be inferred from the table. In some of the families the male members dominate in deciding even the cooking fuel and the women have to simply obey. So in 34 percent of the families, women have no choice in selecting the fuel and mode of cooking.

The biogas generated from the night soil based biogas plant made a dent among the women. By equipping them with the adequate knowledge about the process of bio-methanisation, their attitude might change towards positive side.

Awareness Programme for Rural Women

The observation of fuel practices of rural households in the selected villages necessitated specific action programme to make the women witness, involve and experience the impact in real life situation. To make women to accept the use of biogas in the community kitchen, they should be made aware of its multifaceted uses. If the technology transfer is done successfully, it will get penetrated into the minds of the women which in turn will pay rich dividends in terms of energy conservation. So in order to make large percentage of women who are reluctant towards adoption of this technology, several awareness programmes have been chalked out and executed.

Strength of Community Biogas Plant

- Sustainable eco-friendly energy resource
- Self-promoting and viable indigenous technology and not involving sophisticated device or highly qualified expertise
- Meet ecological and economic demands of future
- Effective means of sanitary disposal of human excreta
- Pollution abatement and reduction of Green House Gas emissions
- Restoration of forest wealth by reducing the practice of indiscriminate felling of trees
- Supplies an efficient, clean burning fuel as it does not contain Sulphur
- Effective utilization of biogas technology readily integrated with rural development
- Cleaner village surroundings resulting in improved sanitation
- Reduces drudgery and provides leisure hours for productive employment to the rural women
- Digested slurry improves soil fertility and increases crop yield
- Mimics environmental cycles – nutrients such as Nitrogen, Phosphorus and Potassium are conserved and recycled back in the form of slurry
- Recovery of valuable resources – fuel, fertilizer and money
- Rural women would highly benefit by the construction of Community Biogas Plant (CBP)

Weakness of Community Biogas Plant

- High initial capital cost and poor financial viability
- Lack of logical promotional strategies and implementation process
- Low efficiency compared to Liquefied Petroleum Gas (LPG)
- Climatic factors affects gas production
- Declining of skilled persons at present for construction of Fixed-Dome type biogas plants

- Technical problems and difficulty in identifying scum formation, blockages and pin-hole leakages
- Improper maintenance of the units constructed in rural areas
- Problem of co-ordination and co-operation among users of Community Biogas Plant (CBP)
- Social taboos and psychological barriers hindering the usage

CONCLUSION

Rural women would highly benefit by the construction of Community Biogas Plant (CBP). Energy and money can be saved and at the same time organic waste can be utilized. Science and technology can be reached to unreached women through this type of biogas plant. Community kitchen practices would gradually become a practice in our culture; thereby promoting green technology for rural women.

REFERENCES

Baby, K. and Govindarajalu, K. (2012), Solid Waste Management – A Case Study of Palakkad Municipality in Kerala, Yojana, Vol.50, No.20, Pp. 52-54.

Govindaraja, H. and Sacratees. J. (2012), Solid Waste Management in Tirunelveli Corporation, Southern Economist, Vol-50, No.20, Pp. 34-38.

Kannaiyan, S. and Lilly, S.S. (1999), Bio Resources Technology for Sustainable Agriculture, Associated Publishing Company, New Delhi. Pp. 355-357.

Sinha, P.C. (2002), Energy Crisis, Anmol Publications Pvt. Ltd., New Delhi, P. 67.

QUALITY OF WORK LIFE AMONG WOMEN EMPLOYEES AT ITES (INFORMATION TECHNOLOGY ENABLED SERVICES) SECTOR IN COIMBATORE

J. Arthi

Dr. J. Arthi, Assistant Professor (SG), Avinashilingam School of Management Technology, Avinashilingam Institute for Home Science and Higher Education for Women, Coimbatore, Tamil Nadu. Email: arthiifm@gmail.com

ABSTRACT

In India over the past few years, the Information Technology Enabled Services (ITES) industry has been growing rapidly and this growth has fuelled a lot of Human Resource (HR) challenges. The biggest challenge of them all is to manage the ambitious and transient work force. Moreover, since the industry is predominantly service oriented, the importance of attracting and retaining talent has become very crucial. Quality of Work life (QWL) is a strategic tool to influence the employees in a positive manner so that their happiness index is increased both in work and family life. QWL has got a rich literature where several studies have been undertaken with variables like organizational commitment, Job performance, Employee Retention, Job Stress, Organizational Citizenship Behavior have been tested and proved to have positive and significant relationship with QWL. A research attempt is made to analyze the Quality of Work life among women employees at ITES in Coimbatore. The sample size of 561 is drawn from 20 organizations in ITES sector in Coimbatore at the operations level. This study is of great importance for a city like Coimbatore where ITES sector has established itself with many companies and starting new ventures in this Coimbatore city.

Keywords: ITES, quality of work life, organizational commitment, job performance, employee retention, job stress, organizational citizenship behavior, women employees

INTRODUCTION

In today's global economy, organizations face various Human Resource (HR) challenges as in recent times there is increasing importance given to human resources. HR departments pay more attention to the aspiration of every employee and evolve strategies to constantly discover their true potential. As Indian employees become more ingrained and connected to foreign organizations, it is important for both the client firm and the Information Technology Enabled Services (ITES) operation to identify applicable Human Resource Development and High Performance Management practices. The present research conducted with the women employees of ITES in Coimbatore assesses the work situations to understand the QWL practices which supports women employees.

Quality Work Life (QWL) - A Review

A wide range of literature consolidates the factors that determine Quality of working Life (QWL) and variables included by different researchers in their studies. The QWL models proposed by certain authors are discussed in this paragraph. Sirgy *et. al.* (2001) listed various factors affecting quality of working life as: Need satisfaction based on job requirements, Work environment, Supervisory behavior, Ancillary programmes and Organizational commitment. They observed QWL as fulfillment of these key needs through resources, activities, and outcomes resulting from participation in the workplace. This model is based at Maslow's needs theory, covering Health and safety, Economic and family, Social, Esteem, Actualization, Knowledge and Aesthetics.

Hackman and Oldham (1976) observed psychological growth needs as crucial determinant of QWL. Several such needs were identified; Skill variety, Task Identity, Task significance, Autonomy and Feedback. They concluded that fulfilment of these needs plays an important role if employees are to experience high QWL. According to (Davis & Cherns, 1975; Sashkin & Burke, 1987),

QWL is not only enhancing the company's productivity but also employee identification and a sense of belonging and pride in their work. Based on various researches we can identify some determinants of QWL which are adequate and fair compensation, safe and health work environment, opportunity for career growth and security, social integration in the work organization which relates to freedom of speech, work and total life space and the social relevance to the work.

QWL is often considered in two directions, one is the removal of negative aspects of work and working conditions and the other direction is the modification of work and working conditions to enhance the capability of employees and to which is important for individual and society (Kotze, 2005). According to Dessler (1981), QWL was seen as the level to which employees are able to satisfy their personal needs not only in terms of material matters but also of self-respect, contentment and an opportunity to use their talents make contribution and for personal growth. So it is very important for an organization to provide employees proper valuation which will satisfy them and will ensure the productivity.

Ali Najafi (2006) concluded that there's a positive and significant correlation between QWL and managers' profiting. This means that as the QWL or quality of work life increases the profits of the organization will also improve. Michael (1992) studied the impact of QWL on organizational commitment, and concluded that after providing quality of work life, changes also take place in commitment.

Quality of Work Life among Women Employees at ITES Sector in Coimbatore

Indian Information Technology Enabled Services and Business Process Outsourcing (ITES-BPO) continue to grow from strength to strength, witnessing high levels of activity - both Onshore as well as Offshore. Continuing pressure on cost bases at a time of growing competitiveness is driving companies to look at offshore outsourcing as a strategic alternative. Coimbatore is also emerging as an IT and BPO city. It is ranked at seventeenth place among the global outsourcing cities. Coimbatore City is one of the top 10 fastest growing cities of India.

Most of the research in ITES has addressed only specific problems related to challenges of Attrition, HRM systems, Job Stress, Job satisfaction etc. The current research is a thoughtful endeavor to explore the QWL practices that are in place to sustain the women workforce.

The QWL dimensions are extracted through Factor Analysis using Principal component analysis with Varimax Rotation and labelled as Reward system, Managerial Style, Organizational support and Job Itself. QWL provides contentment not only in the workplace but reflects highest satisfaction to their extended environment (i.e.,) family. This will increase work commitment, employee involvement, employee retention and reduce employee turnover which is the major challenge in ITES Sector. The job in which an employee is engaged should fulfill his needs thus leading to a longer stay in the organization. The research objective is to identify the major determinants of QWL for the women employees in ITES sector.

METHODOLOGY

For this research, QWL is defined as the perception of the employees on organizational environment that focuses on the well-being at work and it is measured across 25 statements adopted from the instrument of Russell Consulting Inc. named Quality of Work Life Assessment survey.

The demographic profile of individuals includes type of organization, age, marital status, educational qualification and income. The present analysis includes calculating Mean Score Value to ascertain results across the dimensions given. The employees in ITES sector at the operational level and working in day time shift from 20 organizations constitute the universe for the research.

After cases with missing data were eliminated, the final sample consisted of 561 useable responses which yielded a response rate of 62 percent. The samples were selected based on purposive sampling. The results will help to understand that QWL across different dimensions projects the perception of target employees in the respective group. The organizations will get the right inputs to decide the strategies to be designed appropriately to retain as well has make them feel happy in the organizations.

RESULTS AND DISCUSSION

Based on the analysis, the results are presented in the next page.

Figure 1
EXTRACTION OF QUALITY OF WORK LIFE (QWL) DIMENSIONS

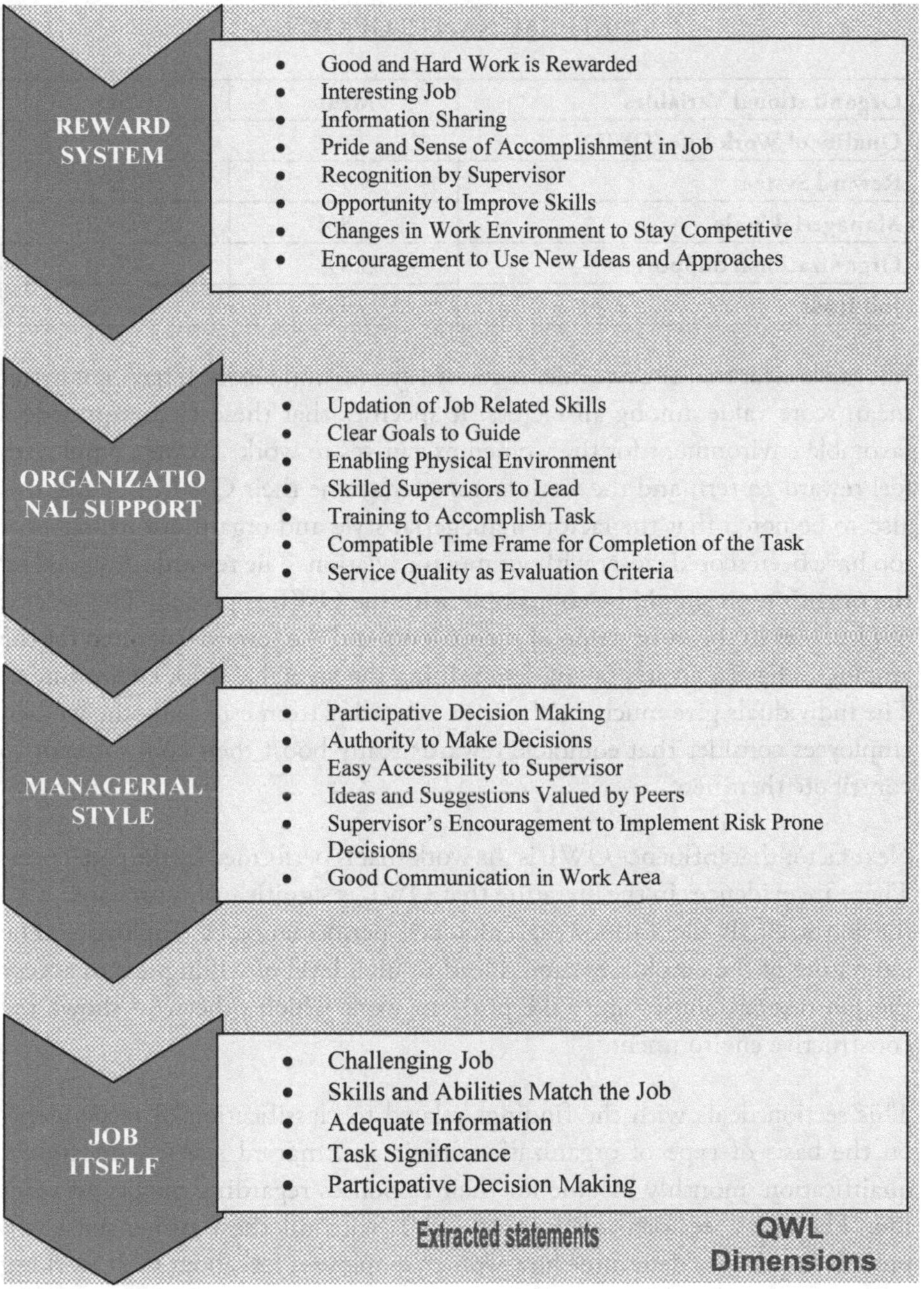

REWARD SYSTEM
- Good and Hard Work is Rewarded
- Interesting Job
- Information Sharing
- Pride and Sense of Accomplishment in Job
- Recognition by Supervisor
- Opportunity to Improve Skills
- Changes in Work Environment to Stay Competitive
- Encouragement to Use New Ideas and Approaches

ORGANIZATIONAL SUPPORT
- Updation of Job Related Skills
- Clear Goals to Guide
- Enabling Physical Environment
- Skilled Supervisors to Lead
- Training to Accomplish Task
- Compatible Time Frame for Completion of the Task
- Service Quality as Evaluation Criteria

MANAGERIAL STYLE
- Participative Decision Making
- Authority to Make Decisions
- Easy Accessibility to Supervisor
- Ideas and Suggestions Valued by Peers
- Supervisor's Encouragement to Implement Risk Prone Decisions
- Good Communication in Work Area

JOB ITSELF
- Challenging Job
- Skills and Abilities Match the Job
- Adequate Information
- Task Significance
- Participative Decision Making

Extracted statements   **QWL Dimensions**

Based on the extracted dimensions, which state the sub factors in each dimension, the results are presented below.

Table I
DETERMINANTS OF QWL

Organizational Variables	Mean	SD
Quality of Work Life (QWL)		
Reward System	3.938	0.694
Managerial Style	3.865	0.682
Organizational Support	3.893	0.670
Job Itself	3.955	0.726

It is made clear that the two factors reward system and job itself have got better mean score value among all factors. It specifies that these factors provide a favorable environment for the women executives to work. Women employees feel reward pattern and the work factors determine their QWL. But still it is also to be noted that the factors managerial style and organizational support too have been scored closer without much deviation. The rewards designed by the organization should be compatible with the QWL approach. The success of ITES lies in the satisfaction of their clients and the rewards planned for the employees have a greater say in determining the favorable work environment. The individuals give much emphasis on reward pattern especially the women employees consider that equitable rewards really boost their commitment to contribute their best.

Next factor that influence QWL is the work that is performed by the employees. There are evidences in the literature that QWL is significantly correlated with the job itself. It determines the enhanced performance of employees. The job nature of the employees should lead to high level of willingness to accept the job responsibilities and take pride to work which otherwise shows the constructive environment.

This section deals with the findings related to classification of respondents on the basis of type of organization, their age, marital status, educational qualification, monthly income for their responses regarding quality of work life. The cross sectional analysis of QWL with all these dimensions will provide impetus to determine how women employees feel about their working environment.

Table II
QWL ACROSS TYPE OF ORGANIZATION

Type of Organization / Organizational Variables	Fin BPO		BPO		MRM		MT	
	Mean	SD	Mean	SD	Mean	SD	Mean	SD
Quality of Work Life								
Reward System	3.781	0.754	3.932	0.493	4.228	0.412	3.976	0.750
Managerial Style	3.743	0.682	4.005	0.496	4.181	0.516	3.831	0.698
Organizational Support	3.736	0.696	3.991	0.518	4.172	0.454	3.922	0.664
Job Itself	3.774	0.730	4.152	0.552	4.397	0.512	4.017	0.734

BPO- Business Process Outsourcing, Fin BPO- Financial BPO, MRM- Medical Records Management, MT- Medical Transcription

Among the types of organizations, it is found that QWL has good scoring with MRM followed by BPO, MT and finally financial BPO. The operations of ITES in Coimbatore predominantly are related to health care and financial services. The City Coimbatore has many organizations involving in Medical Transcription and MRM. The employees trained in Medical records management has specific skills which cannot be otherwise applied so their retention becomes easy. The organizations in the fear of losing the specially trained experts provide better environment so that their international clients are satisfied.

Table III
QWL ACROSS AGE

Factors / Quality of Work Life	20-25 Yrs		25-30 Yrs		30-35 Yrs		35-40 Yrs		40-45 Yrs		Above 45 Yrs	
	Mean	SD	Mean	SD	Mean	SD	Mean	SD	Mean	SD	Mean	SD
Quality of Work Life												
Reward System	4.008	0.628	3.967	0.672	3.917	0.741	3.539	0.852	3.284	0.917	4.062	0.525
Managerial Style	3.913	0.590	3.897	0.695	3.835	0.733	3.671	0.829	3.061	0.863	3.916	0.347
Organizational Support	3.970	0.574	3.926	0.667	3.827	0.734	3.571	0.819	3.169	0.882	3.964	0.552
Job Itself	4.095	0.639	3.948	0.697	3.854	0.791	3.594	0.900	3.046	0.835	4.250	0.540

It is made clear that women executives at lower age group and higher age group perceive better QWL. At young age their expectation towards work environment may not probably be a major factor as they concentrate more on earning money and as they grow their expectations differ. When they attain more than 45 years the QWL is perceived differently as the executives are given flexible options to balance work and life. With increase in age, the expectations too increase and when the fresher's join the organization they carry a mindset about their work expectations and work environment.

Table IV
QWL ACROSS MARITAL STATUS

Factors	Married		Not Married	
	Mean	SD	Mean	SD
Quality of Work Life				
Reward System	3.916	0.768	3.956	0.628
Managerial Style	3.873	0.760	3.858	0.612
Organizational Support	3.862	0.745	3.917	0.600
Job Itself	3.877	0.781	4.020	0.672

It is found that married and unmarried respondents more or less have expressed the same level of perception about QWL which can be inferred as rated high. The marital status does not influence the way employees perceive their QWL in their respective organizations. The employees feel better satisfied when their social needs are taken care of than economic needs. The results portray among both categories it is the reward system and job component that is having high Mean score value.

Table V
QWL ACROSS EDUCATIONAL QUALIFICATION

Factors	UG		PG		Professional		Diploma	
	Mean	SD	Mean	SD	Mean	SD	Mean	SD
Quality of Work Life								
Reward System	3.973	0.640	3.982	0.654	3.683	0.919	4.139	0.386
Managerial Style	3.876	0.637	3.916	0.668	3.685	0.850	3.981	0.461
Organizational Support	3.915	0.644	3.960	0.625	3.651	0.840	3.944	0.340
Job Itself	4.036	0.699	3.971	0.661	3.628	0.900	4.125	0.479

It is vividly shown that people with diploma perceive their environment as very supportive than others. As this category of samples have developed specific skills required for ITES work. It is to be noted that employees with UG qualification have given slightly higher rating for the factor Job Itself. After much educational efforts and placed in an organization whether fresh or experienced, the educational qualification influence the expectations of employees.

Table VI
QWL ACROSS INCOME

Factors	Rs. 5000-10000		Rs. 10000-15000		Rs. 15000-20000		Rs. 20000-25000		Above Rs. 25000	
	Mean	SD	Mean	SD	Mean	SD	Mean	SD	Mean	SD
Quality of Work Life										
Reward System	3.943	0.660	3.945	0.722	3.891	0.787	3.891	0.592	4.052	0.563
Managerial Style	3.825	0.617	3.862	0.730	3.880	0.803	3.970	0.604	4.044	0.516
Organizational Support	3.885	0.624	3.902	0.712	3.862	0.764	3.975	0.633	3.950	0.506
Job Itself	4.005	0.685	3.940	0.766	3.848	0.818	3.967	0.671	4.000	0.537

Based on the level of income, it is clear that people at higher level of earnings have mentioned that the environment is favorable than others. At the same time, it is observed that employees earning between Rupees 15,000 to 25,000 have stated that all the QWL factors equally decide their well being in the organization. QWL is an evaluation that individuals possess comparing his/her desires and dreams and actually how the present environment is.

There is no doubt which is explicitly observed from the results that QWL promotes the effective functioning of the organization.

SUGGESTION

The following suggestive model would help organizations to further enhance their work environment. Considering the results it is found that across all QWL factors, Reward Systems and Job itself had good scoring.

Figure 2
MOTIVATIONAL DRIVERS

Primary Lever	Actions
Reward System	Tie Rewards Clearly to Performance Competitive Payment Sharply Differentiate Good Performers from Average and Poor Performers
Job Factors	Change in Job Quality Job Security Work Autonomy Application of Skills Efforts Measurement Special Training

The organizations can constitute a Work Assessment Committee so that the specific demands of different categories of people can be represented so that it helps not only in increasing commitment levels and retention of employees but also to improve the job performance. Several studies have proved that QWL has been positively correlated with Organizational commitment, Organizational Citizenship Behavior, Employee satisfaction, Job performance, Career growth, Motivational level etc., The other related factors are work life conflict, work overload, job stress which defines QWL as a multidimensional Construct. There are certain facets of QWL still unexplored and further research with different target audience and geographic description will give different results.

CONCLUSION

The ITES organizations need to focus on the work place determinants. The work environment is changing dramatically and demand for the high level of productivity is increasing. To remain competitive in the face of multiple pressures, QWL is crucial. Unless organizations create world-class environment to facilitate the employees, they cannot aspire to reach greater heights. The employees in different organizational set up, different age group, educational level, marital status, Income categories have different perception and the stress level in ITES adds to their perception of having a favorable environment. The employers should give strategic importance in building a better organizational climate to improve organizational effectiveness. From the research among women employees in ITES in Coimbatore, it may be consolidated that Reward

System and the Job factor to the major determining factors for QWL. This insight gives a right path to the organizations to further enumerate their strategies to make employees happy and reduce their stress levels.

India has already become the most privileged destination for BPO/ITES. In order to gain advantage of the demographic dividend the organizations need to gear up to employ skilled workforce and help India to realize its dream of becoming super power economy in the globe.

REFERENCES

Aswathappa, K. (2010). Human Resource and Personnel Management - Text and Cases, Tata McGraw Hill, New Delhi. Pp. 270-283.

Baron, R.A. and Greenberg, J. (1990). "Behaviour in Organizations: understanding and managing the human side of work", 3rd edition, - Allyn & Bacon, Boston. Pp. 202-220.

Cascio, W.F. (1992). "Managing Human Resources: Productivity Quality of Work Life Profits." McGraw Hill Inc., New York. ISBN: 9780072987324.

Cooper, C. (1980). Humanizing the work place in Europe: An overview of six countries. *Personnel Journal*, Vol. 59. Pp. 488-491.

Davenport, J. (1983). "Whatever happened to QWL?" *Office Administration and Automation*, Vol. 44, Pp. 26-28.

Deery, S. and Kinnie, N. "Call centres and beyond: a thematic evaluation." *Human Resource Management Journal*, Vol. 12 No. 4. Pp. 3-14.

Eaton, A.E., Gordon, M.E. and Keefe, J.H. (1992). "The impact of quality of work life programs and grievances system effectiveness on union commitment." *International and Labour Relations Review*, Vol. 45, No.3. Pp. 591-603.

Frenkel, S., Tam, M., Korczynski, M. and Shire, K. (1998). "Beyond Bureaucracy? Work Organization in Call Centres", *International Journal of Human Resource Management*, Vol. 9 No. 6. Pp. 957-979.

Gwendolyn M. Combs, Rachel Clapp-Smith, Sucheta Nadkarni (2010). Managing BPO Service Workers in India: Examining Hope on Performance Outcomes, University of Nebraska - Lincoln

Hannif, Z., Burgess, J., and Connell, J. (2006). "The Quality of Work Life in Call Centres: A Research Agenda". Proceedings of 2006 ACREW Conference, Prato: Italy

Havlovic, S.J., (1991). "Quality of work life and Human resource outcomes", *Industrial Relations*, Vol. 30 No. 3. Pp. 469-479.

Hutchinson, S., Purcell, J., and Kinnie, N. (2000). "The Challenge of the Call Centre". *Human Resource Management International Digest*, Vol. 8 No. 5. Pp. 4-7.

Igbaria, M., Parasuraman, S., & Badawy, M. (1994). "Work experiences, job involvement, and quality of work life among information systems personnel". *MIS Quarterly*, 18. Pp. 175-201.

Jayamma, V. (2006). "Quality of Work Life", Sonali publications, New Delhi. Pp. 134-157.

Shalini Sheel, Bhawna Khosla Sindhwani, Shashank Goel, Sunil Pathak (2012). "Quality of Work life, Employee Performance and Career Growth Opportunities: A Literature Review" Zenith, *International Journal of Multidisciplinary Research*, Vol. 2 Issue 2 (February), ISSN 2231 5780. Pp. 294-297.

S. Subhashini, C.S.Ramani Gopal (2013). "Quality of Work life among Women employees working in Garment Factories in Coimbatore District", *Asia Pacific Journal of Research*, Vol. I Issue XII, ISSN: 2320-5504, E ISSN -2347-4793. Pp. 23.

Svenn Age Dahl, Torstein Neishem, Karen M. Olsen (2009). "Quality of Work - Concept and Measurement", Working Papers on the Reconciliation of Work and Welfare in Europe, RECWOWE Publication, Dissemination and Dialogue Centre, Edinburgh. Pp. 7-18.